BREAKING INTO NEW MARKETS

BREAKING INTO NEW MARKETS

Emerging Lessons for Export Diversification

RICHARD NEWFARMER
WILLIAM SHAW
AND
PETER WALKENHORST
Editors

THE WORLD BANK
Washington, D.C.

1818 H Street, NW
Washington, DC 20433
Telephone: 202-473-1000
Internet: www.worldbank.org
E-mail: feedback@worldbank.org

1 2 3 4 12 11 10 09

ISBN: 978-0-8213-7637-9
eISBN: 978-0-8213-7638-6
DOI: 10.1596/978-0-8213-7637-9

Cover: Design by Edelman Communications Inc. All photo credits: Curt Carnemark/World Bank.

Library of Congress Cataloging-in-Publication Data
Breaking into new markets : emerging lessons for export diversification / editors, Richard Newfarmer, William Shaw, and Peter Walkenhorst.
p. cm.
Includes bibliographical references and index.
ISBN 978-0-8213-7637-9 — ISBN 978-0-8213-7638-6 (electronic)
1. Exports—Developing countries. 2. Foreign trade promotion—Developing countries. 3. Diversification in industry—Developing countries. I. Newfarmer, Richard S. II. Shaw, William, 1953- III. Walkenhorst, Peter.

HF1413.B725 2009
658.8'4091724—dc22

2009005195

CONTENTS

BOXES

FIGURES

TABLES

FOREWORD

Diversifying exports has long been a policy objective of commodity-dependent, low-income countries. This quest is all the more urgent in today's economic context. International trade in 2009 is likely to contract—the first time since 1982—and the outlook is subject to unusual uncertainty. Moreover, customary worries about commodity dependence have intensified with the extreme volatility in commodity prices that threatens to impart terms-of-trade shocks and depress long-term growth. Maintaining growth in incomes in this environment has made export growth an imperative.

This book takes a fresh look at export diversification. It concludes that much of the recent literature, though novel, has focused excessively on simply adding new products to export portfolios. One branch of these studies centers on the "discovery" of exports, and it argues that the threat of entry (imitation) leads to an underinvestment in bringing new products to the global market. Another analytical branch focuses on changing the contents of an export portfolio to mirror the exports of countries with higher incomes on the grounds that these lead to higher productivity. Both strands implicitly point to the need for careful yet active government policies. While such policies are important, this book argues for a more comprehensive view of diversification and hence a more comprehensive trade policy strategy—one that takes into account improving the quality of *existing* exports, breaking into new geographic markets, and increasing services exports.

This publication has been tailored to policy makers, their staffs, and the international development community at large. It is a collection of short articles that summarize major issues and policies on particular topics. Many of the chapters are digests of more formal studies but are presented here with a minimum of underlying econometric and theoretical detail of less interest to policy makers.

As the World Bank increases its efforts on "aid for trade," staff are working with countries to help diversify their exports. Along with other development partners, the Bank is providing enhanced assistance to improve competitiveness, facilitate trade, improve trade-related services, and exploit regional and multilateral initiatives to open markets for developing countries. This book makes a substantial contribution to the efforts of developing countries to use the global economy to spur growth and reduce poverty.

Danny Leipziger
Vice President
Poverty Reduction and Economic Management
World Bank

PREFACE

This book was prepared by staff in the World Bank's Trade Department in response to a challenge given to us by Danny Leipziger, Vice President of the Poverty Reduction and Economic Management network. He wondered if Trade Department staff could distill the new learning on export diversification based on the substantial amount of operational work the department was undertaking with clients in developing countries. In responding, we have benefited from contributions from operational and research staff across the World Bank, from the staff of other international institutions, and from leading experts and academics around the world. All of the contributors gave generously of their time to prepare these chapters, often deferring other urgent work. This compilation would not have been possible without their willingness to share their considerable expertise and experience.

Many of our colleagues and outside reviewers provided extremely useful comments on these chapters. We would particularly like to thank Paul Brenton and Bernard Hoekman of the World Bank, Olivier Cadot of the University of Lausanne, and Jim de Melo of the University of Geneva for their keen insights as they reviewed selected chapters. Uri Dadush, as director of the Trade Department, was persistently supportive, and Mona Haddad, sector manager in the department, generously provided the resources essential to making this book a reality. Moreover, members of the team benefited from extensive discussions of the literature with Marc Bacchetta and Marion Jansen of the World Trade Organization. Bingxing Huo (New York University) and Erik von Uexküll (World Bank) provided excellent research assistance to the production team. Stephen McGroarty, Andrés Meneses, and Janet Sasser of the World Bank's Office of the Publisher efficiently coordinated the editorial production, design, and printing of the final manuscript and the distribution of the book.

Richard Newfarmer
William Shaw
Peter Walkenhorst

CONTRIBUTORS

Editors

Richard Newfarmer	Special Representative to the World Trade Organization and the United Nations, Geneva, World Bank
William Shaw	Consultant, Development Economics Prospects Group, World Bank, Washington, D.C.
Peter Walkenhorst	Senior Economist, Trade Department, World Bank, Washington, D.C.

Other Contributing Authors

Aradhna Aggarwal	Associate Professor, Department of Business Economics, University of Delhi, India
Marc Bacchetta	Counselor, Economic Research and Statistics Division, World Trade Organization, Geneva
Paul Brenton	Senior Economist, Trade Department, World Bank, Washington, D.C.
Olivier Cattaneo	Consultant, Trade Department, World Bank, Washington, D.C.

Torfinn Harding	Research Fellow, Oxford Centre for the Analysis of Resource-Rich Economies (OxCarre), Department of Economics, University of Oxford, United Kingdom; and Research Department, Statistics Norway, Oslo
Heiko Hesse	Economist, Global Financial Stability Division, Monetary and Capital Markets Department, International Monetary Fund, Washington, D.C.
Mombert Hoppe	Trade Economist, Ministry of Trade, Industry, Private Sector Development & President's Special Initiatives, Government of Ghana, Accra; formerly Junior Professional Associate, Trade Department, World Bank, Washington, D.C.
Marion Jansen	Counselor, Economic Research and Statistics Division, World Trade Organization, Geneva
Bailey Klinger	Fellow, Center for International Development, Harvard University, Cambridge, Mass.
Daniel Lederman	Senior Economist, Development Economics Research Group, World Bank, Washington, D.C.
Iza Lejárraga	Economist, Regional Integration and Trade Division, African Development Bank, Tunis, Tunisia
Carolina Lennon	PhD Candidate, Centre d'Economie de la Sorbonne (TEAM), Université de Paris 1 and Paris-Jourdan Sciences Economiques
William F. Maloney	Lead Economist, Latin America and the Caribbean Region, World Bank, Washington, D.C.
Aaditya Mattoo	Lead Economist, Development Economics Research Group, World Bank, Washington, D.C.

Claudia Nassif	Economist, Middle East and North Africa Region, World Bank, Washington, D.C.
Marcelo Olarreaga	Professor, Department of Political Economy, University of Geneva
Lucy Payton	Consultant, Boston Consulting Group, London
Roberta Piermartini	Counselor, Economic Research and Statistics Division, World Trade Organization, Geneva
Martha Denisse Pierola	Consultant, Development Economics Research Group, World Bank, Washington, D.C.
Erik von Uexküll	Consultant, Trade Department, World Bank, Washington, D.C.

ABBREVIATIONS

$	All dollar amounts are U.S. dollars unless otherwise indicated
EBRD	European Bank for Reconstruction and Development
EPA	export promotion agency
FDI	foreign direct investment
GDP	gross domestic product
GMM	generalized method of moments
OECD	Organisation for Economic Co-operation and Development
OLS	ordinary least squares
SEZ	special economic zone
SITC	Standard Industrial Trade Classification
VAR	vector autoregression
VAT	value added tax

EXECUTIVE SUMMARY

Export diversification has suddenly moved back to center stage in development concerns, both because of the new urgency of using exports to regain lost growth momentum and because of the need to reduce income volatility for countries with large populations living in poverty. Dani Rodrik and Ricardo Hausmann have generated a new literature on export diversification focusing on the "discovery" of exports, that is, investing in learning which products can profitability be sold in overseas markets. Their argument is that would-be pioneer companies actually invest too little because of the risk that other firms, seeing their initial profitable activity, will soon enter and capture enough of the market to depress their earnings. This situation leads collectively to underinvestment in bringing new products to the global market. Rodrik and Hausmann argue that an activist industrial policy is necessary to overcome this barrier to discovery. An extension of this argument is that governments should attempt to match the contents of their export portfolios to those of richer countries because these goods are characterized by high productivity and hence growth potential.

This book argues for a more comprehensive view of diversification. While efforts to stimulate entry into new product markets might well be one target of policy, a more comprehensive trade policy strategy has to discern ways to improve the quality of *existing* exports, focus on ways for existing exports to break into new geographic markets, and promote services exports. Three findings underpin this conclusion.

First, the evidence suggests that the "acceleration" phase of the export product cycle is more important than the "discovery" phase. Most export growth over time occurs in already existing products rather than in new exports. This export expansion is rooted in improvements in productivity that confer either a cost advantage over competitors and/or improve the quality of the products. In contrast to the discovery hypothesis, the problem for low-income countries is not insufficient "births" of new exports. In fact, producers in these countries give rise proportionately to about the same number of new export products as do producers in middle-income countries. Rather, the problem is that low-income countries experience a much higher "death rate" for new exports. So attention to sustaining and growing viable products—through improvements in quality and progressive reductions in costs associated with economies of scale and increases in productivity—can have a high payoff. For policy makers, this means looking at market failures, institutional obstacles, and policy shortcomings that would otherwise strangle success in its infancy, a policy message similar to the discovery literature, if cast here somewhat more broadly.

Second, low-income countries take advantage of only a small portion of potential overseas markets for the products that they already produce and export. On average in 2006, their exports reached only 6.5 percent of the nations importing those same products. This contrasts sharply with the fastest-growing countries, which reached some 26 percent of the nations importing the products they produce. Moreover, analysis in this volume shows that this geographic diversification, like product diversification, can moderate the transmission of adverse international shocks. Finally, traditional markets in the Western industrial countries are rapidly relinquishing their preeminence in world trade with shifts to the faster-growing markets of developing countries themselves. Thus, policy attention to promoting export sales in new markets can have a high payoff. This underscores the importance of a pro-active role for government to help introduce prospective exporters to foreign markets, encourage adoption of sophisticated international standards, and develop trade-related infrastructure.

Third, services exports are routinely overlooked in the analysis of diversification. Most economic studies are constructed solely on an analysis of merchandise exports. Yet services exports—business services, labor services, and tourism, to name a few—are rapidly growing in low-income countries as well as in middle-income countries, and they have become one of the most dynamic areas of the global economy. Policy makers too have tended to ignore the services path to diversification. Ministries of trade rarely control the policy levers that would propel services exports; transportation and telecommunications ministries are far more important but rarely orient their activities around goals of international competitiveness. Promoting services exports, much as with implementing a broader strategy of competitiveness itself, requires interministerial collaboration. Moreover, competitive backbone services—such as telecommunications, transportation, and even electric power—are fundamental to the overall competitiveness of manufactured and primary exports.

A comprehensive array of policies can help a country's exporters upgrade existing products, break into new geographic markets, and launch and consolidate new lines of business abroad. This array spans three broad areas: getting the incentive structure right to reduce or eliminate policy-induced bias against exports in relative prices; lowering the costs of trade-related services, including telecommunications, ports, transport, and customs administration; and instituting proactive interventions by governments, including notably export promotion and standards. Industrial policies can help, but they have to be carefully designed and administered to avoid private capture. The overall objective must be to improve international competitiveness and support the most productive firms in overcoming market and policy failures that constrain their capacity to exploit potential export opportunities.

A corollary is that a country's trade strategy cannot be limited to the domains under the traditional purview of a trade minister. For example, the most important obstacle to diversification and improved competitiveness may be a telecommunications or port monopoly or pricing in an agricultural marketing board. A program to improve competitiveness necessarily involves all economic ministries and must be guided by the economic cabinet itself to achieve success.

CHAPTER 1

BREAKING INTO NEW MARKETS: OVERVIEW

Paul Brenton, Richard Newfarmer, William Shaw, and Peter Walkenhorst

Expanding international trade has been an important avenue for growth in many developing countries. And export diversification is seen by many as an important channel through which trade fuels economic growth: by facilitating improvements in productivity, by capturing economies of scale, and by curbing volatility. Since the 1950s, when Raul Prebisch and Hans Singer argued that specialization in primary products would lead to secular falls in the purchasing power of primary exports, diversifying out of primary products into manufactures has been a major policy objective of developing countries (Prebisch 1950).

Indeed, in the past 25 years, many developing countries have become less dependent on a narrow range of primary products. But new questions concerning export diversification have emerged in the recent literature—and with important policy implications:

- What is the role of export diversification in the growth process? Is export diversification a natural structural outcome of the growth process, meaning that as countries become richer they tend to become more diversified?
- If diversification is associated with growth, can policies actually promote more rapid diversification and therefore more rapid growth?
- What are the main constraints that prevent countries from diversifying? Is it macroeconomic stability and exchange rate management, the quality of institutions, or market failures that, for example, lead firms to underinvest in efforts to reach new markets?

- If diversification is an important development objective, what policies are most suitable for countries at different stages of development and diversification?
- Should governments seek to move their economies toward products with particular characteristics?

This book explores the policy implications of exciting new research on the diversification process. This introductory chapter reviews recent literature on diversification, weaving in the findings of the chapters in this volume. Diversification can take the form of breaking into new product markets or into new geographic markets. Two main threads unite the chapters. The first traces the importance of diversification for development and shows that while developing countries have achieved significant export diversification, there is enormous potential for further progress—progress that if realized would likely lead to faster sustained growth. In one sense, the causality runs from growth to diversification, almost by definition (at least up to some level of income, as shown later). But in another sense, diversification into new products and geographic markets can lead to higher sustained growth to the extent that diversification unleashes productivity-inducing externalities and facilitates progressively more rapid moves into higher value-added production, less macroeconomic volatility, and less elite misappropriation of rents associated with a narrower economic base.

The second theme is the presumption that policy can make a difference. While there is no magic recipe to promote diversification, a broad array of policies, ranging from getting the incentive structure right, to lowering the costs of trade-related services, to proactive policies, can help a country's exporters upgrade existing products, break into new geographic markets, and launch and consolidate new lines of business abroad.

THE EXTENT OF DIVERSIFICATION IN DEVELOPING COUNTRIES

Many developing countries, including some of the poorest, have achieved significant export diversification over the past two decades, spurred by changes in technology and investments in infrastructure. Chandra, Boccardo, and Osorio (2008) observe that some degree of export diversification, as measured by the Herfindahl index, has been widespread: almost 60 percent of the developing countries diversified their export baskets in the past

30 years to some extent, and export diversification was evident in both middle- and low-income countries. Many countries have failed to take advantage of the great potential for further diversification, however, as evidenced by the limited penetration of countries' existing products into new markets (see below). Moreover, a few poorly performing low-income countries have made almost no progress in diversification, while a few initially upper-middle-income countries, like the Republic of Korea and Singapore, have begun specializing in high-tech exports.

An important qualification to nearly all of the literature on diversification is its rather blind focus on merchandise exports. Even though, as the chapters in this volume show, export of services is an important avenue of diversification for developing countries (as well as a critical input into goods production), in virtually none of the academic cross-country studies are services taken into account. One reason for this oversight may be the difficulty of quantifying services exports. Both the traditional balance of payments definition and the World Trade Organization negotiating definitions have severe drawbacks. Moreover, in both cases, services export data for most countries are insufficiently disaggregated to provide for meaningful analysis of diversification within services across countries.

Export diversification appears to have an inverted-U-shaped relationship with income levels: diversification increases with income until economies reach the lower rung of the high-income countries, and thereafter diversification falls as income rises.[1] For developing countries, Cadot, Carrère, and Strauss-Kahn (2008) find that exports become less concentrated as average income rises to $20,000–$22,000 per capita—roughly the levels of income of New Zealand and Portugal. (All dollar amounts are U.S. dollars unless otherwise indicated.) By contrast, high-income countries show a rise in concentration ratios driven by the reduction in the number of products they export. Data on Africa indicate that export diversification increases with income (UNECA 2007), while Bebczuk and Berrettoni (2006) find an inverted-U-shaped relationship between export diversification and income, across a group of countries that includes both developing and developed countries. In this volume, Hesse (chapter 3) and Klinger and Lederman (chapter 5) confirm that the relationship between export diversification and per capita income is positive for developing countries. The relationship between income and export diversification across countries is illustrated. In figure 1.1, the number of new export products continues to rise until just below income levels of $10,000 per capita (although the value of these new products remains relatively low).

Figure 1.1 New Products and Their Average Value: Nonparametric Curves

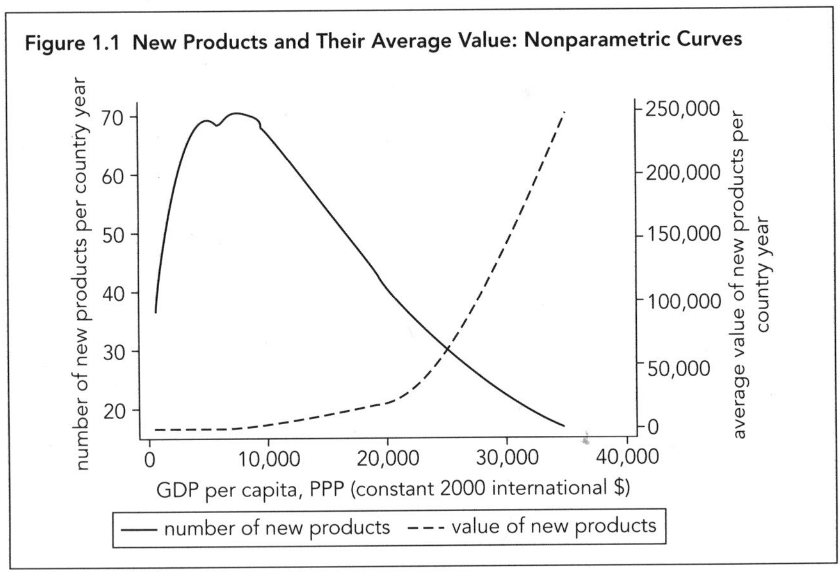

Source: Cadot, Carrère, and Strauss-Kahn 2008.

It is easy to misconstrue the role of diversification in export growth. In fact, time series data indicate that the primary source of export growth in developing countries has been from increases in existing bilateral trade flows (the intensive margin) rather than increases in new products or in old products to new geographic markets (the extensive margin). Within the extensive margin, the export of existing products to new geographic markets has accounted for a greater share of developing countries' export growth than the export of new products. Evenett and Venables (2002) find that selling existing products to new markets accounted for only about one-third of export growth for 23 developing countries, while Besedes and Prusa (2007) find that (for their sample of 26 developing countries) about a quarter of all export relationships from 1975 to 2003 were new in any given year, but almost all of these new relationships were short lived. Brenton and Newfarmer (chapter 6 in this volume) show that from 1995 to 2004 for 99 developing countries, the intensive margin contributed more to export growth (80.4 percent) than did the extensive margin (19.6 percent). Within the extensive margin, the export of existing products to new markets accounts for about 18 percent of total export growth, while the contribution of the export of new products is negligible.[2] Similarly, Amurgo-Pacheco and Pierola (2007) find that in all of the developing regions, the intensive margin provides the dominant source of export growth (figure 1.2). Amiti and Freund (2007) find that no more than 15 percent of China's phenomenal export growth to the United States from 1992 to 2005 reflected new products.

These studies have important implications for policy makers. First, as Brenton and Newfarmer conclude, an export strategy that ignores the scope for expanding exports at the intensive margin will miss important opportunities for export expansion—and for propelling growth. This means public and private efforts that focus on continually upgrading

Figure 1.2 Share of Export Growth Contributed by Intensive and Extensive Margins, 1990–2005

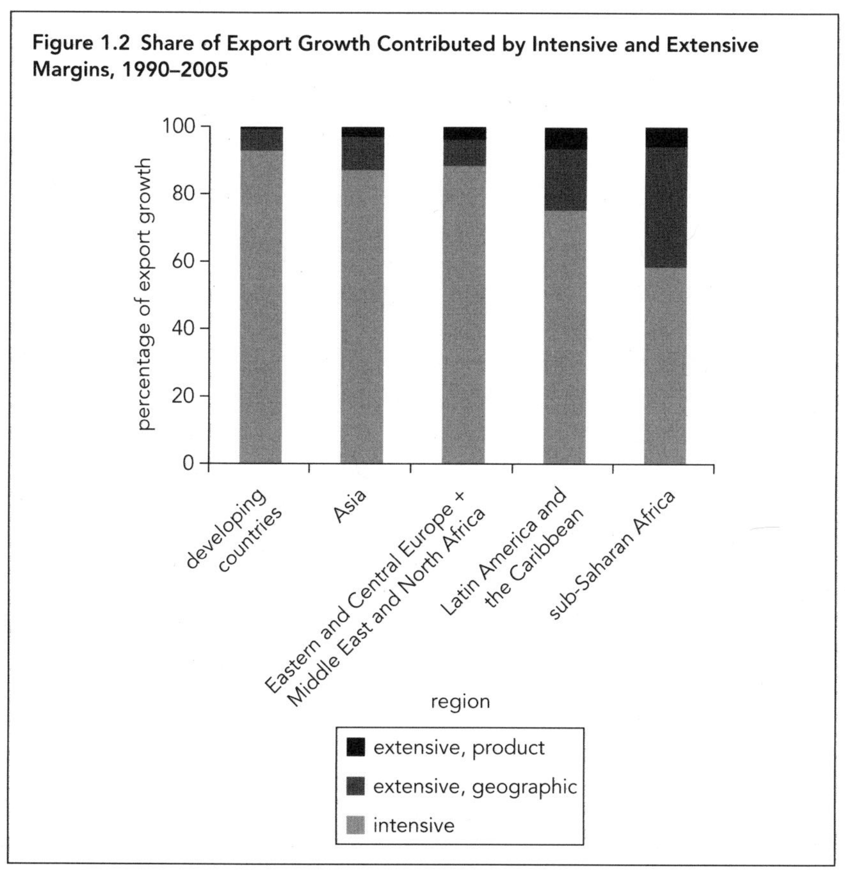

Source: Amurgo-Pacheco and Pierola 2007.

Note: See text for definitions of the intensive and extensive margins.

quality, reducing costs, and increasing productivity have a high payoff. Second, in general, promoting diversification of existing products into new markets is likely to be more effective as a growth stimulus, and arguably easier to achieve, than focusing on developing new products for export to new markets. Third, learning from survival and death patterns of new exports could lay the basis for more effective export promotion. Finally, growth of new products and markets may have a significant impact on economic growth by disseminating information on new technologies, helping firms capture economies of scale, and reducing terms-of-trade volatility.

DOES DIVERSIFICATION MATTER? EXPORT DIVERSIFICATION AND DEVELOPMENT

Export diversification may improve growth through several channels. In particular, cumulative investment in traditional products will in most cases eventually exhaust the activity-specific economies of scale and lead to stagnating or decreasing returns. Building up nontraditional outputs then represents a better use for domestic production factors at the margin. The switch to suitable alternatives among the large range of modern activities is not frictionless, though, due to risk aversion of entrepreneurs (Hoff 1997) or the existence of market failures (Hausmann and Rodrik 2003). In fact, economic growth can be seen as depending on the extent and speed with which an economy shifts to the mix of activities that provides the best returns to available production factors.

Diversification also makes countries less vulnerable to adverse terms-of-trade shocks by stabilizing export revenues (Ghosh and Ostry 1994) and makes it easier to channel positive terms-of-trade shocks into growth. The issue is not necessarily that exports are concentrated but that they are usually concentrated on homogeneous products, with individual exporting countries facing a highly inelastic demand curve. Thus, changes in global supply or demand are translated into significant price volatility, with low-income countries often suffering terms-of-trade shocks that adversely affect investment and even consumption (Jansen 2004). This volatility can reflect changes in global prices, as well as changes in demand from specific markets, where switching to new markets is difficult owing to fixed entry costs (see Bacchetta, Jansen, Lennon, and Piermartini, chapter 4 in this volume). The magnitude of terms-of-trade shocks is raised by trade openness but lowered by financial openness (Loayza and Raddatz 2007). Further, income volatility caused by terms-of-trade shocks has depressed long-term growth, in part by impairing human capital through ratchet effects, as unemployed workers lose contacts and skills and younger workers forgo education to support themselves during downturns (Lutz and Singer 1994; Easterly and Kraay 2000). Finally, knowledge spillovers (such as information on the size of foreign demand and quality specifications, as well as on new production processes and management techniques) from exporters, combined with increasing returns to scale, create learning opportunities that lead to new forms of comparative advantage (see Amin Guttiérez de Piñeres and Ferrantino 1999 for the example of Colombia). Such spillovers tend to be more common in manufactures than in primary commodities, placing a premium on diversification into manufactures.

Another channel through which dependence on a few exports may inhibit growth, if these exports are oil or minerals, stems from the way rents are captured and reinvested. Pritchett and others (2002) have argued that rents from primary commodities are associated with poor governance, and Collier and Hoffler (2002) have noted that they are also associated with civil wars, as contending groups struggle for the state and capture of resource rents.

Some studies have found an empirical relationship between export diversification and growth. Al-Marhubi (2000) finds that export diversification boosts growth (using cross-section data), Amin Guttiérez de Piñeres and Ferrantino (2000) find that export diversification is associated with income growth in Latin America (using panel data), and Feenstra and Kee (2004) estimate that export product variety explains 13 percent of productivity gains in 34 industrial and developing countries. Ben Hammouda and others (2008) find that deepening diversification has been associated with increases in total factor productivity in sub-Saharan Africa. In Bangladesh and Nepal, export diversification is estimated to raise export growth, which increases GDP growth (Hasan and Toda 2004). Herzer and Nowak-Lehnmann (2006) find that export diversification played an important role in growth in Chile. In this volume, Hesse (chapter 3) provides robust empirical evidence of a positive effect of export diversification on growth of per capita income in developing countries, while Lederman and Maloney (chapter 2) present econometric evidence that slow growth associated with dependence on natural resources is likely a result of export concentration, rather than dependence on natural resources per se.

A DIGRESSION: DOES THE SOPHISTICATION OF EXPORTS MATTER?

While concentration of exports creates vulnerabilities, two opposing strands of thought have emerged on whether the kinds of products exported—controlling for the concentration of exports—matters for trade performance. The first, represented by de Ferranti and others (2004), studied Latin America's export performance, including supplementary studies worldwide, and concluded that what was important was not *what* a country produced but *how* it produced it. This study emphasized that productivity improvements in production could keep export prices competitive while improving quality and providing an ever-higher return to workers.

A recent and slightly different argument suggests that countries exporting goods associated with higher productivity levels will grow more rapidly than countries with exports associated with lower productivity levels. Hausmann, Hwang, and Rodrik (2006) measure this "notion of the productivity" of products using the income levels of countries that export a particular product, weighted by each country's revealed comparative advantage in that product (defined as the variable *PRODY*). For each exporter, they then calculate a measure of the overall productivity of the export bundle by weighting each of the *PRODY*s by the share of the product in that country's total exports. They find a strong correlation between this measure of the productivity of a country's export bundle and per capita income and between initial values of the measure and subsequent growth. Rodrik (2006) suggests, on the basis of this measure, that China is an outlier in its export sophistication in that it exports products that are normally associated with countries that have per capita incomes three times higher. This apparent capacity to make advanced, high-productivity products is then seen as having been an important factor in China's recent strong growth.

However, recent studies have challenged this view by taking into account differences in product quality. By ignoring the quality of products, the Hausmann-Hwang-Rodrik measure tends to overestimate the importance of sophisticated products in low-income country exports. Because product quality is correlated with income, correlations between the measure of export productivity and per capita income are likely to be biased, it is argued. For example, Xu (2006) conditions the Hausmann-Hwang-Rodrik measure by relative unit values of exports, which are used to proxy relative quality. This analysis shows that once product quality is taken into account, the structure of China's exports appears consistent with its level of development. Minondo (2007) finds that the relationship between initial export sophistication and subsequent economic growth no longer holds once differences in quality are taken into account.

In addition, emerging global production chains complicate the analysis of an export basket as in the Hausmann-Hwang-Rodrik measure. Technological change and declining transport costs have led to a splitting of the production chain for many processed products and the reallocation of production throughout the world. Successful exporting in many developing countries, especially those in East Asia, has been driven by the importation of parts and components for further processing and assembly. However, the trade data used in these measures of diversification and export sophistication relate to gross exports and do not capture the impact of outsourcing. For example, China's export of sophisticated iPods largely reflects assembly activities, while most of the advanced, high-productivity activities that are combined to produce the iPod take place in other countries (box 1.1). Similarly, Moldova exports Max Mara coats, which are very expensive products, but most of the value is embodied in the fabrics that are imported into Moldova and assembled into the final product and then exported.

Box 1.1 Global Production and the iPod

Global production chains can make it difficult to determine the location of the value added in sophisticated export products. Take, for example, just one component of the iPod nano, the central microchip that is provided by the U.S. company PortalPlayer. The core technology of the chip is licensed from the British firm ARM and is modified by PortalPlayer's programmers in California, Washington State, and Hyderabad. PortalPlayer then works with microchip design companies in California that send the finished design to a "foundry" in Taiwan, China, that produces "wafers" (thin metal disks) imprinted with hundreds of thousands of chips. These wafers are then cut up into individual disks and sent elsewhere in Taiwan, where each one is tested. The chips are then encased in plastic and readied for assembly by Silicon-Ware in Taiwan and Amkor in the Republic of Korea. The finished microchip is warehoused in Hong Kong before being transported to mainland China, where the iPod is assembled.

Sources: C. Joseph, "The iPod's Incredible Journey," *Mail on Sunday*, June 15, 2006; A. S. Mutschler "Meet the iPods's 'Intel' " *Business Trends* 32, no. 4 (April 1, 2006).

OVERCOMING OBSTACLES TO DIVERSIFICATION: LESSONS FROM EXPERIENCE

Export diversification is encouraged by ensuring the quality of institutions that support trade, by relying on the market to determine prices where private firms internalize all costs and benefits, and by addressing market failures where feasible. Building the institutions required for export success is a slow process, but the major issues are well understood: access to efficient transportation and modern telecommunications infrastructure are essential to reduce costs and improve speed and reliability; well-functioning tax and customs services (including duty drawbacks and bonded warehouse facilities) are necessary to facilitate transactions and ensure that exporters face world prices for their inputs; and access to modern communications, metrology, testing, and conformity assessment facilities are essential to help exporters meet quality standards in foreign markets. Stable macroeconomic policies, an efficient financial sector, a properly valued exchange rate, open trade policies with low tariff and nontariff barriers, and a regulatory climate that encourages private sector development are key to successful exporting and domestic production.

In contrast to the basic requirements for sound institutions and market determination of prices, the market failures that affect exporting are more difficult to define precisely and more controversial to address. They are the focus of the articles in this volume.

Market Failures in the Discovery Phase

In developing countries, within-the-frontier innovations can generate valuable social knowledge. Demonstrated success in exporting a product for the first time (from a given country) generates valuable information on the structure of foreign demand and production costs and facilitates imitation. While imitation has a positive social benefit, it can also reduce the return to first movers, who in the case of within-the-frontier discoveries cannot be protected by intellectual property rights. The result is a tendency to underinvest in innovation. Klinger and Lederman (chapter 5 in this volume) develop an ingenious empirical test of the existence of market failures affecting discovery and find that while export growth (a proxy for the returns to exporting) is associated with increased export discoveries, the magnitude of the effect rises with barriers to entry.[3] Thus, countries where high barriers to entry discourage imitators show a greater response (in terms of export discoveries) to increased returns to exporting.

As Klinger and Lederman (chapter 5) recognize, however, erecting policy barriers to entry into exporting would be an extremely inefficient (indeed paradoxical) approach to improving the returns to first movers and thereby promoting export diversification. If lack of discovery is a genuine problem, then public efforts to improve access to information about technologies and markets as well as subsidies and investment in upstream innovation capacities can aid the process.

The threat of new imitative entry may not in fact reduce first-movers' profits or discourage discovery. If demand in global markets is virtually limitless—normally the case for an exporter in a developing country—then expanding the supply from new entry will have minimal, if any, adverse implications for the first-movers' profits. Moreover, new entry often brings economies of agglomeration and lowers transportation costs for all firms in the industry. It is precisely these economies that have led Michael Porter (1990) to advocate the creation of business clusters. Thus, the presence of a critical mass of firms producing similar products or using common inputs allows firms to move down the long-run cost curve and expand and diversify exports. For example, scale economies are found to be an important channel for the productivity improvements generated by exporting in nine African countries (Van Biesebroeck 2003). In Peru, the success of the initial asparagus producers demonstrated the industry's viability, attracting many new farmers into the industry, and the greater scale consequently lowered costs of transportation, standards administration, and logistics for all farmers. In Kenya, pioneer call-center operators reported that new entry would help them by widening the pool of available, flexible labor to respond to fluctuating demand.

In chapter 8 of this book, Nassif provides a detailed analysis of the market failures and policy response governing exporters from the Middle East and North Africa. She presents survey evidence that imitation is not a major concern of exporters, and indeed exporting firms are eager to share information to achieve economies of agglomeration. Major avenues toward increasing export diversification in the countries she studied include the following:

- Improving information transparency, which is particularly important for new exporters, who typically encounter discrimination in the provision of public support for exporting in the Middle East and North Africa
- Reducing the cost of experimentation through strengthening the national innovation system, including business incubators, technology parks for more mature firms, technology support services (although the

quality of many existing service providers is low), and stronger links between research centers and firms
- Improving the supply of financial services to risky, innovative firms; such financial services may include business-angel networks, provision of mixed debt and equity financing, and government support in facilitating access to bank financing for risky ventures, such as innovation-oriented credit guarantee schemes and assistance to small firms in dealing with commercial banks
- Addressing coordination failures through clusters and networks, including encouraging local producers to link into international production chains and making use of the diaspora
- Improving export promotion by emphasizing new activities, targeting market failures, subsidizing activities with spillover and demonstration effects, incorporating sunset clauses for all subsidy activities, rewarding rather than picking winners, and bundling support (research and development, product development, design, management process, and upscaling to marketing).

Market Imperfections in Other Phases of the Export Cycle

Discovery is only one phase of the export cycle. Once a new export has been sold abroad, ensuring that it grows and can eventually be placed in other markets may be the more important obstacle. Indeed, Brenton, Pierola, and von Uexküll (chapter 7 in this volume) find that from 1985 to 2005, while the birth of new export flows was larger (relative to income) in low-income than in middle- and high-income countries, average death rates were also larger (figure 1.3).[4] This finding is consistent with the very limited information on the dynamics of exporting at the firm level. Eaton, Dekle, and Kortum (2007) show that the majority of new entrants into exporting in Colombia exit the following year. Nevertheless, firms that enter into exporting and survive tend to grow rapidly.

The reasons for the high death rates in what should be the growth phase of an export product have not been fully researched. The prevalence of short-term entry into exporting appears inconsistent with previous studies that have found significant costs for entry into exporting (Roberts and Tybout 1997). However, it may be that the costs of securing long-term export contracts are substantial relative to the costs of "testing the waters" (Eaton, Dekle, and Kortum 2007). Hence, the low survival

Figure 1.3 Ten-Year Survival Rate of New Export Products Relative to per Capita Income, 2004

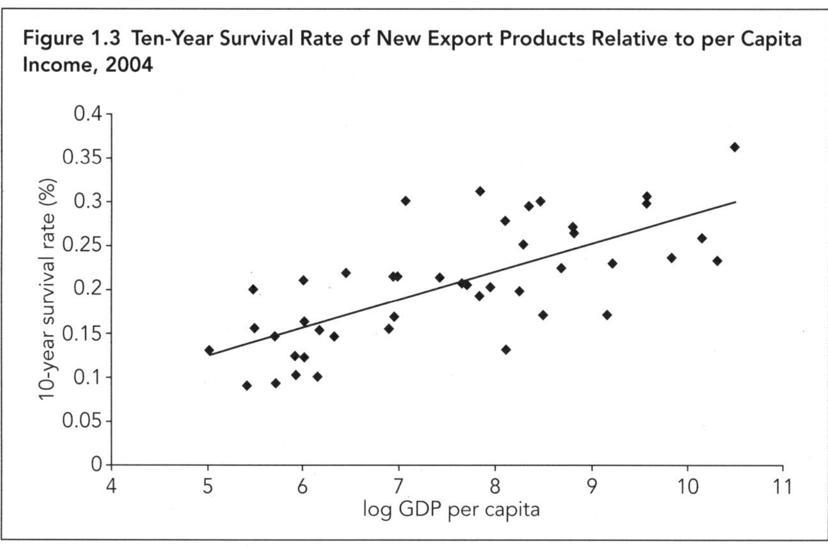

Source: Brenton, Pierola, and von Uexküll, chapter 7 in this volume.

rate of new export activities may result from the high costs of obtaining information: uncertainty concerning the fixed costs of exporting may result in firms that discover they are unable to cover their relatively high entry costs into a market; firms may enter a market primarily to discover costs, resulting in frequent entry and exit; uncertainty over suppliers' ability to deliver large orders to the buyer's specifications may induce buyers to start with small orders to determine which suppliers would benefit from training, while terminating other purchases; and weak contract enforcement may provide an incentive for sellers to begin with small orders that increase over time as the buyer builds credibility (Rauch and Watson 2003). Another cause for the premature death of exports may be instability in the business environment, including, for example, unpredictable delays in customs, changes in tax policy, or unanticipated rent-seeking officials expecting payments. The low survival rate for initially small flows suggests caution in public policy interventions that are aimed specifically at exporters that start small.

When information on the costs of exporting is well known, or can be obtained at little cost, then entry on a larger scale is more likely, and exit after a short period should be less prevalent. Cost information is likely to be easier to obtain, the greater the presence of exporters of other products to the particular overseas market and the greater the overall experience in exporting the specific product. In chapter 7, Brenton, Pierola, and von Uexküll find that the larger the initial export flow, the lower the percentage of export relationships that disappear quickly (the hazard rate). Variables included to proxy market information, search costs, and ease of matching (trading with a neighbor, common language, and colonial ties) all significantly influence the survival of export flows.[5] These authors find that total exports of a product are important in sustaining entry into new markets and that the higher the overall level of trade is, the lower will be the hazard rate.

Thus, policy measures that create a bias against exports of existing key products may be undermining opportunities for new exports. For example, an export tax on a raw material or intermediate export, designed to support exports of the finished product, may actually act to constrain export diversification by limiting the flow of information from overseas markets as well as the experience of exporting. Similarly, taxing existing exports to fund an export promotion agency may not be appropriate.

Macroeconomic factors could also play an important role in the high death rates afflicting exports from low-income countries. In small economies subject to volatile commodity prices or sharp swings in capital inflows, sudden exchange rate appreciations may be sufficient to choke off small volumes of exports through "Dutch disease" effects. Likewise, these same effects of volatility can occur through growth swings in the domestic market: a sudden downturn may precipitate a search for external markets (a type of vent for surplus), while a sudden domestic expansion may induce sellers to focus their activities in the domestic market. This underscores the importance of sound management of the macroeconomy—and the exchange rate.

Even though time series information points to the predominance of the intensive margin in export growth, the main action at the extensive margin is the sale of existing products to new geographic markets—an approach that low-income countries have barely explored. The potential for further geographic diversification is enormous, given how few markets these exporters have actually exploited. Brenton and Newfarmer (chapter 6 in this book) derive an index of export market penetration (IEMP) that measures the extent to which a country is actually exploiting the market opportunities from its existing set of export products. For the given range of products that a country exports, the IEMP will be higher for countries that reach a large proportion of the international markets that import the type of products they export.

The IEMP index is positively correlated with GDP per capita (figure 1.4). Countries with relatively low per capita incomes tend to do less well in exploiting the available markets for the goods that they export. For example, Korea (income per head of $14,135 in 2004) has been much more effective in covering potential export markets than Kenya (income per head of $480). The value of the IEMP for Korea increased from 21.3 percent in 1985 to 42 percent in 2005. By contrast, the index for Kenya increased from just 5.9 percent in 1985 to 8.5 percent in 2005, with much of this increase occurring in the past five years.[6]

These results may reflect asymmetries in the costs of accessing overseas markets. Kenyan exporters may face higher transaction and informational costs in entering an equidistant market than do their Korean counterparts. These findings point to the importance of improvements in trade facilitation[7] and to the role of export promotion agencies and commercial attachés in identifying and reaching third-country markets. The high-income countries have for decades used embassies to expand exports into new markets. Brazil in the 1970s and 1980s started hiring economists instead of foreign policy experts to staff the commercial sections of its embassies, a move that aided its rather spectacular export performance, particularly of manufactures.

Regional trade arrangements can help overcome informational gaps. Borchet (2007), for example, found that bilateral trade agreements can trigger increases in exports to third markets outside the preferential

Figure 1.4 Export Market Penetration Relative to per Capita Income

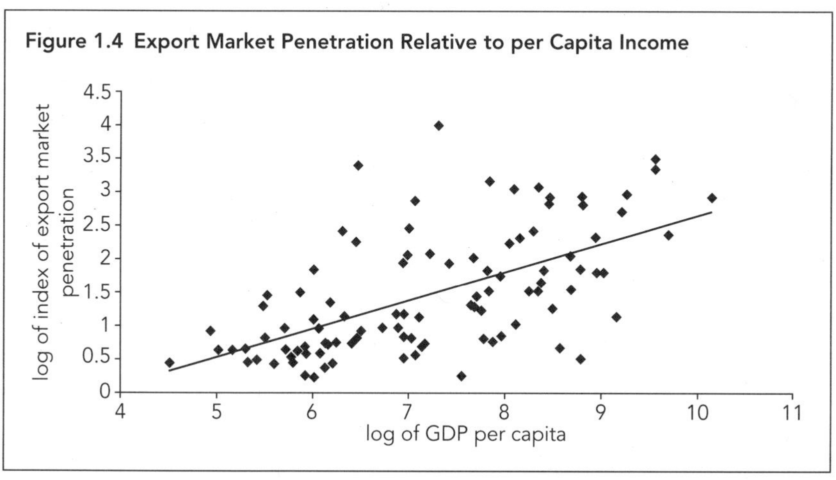

Source: Brenton and Newfarmer, chapter 6 in this volume.

trading area. Exporting may involve initial, product-specific fixed costs of obtaining information, for example, on packaging appropriate for foreign markets, complying with customs procedures, defining quality control, and observing product standards. Once these costs are absorbed, then the marginal cost of exporting to third markets declines.

Services: A Potentially Important Source of Export Diversification

Advances in information and communication technologies are increasingly permitting cross-border services trade through digitization and fragmentation of the offer across suppliers from different countries. These developments have been turning services exports into an ever more important component in the balance of payments and potentially a major source of economic growth. Services can contribute to growth and export diversification in several ways: by expanding exports of existing services activities to existing markets; by developing new services exports or starting to export existing services activities to new markets; and by lowering input and transaction costs to make merchandise products more competitive in international markets.

Services exports have grown dynamically across all modes of supply. These developments are reflected in the services trade statistics (figure 1.5); and foreign direct investment (FDI), that is, services trade under mode 3 (commercial presence), has been even more dynamic. The ongoing trend of outsourcing back office and information technology functions to take advantage of advanced skills and lower labor costs of specialized service providers has opened new export paths for a growing number of developing countries. Most of the contracting-out is still undertaken with companies in the country of origin ("onshoring"), but cross-border arrangements ("offshoring") have become increasingly common. Also, regional trade in services among developing countries is gaining in importance, with South-South transactions estimated to amount to about 10 percent of world services exports (Dihel, Eschenbach, and Shepherd 2006).

As Mattoo argues in chapter 9 of this volume, many of the endowments that drive countries' comparative advantage in cross-border services trade are amenable to policy action. Key conditions for success are competition in "delivery" services such as telecommunications and transport, higher education systems that are capable of providing a large number of graduates with advanced skills, and regulatory institutions that can credibly signal quality to foreign buyers. He contrasts the successes of Brazil and India in

Figure 1.5 Global Expansion of Services Exports, 1995–2006

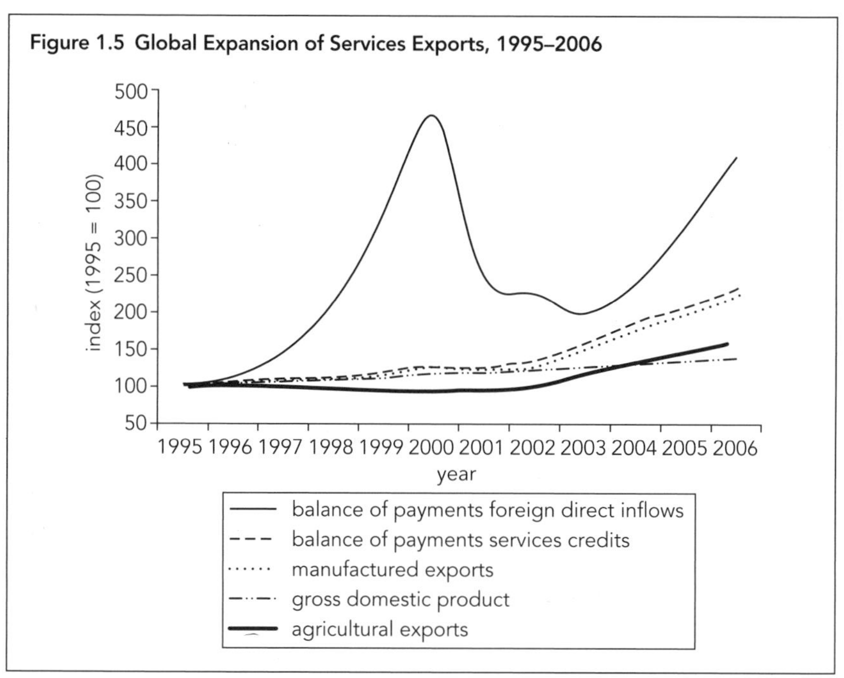

Source: World Trade Organization 2006.

growing exports of business services with the relatively poor performance of Pakistan, Sri Lanka, and Zambia where, respectively, the telecommunication infrastructure is deficient, the pool of highly qualified individuals is shallow, and the financial sector and business climate are insufficiently developed. Addressing and overcoming these impediments is of crucial importance for developing an export-oriented services sector.

While cross-border services exports have attracted considerable interest in the recent past, opportunities are also arising for developing countries by attracting foreign services consumers (mode 2) or by moving service providers abroad (mode 4). Important obstacles with trading partners have to be overcome, though. Mattoo points, in particular, to powerful political barriers in developed countries that limit the reimbursement by health insurance companies of medical treatment abroad, impose cumbersome and costly qualification and licensing requirements on foreign professionals, and restrict the number of visas issued to temporary workers in industries ranging from construction to information technology. Little progress on facilitating the temporary movement of workers has been made so far in the multilateral context of the General Agreement on Trade in Services, but bilateral cooperation agreements between source and destination countries that take into account the particular interests and sensitivities of the trade partners might be a promising alternative to arrive at mutually beneficial outcomes.

A large portion of benefits from services liberalization derives not from seeking better market access abroad, but from the increased competitiveness and efficiency of the domestic market (Nielson and Taglioni 2004). Services trade through mode 3, that is, FDI, appears particularly important (Hoekman and Mattoo 2008). Results from simulation models have predicted substantially higher gains from liberalization of services sectors than goods sectors, even in countries with high tariff barriers such as Tunisia (Konan and Maskus 2006). Moreover, if endogenous productivity effects are taken into account, the long-run benefits from services liberalization can reach a multiple of the static benefits, as recently demonstrated for Russia (Jensen, Rutherford, and Tarr 2007) and Kenya (Balistreri, Rutherford, and Tarr 2008). In the same vain, Arnold, Javorcik, and Mattoo (2007) analyze econometrically the effects of allowing foreign providers greater access to services industries on the productivity of manufacturing industries that rely on services inputs. The results, based on firm-level data from the Czech Republic for the period 1998–2003, show a positive relationship between FDI in services and the performance of domestic firms in manufacturing.

Yet growth in services has stagnated in many developing countries with considerable potential because they have focused on eliminating barriers to entry but have paid inadequate attention to the development of regulations to deal with market failures and access-widening policies. The poor integration in the domestic economy of foreign-owned firms that often carry out a large share of export-oriented activities seems to be another issue, and econometric analysis shows that for developing countries, the services exports–GDP growth nexus is indeed weaker than for developed countries (Gabriele 2006). Also, many services, such as telecommunications, require specialized distribution networks that give rise to natural monopolies or oligopolies. Liberalization then calls for procompetitive regulation or independent regulators to ensure equal access to established networks. In many developing countries, however, the enforcement of competition law and equal access regulation is often insufficient. For example, a large part of the very high maritime transport costs that exporters in sub-Saharan Africa face can be attributed to private sector collusion; Fink, Mattoo, and Neagu (2001) estimate that the dissolution of conference and other price-setting agreements would lead to a reduction in transport prices by almost 40 percent.

Moreover, services exports to new markets are often hampered by regulatory diversity. Regulatory measures affect the fixed cost of entering a market as well as the variable costs of servicing that market. Moreover, differences in regulations among countries often imply that firms have to incur entry costs in every new market. Kox and Nordås (2007) introduce indicators of regulatory intensity and heterogeneity into a gravity model, and estimate the impact of these indicators on market entry and subsequent trade flows for total services, business services, and financial services, using information on bilateral trade in services as the dependent variable. They find that regulatory heterogeneity has a relatively large negative impact on both market entry and subsequent trade flows. Furthermore, regulatory barriers have a negative effect on the local services sectors' export performance. Finally, they find that regulations aimed at correcting market failure can have a positive impact on trade. Hence, services trade liberalization and regulatory reforms are complementary in creating competitive services markets.

In other cases, governments are playing a more active role. Some countries, including China whose services exports have grown strongly from a low base, have shown interest in using regional trade agreements to open markets for their services providers. While such agreements cannot replace supportive domestic policies toward diversification into services, they can play a complementary role, in particular if they are ambitious and based on a negative-list approach, as first practiced in the North American Free Trade Agreement. Other proactive international policies include efforts to conclude bilateral open skies agreements, as in the case of Dubai.

There are so many interactions between services and manufacturing that the distinction between the two sectors is beginning to blur. Indeed, by one estimate as many as half of all manufacturing workers in industrial countries are performing jobs that would be classified as services if performed by separate companies (Pilat and Wölfl 2005). Moreover, many services, such as finance, telecommunications, and transport, provide vital inputs to manufacturing firms that substantially influence their international competitiveness and hence their potential to export and grow.

For example, Harding reports in chapter 14 of this volume that better infrastructure services can lead to improvements in the quality of merchandise products that, in turn, make it possible for exporters to charge higher prices. Two mechanisms are at the source of these interactions between services provision and goods diversification. First, better infrastructure services, such as fewer electricity outages or more extensive and reliable telecommunications networks, may increase manufacturing productivity and foster the production to higher-quality outputs. And second, where better transport infrastructure reduces delivery times, exporters might be able to respond more swiftly to changing demand and, as a result, command higher unit prices.

Harding finds evidence for both transmission mechanisms when evaluating changes in infrastructure provision in 10 Eastern European countries that recently joined the European Union. Using indicators of services sector reform during the period of economic transition as instruments for infrastructure quality, he reports that better infrastructure in the electric power, telecommunications, and road transport sectors is positively associated with higher unit export values. Better road transport facilities led to higher export prices for differentiated products, while the effects of higher-quality electric power and telecommunications services were found to affect both homogeneous and differentiated goods.

Efficient services are also crucial for taking advantage of modern distribution channels. Chinese producers have shown the way in which firms in developing countries can advertise their products over the Internet or even sell directly to consumers in industrial countries through Web-based outlets, such as eBay. This type of direct selling greatly reduces the costs of establishing an elaborate distribution infrastructure overseas or paying a foreign partner for its distribution services. At the same time, it requires an internationally integrated financial system, reliable postal delivery, and well-performing telecommunications operators.

Tourism's Potential for Encouraging Diversification of Foreign Exchange Earnings

Tourism can be an important element of export diversification because it essentially reduces many of the informational costs involved in earning foreign exchange (see Lejárraga and Walkenhorst, chapter 11 in this volume). It provides a local source of foreign demand to assist producers in learning about demand preferences and adapting to higher standards in developed-country markets (as well as increasing the demand for more sophisticated goods and for exotic, cultural goods). Tourism reduces the costs of discovery because the minimum scale is typically lower than for most modern manufacturing products, while transaction costs generated by border barriers, administrative barriers, transportation, time, and distance are also lower. Moreover, the demonstration effects of tourism may be greater and more immediate than for other exports as potential entrepreneurs can easily view results. Examples of tourism-related export discoveries include macadamia nuts from Hawaii, butterfly chrysalises from Costa Rica, and traditional spices from Jamaica. Many other export discoveries, ranging from agricultural products (such as organic fruit from the Dominican Republic) to handicraft (such as Tinga-Tinga paintings from Tanzania), have their likely origin in tourist demand, even though the links that inspired the innovators are difficult to pin down over time. Citing the example of Mauritius, Cattaneo (chapter 10 in this volume) underlines the proactive role that government can play in encouraging tourism development, through ensuring a stable and secure business environment, establishing a sound regulatory framework for the sector, providing a coordinating role, and protecting the environmental resources essential for successful tourism.

Lejárraga and Walkenhorst also present evidence that tourism is associated with the diversification of export goods: tourism is associated with a greater occurrence of new products and exports as well as a more even distribution of production across sectors. Controlling for time-invariant country characteristics, a 1 percent rise in tourism specialization from 1993 to 2000 was associated with a 0.11 percent rise in an index of export diversification. These findings suggest that policy makers may want to devote increased attention to fostering links between the tourism sector and the domestic economy to stimulate the discovery process and promote economic diversification and growth.

The impact of tourism on export diversification depends, however, on establishing links with domestic firms. What country-specific factors matter most for creating or enhancing these links? Lejárraga and Walkenhorst find that fixed or semifixed factors of production, such as land, labor, or capital, have less influence on the extent of tourism links than is generally supposed.[8] In contrast, variables related to entrepreneurial capital and the business environment of the host economy are of notable explanatory significance. In particular, high corporate taxes in the host economy have the most significant adverse effect on the formation of links, in conformity with the lower-cost motivation underlying tourism-led discovery. Also, widespread use of the Internet has a positive effect on the ability to orchestrate coordination. Another notable observation concerns institutions for policing and vigilance. As would be expected, the results show that countries with a higher incidence of violence or crime have significantly less tourism and therefore fewer opportunities for forging links with domestic producers. Finally, the results suggest that maintaining an open trade regime is critical for the emergence of links. This underscores the importance of not protecting inefficient activities and of opening potential products for tourism demand to competition. Although trade barriers may indeed serve to prod investors in the tourism economy to procure domestic goods, they will also hinder the competitiveness of local producers. Shielded from imports, local producers will not have the incentives to meet the international quality standards of the products needed by the tourism economy.

The Role of Export Promotion Agencies in Posting Export Growth

The significant productivity enhancements from exporting argue for government interventions to subsidize some export activities, and many governments in both developing and high-income countries have set up export promotion agencies. The recent literature on firm heterogeneity and exports suggests that exporters tend to be relatively large, have subsidiaries in other countries, and have to overcome considerable sunk costs when starting to export (Greenaway and Kneller 2007). All these properties put developing countries with their small-scale firms, paucity of multinationals, and high costs of finance at a disadvantage and suggest that some proactive government policies might be warranted to kick-start the exporting process.

In an influential study, however, Hogan, Keesing, and Singer (1992) noted several weaknesses that impeded the performance of export promotion agencies in developing countries. The major impediments to success concerned staffing with poorly trained civil servants who often had insufficient private sector experience, lack of incentives for staff to provide high-quality services to exporters, and excessive focus on marketing-related aspects while neglecting other supply constraints for exporters. More recently, Alvarez (2004) provided evidence from a survey of almost 300 small and medium exporters in Chile on the importance of an appropriate setup of export promotion efforts. He finds that the establishment of exporter committees, composed of firms in similar industries to encourage cooperation in research, marketing, and promotion, was more likely to be successful than the organization of trade shows and trade missions.

In chapter 12 of this volume, Lederman, Olarreaga, and Payton provide evidence that export promotion agencies have strong, statistically significant impacts on exports—they find that each dollar spent on export promotion yields a $40 rise in exports for the median export promotion agency (similarly, Nassif in chapter 8 cites an estimate that a $1 expenditure by the Tunisian export promotion agency generated $20 in additional exports). Export promotion is subject to strong diminishing returns, though, with a negative effect on exports for expenditures over $1 per capita. Lederman, Olarreaga, and Payton also find considerable heterogeneity across regions (in particular, agencies in the Middle East and North Africa have a relatively low impact on exports), levels of development (the effectiveness of export promotion rises with the level of income), and the types of instruments used. Major recommendations arising from their study are the following: draw the majority of export promotion board members from the private sector but finance export promotion activities through general revenues rather than taxes on exports; centralize export promotion activities and avoid a proliferation of small agencies; and focus on nontraditional exports and on large firms that are not yet exporters. In addition, poorer countries should devote their limited resources to onshore activities rather than financing permanent representation in export markets.

Export Processing Zones: Mixed Record

Many developing countries have chosen to protect exporters from distorted tax and trade policies, ineffective or burdensome regulatory regimes, and poor infrastructure services by establishing export processing zones. Exporting firms in these zones can operate free of tariffs on their inputs; are often exempted from regulatory strictures that limit their freedom of operation; and are ensured favored access to electricity, transportation, and customs services (FIAS 2008). Some studies have found that export processing zones confer limited benefits in easing the impact of distorted economic policies but remain inferior policies compared with overall liberalization.[9] Country experiences vary—for example, Jayanthakumaran (2003) found that export processing zones in China, Indonesia, Korea, Malaysia, and Sri Lanka, although not in the Philippines, generated substantial welfare gains. Moreover, export processing zones may generate dynamic benefits to the general economy through backward links (Din 1994) and demonstration effects (Johansson and Nilsson 1997).

In chapter 13 of this volume, Aggarwal, Hoppe, and Walkenhorst describe the favorable fiscal, regulatory, and infrastructure conditions of export processing zones in Bangladesh, India, and Sri Lanka. These zones have attracted substantial FDI and generated significant economic opportunities; however, export performance differs significantly across these zones. Variations in access to air and seaports, and the establishment of zones in backward regions that tend to be less successful than those in prime industrial locations, lead to diversity in operating conditions and export performance that appears to be more pronounced across different zones in each of the three countries than across country averages. And the effect of export processing zones varies by sector and activity. In some sectors, the zones add to existing exports, in others they simply replace existing production in the domestic economy, and in still others they bring entirely new production processes to the country.

Export processing zones can retard economic reform and modernization by generating economic activity and employment opportunities at the margin, thereby reducing the need to tackle poor regulatory systems and rent-seeking coalitions on a broader scale. On the other hand, the zones can also act as reform pilots that make it possible to test new regulations or sets of new regulatory measures in a spatially confined area before introducing those policies that have proven beneficial to the wider domestic economy (Litwack and Qian 1998). China with its many and differently structured special economic zones seems to be a case where the zones have played a major role in the country's successful economic transformation over the past two decades. The zones have made it possible for Chinese producers to tap into international production networks, with effects on the entire East Asia region. The resulting fragmentation of production has intensified intraregional trade but without reducing extraregional trade in final goods. While production networks centered on China have contributed significantly to growth in East Asia, they have not generated large technology spillovers and have bred some vulnerabilities stemming from an extreme interdependence across East Asian countries (Haddad 2007).

CONCLUSION: DIVERSIFICATION IS A WORTHY BUT NOT OVERRIDING POLICY OBJECTIVE

This discussion and the chapters in the book shed light on the questions posed at the outset. There is some evidence that, on average, as countries move from low-income status to high-income status they become more diversified. But firm conclusions about whether it is possible to infer definitively a "stages of growth" argument await confirmation from more rigorous historical and time series analyses. In any case, at any given income level, the level of diversification varies widely around the average, so locating a given country on a graph is of only limited help to policy makers.

Second, there is enough evidence on the relationship between diversification of exports, exports growth, and economic growth to support developing countries, especially low-income countries, in implementing an explicit policy of diversifying exports. Particularly important should be attention to services exports, an often overlooked source of growth in developing countries.

Third, this conclusion notwithstanding, evidence about the importance of growth at the intensive margin, increasing the quality of exports, and increasing productivity in existing exports points to the fact that policy makers would be ill-advised to make diversification an overriding objective that preempts attention and policy support to the intensive margin. Two findings underscore this point. Evidence is convincing that poor countries have underutilized geographic diversification, and suggests that policy efforts to increase the productivity and quality of old products, and promoting their entry into new national markets would pay high dividends. Moreover, the higher rate of "product deaths" in poor countries also suggests that perhaps some policy attention may be warranted to the growth phase of the export cycle as well as to the discovery phase.

Fourth, though not a central focus here, the major constraints to diversification clearly include weak systems of support for national innovation and technology, problematic access to finance, underdeveloped infrastructure and trade-related institutions that impose a heavy tax on exporters, and inadequate mechanisms to inform exporters about opportunities in foreign markets. Dealing solely with discovery phases of the export cycle and none of these problems that limit steady improvements in productivity growth of extant exports or their spread toward third markets is doomed to failure.

Finally, evidence about the "higher productivity" basket of exports is still preliminary—and not sufficiently strong to reject the conclusion of de Ferranti and others (2002) that "it is not *what* you produce, but *how* you produce it" that matters. To the extent that methodologies can be devised to draw policy implications for a given country about the "productivity of its exports," it seems desirable to ground these conclusions in substantial supplementary evidence before embarking on a particular policy path.

A PORTFOLIO APPROACH TO ADDRESSING CONSTRAINTS TO EXPORT DIVERSIFICATION

How can countries best position themselves to take advantage of new opportunities in the global market? We suggest a portfolio of policies that focus on facilitating trade and improving competitiveness and which focuses on both the intensive and extensive margins. Weighting and selection from the portfolio will depend on a country's level of income, initial policy framework, supply-side assets, and binding constraints.

The First Order of Business: Policies That Affect All Firms and Consumers

Three critical elements of a *general framework* are clearly essential in shaping a country's ability to compete in international markets: the incentive framework, lowering the cost of services, and proactive policies.

The incentives regime. A key challenge for policy makers is ensuring that domestic resources are channeled to their most productive activities. If private investors can make more money by investing in highly protected local markets, they will do so, and opportunities to invest in servicing markets abroad will be lost. Creating a modern incentive framework that spurs national competitiveness requires careful analysis to ensure that land, labor, capital, and technology are moving to sectors in which the country has a long-term capacity to compete and to the most productive firms within sectors. This necessitates a clear understanding of how trade, tax, investment promotion, and labor market policies interact to affect investment and trade decisions. In many small, low-income countries, the economy tends to be dominated by a small number of sectors, so many of the key issues regarding the allocation of resources can be unearthed by analyses that focus on these sectors.

One of the most important aspects of the incentive framework is the price of exports, and tradables generally, compared with nontradables—and therefore the exchange rate policy. In small open economies, export price booms and sudden capital inflows can appreciate the local currency and cut off incipient exports, so macroeconomic management has to make it an objective to maintain a competitive real exchange rate over some long period.

Lowering the costs of backbone services and of doing business in general. Of great importance in today's globalized economy is the access of domestic firms to efficiently produced, critical "backbone" services inputs. Firms that have to pay more than their competitors for energy, telecommunications, transport and logistics, finance, and security will find it hard to compete in domestic and overseas markets. Reducing policy barriers to competition and improving regulatory effectiveness in these services industries lie at the heart of the policy challenge. In many developing countries, lack of infrastructure is a critical constraint on the availability and cost of backbone services. Other critical services are those related to the education and training necessary to ensure a supply of the type of labor required by the more productive expanding sectors in the economy and to foster a process by which value is increasingly added to the products and services produced in the country.

As countries develop and industries' technological requirements permit, services liberalization can play a larger role in meeting supply requirements. Permitting foreign direct investment (mode 3) in telecommunications has markedly increased the supply and quality of telecommunications throughout the developing world. Similarly, some countries have succeeded in expanding their electrical grid through foreign-provided power or by permitting ports to be privately operated. Markets do not work well without a sound regulatory framework, and regulations that permit entry and induce competition among private providers generally produce the best results.

Proactive policies to support trade. Both market and government failures tend to afflict low-income countries as they seek to expand exports and growth. Laissez-faire policies combined with low tariffs are rarely sufficient to prompt dynamic export drives or overcome obstacles in other areas. In many cases these constraints to competitiveness require specific interventions and institutions:

- In tackling government and market failures, trade ministries are typically weak and their policy purview is limited to border barriers. Large domains of policy that affect competitiveness reside outside the normal trade minister's ambit—investment policies, infrastructure services, and transport, to name a few. It is important to bring these initiatives together within *a strategy for competitiveness* rather than as a series of unconnected interventions. In isolation these agencies tend to focus on narrow objectives, some of which may even be inconsistent with a broader competitiveness strategy. Incorporating competitiveness broadly into a national development strategy may require more effective mechanisms to review and coordinate policies. One option is to create an *intra-ministerial council on competitiveness* with the mandate of analyzing the existing policy framework and reviewing policies before they are put in place. A second approach is to set up a consultative group that involves the private sector in identifying policies that impede diversification or information or coordination gaps that the government could fill. These mechanisms have helped in East Asia.
- In identifying the role of product deaths and weak performance in the index of export market penetration, this study underscores the importance of *export promotion agencies*—and even economic officers in foreign embassies—in overcoming informational asymmetries. This is particularly important for overcoming impediments to the private sector in gaining information in the search for additional markets. Of similar importance are likely to be *investment promotion agencies, standards bodies, customs, agencies to support innovation and clustering, export processing zones, and duty refund schemes.*
- *Investment in infrastructure* is essential to export diversification. Cadot (2004) makes this point eloquently using the example of energy in Africa. Because of poor and unreliable supplies of electricity, firms have to install their own generators, driving up their costs and keeping them from being competitive on global markets. This is no less true for seaports, airports, and transportation systems. The public role in infrastructure provision may be indirect in more advanced economies, but in many small, low-income economies, for reasons of scale and risk, the government itself will have to supply crucial infrastructure.

Using Subsidies to Specific Industries to Promote Structural Change

Rodrik (2004, 2007) has argued that market imperfections such as those described in this chapter require government intervention to offset market shortcomings. Indeed, that has been the recommendation in several sections of this chapter. The trick is to identify the shortcomings of the marketplace and then tailor the right combination of tax, tariff, and subsidy policies to offset those shortcomings and promote growth. Said differently, selecting the right prices to "make wrong" is the challenge. Rodrik's suggestions for designing industrial policies revolve around three elements: a *strategic collaboration* between the government and the private sector with the aim of identifying bottlenecks to growth, designing effective interventions to overcome them, and learning from mistakes; *carrots-and-sticks incentives* that encourage investments in bottleneck areas or nontraditional domains but that have sunset provisions and weed out investments that fail; and *accountability* mechanisms that ensure that agencies administering programs and their political masters can be called to task if programs are ineffectual.

In fact, most countries have some de facto policies that stimulate specific economic activities. Often, however, only some of these policies promote structural change; others have the effect of impeding it. This suggests a four-step process for dealing with particular industries through tax, credit, and budget subsidies:

- Any program to diversify exports could usefully start with an analysis of ways the current policy framework uses regulations, taxes, and subsidies to favor private investment in some activities and discourage it in others.
- A second step would be to quantify these investments of taxpayer and consumer resources and make them transparent. New Zealand, for example, put tax subsidies to promote particular activities in its annual budget, to be reviewed as part of the budget process.
- A third step would be to assess whether collectively and individually, these programs and expenditures are achieving their stated objectives. This is useful because too frequently the purpose of many programs adopted for political reasons is not clearly stated, much less evaluated later against stated purposes.
- A final step would be to reconfigure programs around objectives formulated in a national program of competitiveness.[10]

One Size Does Not Fit All

Competitiveness diagnostics can highlight whether binding constraints to export performance reside in low discovery, low geographic diversification, low product quality, or low services exports (or some combination). Each may have slightly different policy remedies. For example, if the problem is discovery, an examination of the innovation framework may be warranted.[11] If the problem is lack of reach into new markets, an examination of the effectiveness of export promotion may be warranted. Failure to improve quality or introduce differentiated products requires consultation with the poorly performing industry to identify policy and economic constraints and areas for support (if any). Moreover, most low-income countries have supply-side constraints in infrastructure that require both policy action and new public investments. Finally, services offer a broad array of opportunities both for diversification of exports and as sources of dynamic diversification locally, and should play a central role in the analysis of nearly every country.

Recent research has made important contributions to our understanding of the process of export growth and diversification. It has shown that opportunities for diversification and growth lie not only at the extensive margin of goods trade but also in the intensification of existing exports flows and in services exports. A focus on firms rather than industries is now paramount, yet there are few detailed firm-level studies of exporting in developing countries. In developed countries, it is large multiproduct, multicountry firms that dominate exports (Bernard, Redding, and Schott 2006). Is size a prerequisite for export survival and success in developing countries? The analysis by Brenton and others in this volume suggests that the larger the initial size of a new trade flow, the greater the chance that flow will survive, but we do not know if this reflects the underlying presence of large firms or a group of smaller successful firms.

Diversifying exports is a complex process and obstacles are specific to countries. For these reasons, policy makers in every country have to craft a group of policy and institutional reforms most likely to yield results.

NOTES

1. Thus, export diversification follows a pattern similar to that documented for domestic production by Imbs and Wacziarg (2003).

2. Amurgo-Pacheco and Pierola (2007) use a data set with more product detail (around 5,000 products) over the longer period of 1990 to 2005, but with smaller country detail (24 developed and developing countries); they confirm that export growth is dominated by the expansion of the intensive margin. These time series studies contrast with cross-section approaches that seek to explain differences in the structure of the exports between large and small countries, which give primacy to the extensive margin of trade (Pham and Martin 2007).
3. Their proxy for entry barriers is the time required to register a firm, which will measure entry barriers imperfectly if most exporting is done by existing firms.
4. An export birth occurs when positive exports are recorded for a product-country flow that was zero in the previous year.
5. Search costs may be higher, and matching more difficult, for differentiated products that are the target of efforts at export diversification, compared with products traded on organized international exchanges (Rauch 1999).
6. The existence of this relationship does not establish causation. Higher incomes may facilitate greater export market penetration, or countries with better policies may achieve both greater market penetration and higher income growth.
7. For example, Korea is ranked 25th in the World Bank's Logistics Performance Index while Kenya has a rank of 76 (www.worldbank.org/lpi).
8. Data are drawn from the Tourism Satellite Accounts research from the World Travel and Tourism Council.
9. See Madani (1999) for a review of export processing zones in developing countries, and Warr (1989) on zones in Indonesia, Malaysia, the Philippines, and the Republic of Korea.
10. This essentially is what Mauritius did in 2006. The government found that the policy framework subsidized capital-intensive techniques over labor-intensive ones and favored investment in domestic activities over export markets, large firms over small firms, and domestic over foreign firms—when in fact the government wanted to do the opposite. See "Mauritius—From Preference Dependence to Global Competitiveness," Report of the Aid for Trade Mission, World Bank, April 2006, and Budget Speech of the Prime Minister, Government of Mauritius, June 2006.
11. For a rich inventory of policies to review, see World Bank (1998) and de Ferranti and others (2002), among others.

REFERENCES

Al-Marhubi, F. 2000. "Export Diversification and Growth: An Empirical Investigation." *Applied Economics Letters* 7: 559–62.

Alvarez, Roberto. 2004. "Sources of Export Success in Small and Medium-Sized Enterprises: The Impact of Public Programs." *International Business Review* 13: 383–400.

Amin Guttiérez de Piñeres, Sheila, and Michael Ferrantino. 1999. "Export Sector Dynamics and Domestic Growth: The Case of Colombia." *Review of Development Economics* 3 (3): 268–380.

———. 2000. *Export Dynamics and Economic Growth in Latin America: A Comparative Perspective.* Aldershot, U.K.: Ashgate.

Amiti, M., and C. Freund. 2007. "An Anatomy of China's Export Growth." Paper prepared for Global Implications of China's Trade, Investment and Growth Conference, International Monetary Fund Research Department, April 6, 2007.

Amurgo-Pacheco, A., and D. Pierola. 2007. "Patterns of Export Diversification in Developing Countries: Intensive and Extensive Margins." Graduate Institute of International Studies, Geneva.

Arnold, Jens Matthias, Beata Smarzyńska Javorčik, and Aaditya Mattoo. 2007. "The Productivity Effects of Services Liberalization: Evidence from the Czech Republic." Policy Research Working Paper 4109, World Bank, Washington, DC.

Balistreri, E., T. Rutherford, and D. Tarr. 2008. "Modelling Services Liberalization: The Case of Kenya." Policy Research Working Paper 4544, World Bank, Washington, DC.

Bebczuk, Ricardo N., and N. Daniel Berrettoni. 2006. "Explaining Export Diversification: An Empirical Analysis." Universidad Nacional de La Plata, Argentina.

Ben Hammouda, Hakim, Stephen N. Karingi, Angelica E. Njuguna, and Mustapha Sadni Jallab. 2008. "Growth, Productivity and Diversification in Africa." United Nations Economic Commission for Africa, Addis Ababa.

Bernard, Andrew B., Stephen J. Redding, and Peter K. Schott. 2006. "Multi-Product Firms and Trade Liberalization." Tuck School of Business Working Paper 2008–44, Dartmouth College, Hanover, NH.

Besedes, T., and T. Prusa. 2007. "The Role of Extensive and Intensive Margins and Export Growth." NBER Working Paper 13628, National Bureau of Economic Research, Cambridge, MA.

Borchert. Ingo. 2007. "Preferential Trade Liberalization and the Path-Dependent Expansion of Exports." Discussion Paper 2007–06, University of St. Gallen, Department of Economics, St. Gallen, Switzerland.

Cadot, Olivier. 2004. "Poor Energy Infrastructure Hobbles Export Diversification." *Economic Report on Africa, 2004*, ch. 4. Addis Ababa: United Nations Economic Commission for Africa.

Cadot, Olivier, Celine Carrère, and Vanessa Strauss-Kahn. 2008. "Export Diversification: What's behind the Hump?" CEPR Discussion Paper DP6590, Centre for Economic Policy Research, London.

Chandra, Vandana, Jessica Boccardo, and Israel Osorio. 2008. "A Technological Capability Story behind Exports of Fish Fillet and iPods." Poverty Reduction and Economic Management Network Working Paper, World Bank, Washington, DC.

Collier, Paul, and A. Hoffler. 2002. "Greed and Grievance in Civil Wars." Working Paper 2002–01, Centre for the Study of African Economies, Oxford University, Oxford.

de Ferranti, David, Guillermo E. Perry, Francisco H. G. Ferreira, and Michael Walton. 2004. *Inequality in Latin America: Breaking with History?* Washington, DC: World Bank.

de Ferranti, David, Guillermo E. Perry, Daniel Lederman, and William F. Maloney. 2002. *From Natural Resources to the Knowledge Economy.* Washington, DC: World Bank.

Dihel, Nora, Felix Eschenbach, and Ben Shepherd. 2006. "South-South Services Trade." Trade Policy Working Paper 39, Organisation for Economic Co-operation and Development, Paris.

Din, M. 1994. "Export Processing Zones and Backward Linkages." *Journal of Development Economics* 43 (2): 369–85.

Easterly, W., and A. Kraay. 2000. "Small States, Small Problems? Income, Growth, and Volatility in Small States." *World Development* 28 (11): 2013–27.

Eaton, Jonathan, Robert Dekle, and Samuel Kortum. 2007."Unbalanced Trade." NBER Working Paper 13035, National Bureau of Economic Research, Cambridge, MA.

Evenett, Simon, and Anthony Venables. 2002. "Export Growth by Developing Economies: Market Entry and Bilateral Trade." Working paper, St. Gallen University, Berne.

Feenstra, Robert, and Hiau Loo Kee. 2004. "Export Variety and Country Productivity." Policy Research Working Paper 3412, World Bank, Washington, DC.

FIAS (Foreign Investment Advisory Services). 2008. *Free Zones: Performance, Lessons Learned and Implications for Zone Development*. Washington, DC: World Bank.

Fink, Carsten, Aaditya Mattoo, and I. Cristina Neagu. 2001. "Trade in International Maritime Services: How Much Does Policy Matter?" *World Bank Economic Review* 16 (1): 81–108.

Gabriele, Alberto. 2006. "Exports of Services, Exports of Goods, and Economic Growth in Developing Countries." *Journal of Economic Integration* 21 (2): 294–317.

Ghosh, Atish R., and Jonathan Ostry. 1994. "Export Instability and the External Balance in Developing Countries." Working Paper 94/8, International Monetary Fund, Washington, DC.

Greenaway, David, and Richard Kneller. 2007. "Firm Heterogeneity, Exporting and Foreign Direct Investment." *Economic Journal* 117 (517): F134–61.

Haddad, M. 2007. "Trade Integration in East Asia: The Role of China and Production Networks." Policy Research Working Paper 4160, World Bank, Washington, DC.

Hasan, M. Aynul, and Hirohito Toda. 2004. "Export Diversification and Economic Growth: The Experience of Selected Least Developed Countries." ST/ESCAP/2314, United Nations Economic and Social Commission for Asia and the Pacific, Bangkok.

Hausmann, Ricardo, Jason Hwang, and Dani Rodrik. 2006. "What You Export Matters." CEPR Discussion Paper 5444, Centre for Economic Policy and Research, London.

Hausmann, Ricardo, and Dani Rodrik. 2003. "Economic Development as Self-discovery." *Journal of Development Economics* 72: 603–33.

Herzer, Dierk, and Felicitas Nowak-Lehnmann. 2006. "What Does Export Diversification Do for Growth? An Econometric Analysis." *Applied Economics* 38: 1825–38.

Hoekman, B., and A. Mattoo. 2008. "Services Trade and Growth." Policy Research Working Paper 4461, World Bank, Washington, DC.

Hoff, Karla. 1997. "Bayesian Learning in an Infant Industry Model." *Journal of International Economics* 43: 409–36.

Hogan, Paul, Donald Keesing, and Andrew Singer. 1992. *The Role of Support Services in Expanding Manufactured Exports in Developing Countries*. Washington, DC: Economic Development Institute, World Bank.

Imbs, Jean, and Bernard Wacziarg. 2003. "Stages of Diversification." *American Economic Review* 93 (1): 63–86.

Jansen, Marion. 2004. "Income Volatility in Small and Developing Economies: Export Concentration Matters." Discussion Paper 3, World Trade Organization, Geneva.

Jayanthakumaran, K. 2003. "Benefit-Cost Appraisals of Export Processing Zones: A Survey of the Literature." *Development Policy Review* (Overseas Development Institute) 21 (1): 51–65.

Jensen, J., T. Rutherford, and D. Tarr. 2007. "The Impact of Liberalization Barriers to Foreign Direct Investment in Services: The Case of Russian Accession to the World Trade Organization." *Review of Development Economics* 11 (3): 482–506.

Johansson, H., and L. Nilsson. 1997. "Export Processing Zones as Catalysts." *World Development* 25 (12): 2115–28.

Konan, Denise Eby, and Keith E. Maskus. 2006. "Quantifying the Impact of Services Liberalization in a Developing Country." *Journal of Development Economics* 81 (1): 142–62.

Kox, H., and H. K. Nordås. 2007. "Services Trade and Domestic Regulation." Trade Policy Working Paper 49, Organisation for Economic Co-operation and Development, Paris.

Lederman, D., and W. F. Maloney. 2007. *Natural Resources: Neither Curse Nor Destiny*. Stanford: Stanford University Press.

Litwack, J., and Y. Qian. 1998. "Balanced or Unbalanced Development: Special Economic Zones as Catalysts for Transition." *Journal of Comparative Economics* 26 (10): 1–25.

Loayza, Norman, and Caludio E. Raddatz. 2007. "The Structural Determinants of External Vulnerability." *World Bank Economic Review* 21 (3): 359–87.

Lutz, Matthias, and H. W. Singer. 1994. "The Link between Increased Trade Openness and the Terms of Trade: An Empirical Investigation." *World Development* 22 (11): 1697–1709.

Madani, D. 1999. "A Review of the Role and Impact of Export Processing Zones." Policy Research Paper 2238, World Bank, Washington, DC.

Mattoo, A., and L. Payton. 2007. *Services Trade and Development: The Experience of Zambia*. Basingstoke, U.K.: Palgrave.

Minondo, Asier. 2007. "Exports' Quality-Adjusted Productivity and Economic Growth." Universidad de Deusto-ESTE, San Sebastian, Spain.

Nielson, Julia, and Daria Taglioni. 2004. "Services Trade Liberalisation: Identifying Opportunities and Gains." Trade Policy Working Paper 1, Organisation for Economic Co-operation and Development, Paris.

Pham, C., and W. Martin. 2007. "Extensive and Intensive Margin Growth and Developing Country Exports." Working paper, Development Research Group, World Bank, Washington, DC.

Pilat, Dirk, and Anita Wölfl. 2005. "Measuring the Interaction between Manufacturing and Services. Science, Technology, and Industry." Working Paper 2005/5, Organisation for Economic Co-operation and Development, Paris.

Porter, Michael E. 1990. *The Competitive Advantage of Nations.* New York: Simon and Schuster.

Prebisch, Raul. 1950. *The Economic Development of Latin America and Its Principal Problems.* New York: United Nations.

Pritchett, Lance, J. Isham, M. Woolcock, and G. Busby. 2002. "The Varieties of Rentier Experience: How Natural Resource Export Structures Affect the Political Economy of Economic Growth." Von Hugh Institute Working Paper 2002–05, Cambridge University, Cambridge, U.K.

Rauch, J. 1999. "Networks versus Markets in International Trade." *Journal of International Economics* 48: 7–35.

Rauch, J., and J. Watson. 2003. "Starting Small in an Unfamiliar Environment." *International Journal of Industrial Organization* 21: 1021–42.

Roberts, Mark J., and James R. Tybout. 1997. "The Decision to Export in Colombia: An Empirical Model of Entry with Sunk Costs." *American Economic Review* 87 (4): 545–64.

Rodrik, Dani. 2004. "Industrial Policy for the 21st Century." Paper prepared for the United Nations Industrial Development Organization, Geneva, September.

———. 2006. "What's So Special about China's Exports," NBER Working Paper 11947, National Bureau of Economic Research, Cambridge, MA.

———. 2007. "Normalizing Industrial Policy." Paper prepared for Commission on Growth and Development, New Haven, CT, September.

UNECA (United Nations Economic Commission for Africa). 2007. *Economic Report on Africa*. Addis Ababa.

Van Biesebroeck, Johannes. 2003. "Exporting Raises Productivity in Sub-Saharan African Manufacturing Plants." NBER Working Paper 10020, National Bureau of Economic Research. Cambridge, MA.

Warr, P. G. 1989. "Export Processing Zones: The Economics of Enclave Manufacturing." *World Bank Research Observer* 4 (1): 65–88.

World Bank. 1998. *World Development Report on the Knowledge Economy.* New York: Oxford University Press.

World Trade Organization. 2006. *International Trade Statistics 2005.* Geneva.

Xu, B. 2006. "Measuring the Technology Content of China's Exports." China Europe Business School, Shanghai.

PART I

DOES DIVERSIFICATION MATTER?

Chapters 2–6 explore the link between export diversification and growth in developing countries (with empirical work on Latin America and more general, cross-country analysis) and the role of export diversification in reducing income volatility.

CHAPTER 2

TRADE STRUCTURE AND GROWTH

Daniel Lederman and William F. Maloney

Are countries that are dependent on exports of a few natural resources condemned by their trade structure to experience a lower economic growth rate? And if so, is it exporting natural resources per se that tends to slow growth or is it the countries' dependency on only a few exports? The short answer to the first question is yes: regardless of the econometric technique employed, we find that trade structure is an important determinant of growth rates. However, econometric tests of the impact of natural resource specialization on growth indicate that other factors besides trade structure can offset—or compound—the effects of trade structure. These independent effects are most likely to work through productivity changes.

It is important to distinguish the growth effects of exporting natural resources from the effects of reliance on only a few products. Concentration of export revenues reduces growth by hampering productivity, and it is this overreliance on a few products, rather than natural resources per se, that drives Sachs and Vial's (2001) finding of a negative impact of natural resource exports on total exports. In sum, we find no evidence of a resource curse using any of these three measures of resource abundance.

This chapter summarizes an extensive investigation into the effects of natural resource dependence on growth (Lederman and Maloney 2007). We first present a brief review of the literature and then the results of several econometric tests in an effort to sort out several complex relationships. A final section draws some policy implications.

NATURAL RESOURCE ABUNDANCE AND GROWTH

Numerous channels have been suggested to explain why an abundance of natural resources may have a detrimental impact on growth. First, natural resources may be associated with lower accumulation of human and physical capital, lower productivity growth, and lower spillovers. However, Martin and Mitra (2001) find total factor productivity growth to be higher in agriculture than in manufactures in a large sample of advanced and developing countries, while natural resource sectors were found to be dynamic and knowledge-intensive industries in some countries (see Irwin [2000] and Wright and Czeelusta [2007] for mining in the United States, and Blomstrom and Kokko [2007] for forestry in Scandinavia).

Second, Prebisch (1959), among others, popularized the idea that the terms of trade of natural resource exporters would experience a secular decline over time relative to those of exporters of manufactures. However, Cuddington, Ludema, and Jayasuriya (2007) find they cannot reject the hypothesis that commodity prices have followed a random walk across the 20th century, with a single break in 1929.

Other channels posit that high export concentration may lead to higher export price volatility and hence greater macroeconomic volatility; that the rents associated with resource extraction may lead to institutional failures (Easterly and Levine 2002); and that imperfect capital markets may allow countries experiencing commodity price booms to overborrow, eventually requiring policies that restrict growth when credit dries up in the inevitable downturn.

There is as yet limited consensus on the appropriate empirical proxy for measuring natural resource abundance. Leamer (1984) argues that standard Heckscher-Ohlin trade theory dictates that the appropriate measure is net exports of resources per worker. Although this measure has been the basis for extensive research on the determinants of trade patterns (for example, Trefler 1995; Antweiler and Trefler 2002; Estevadeordal and Taylor 2002), to date there has been essentially no empirical work testing its impact on growth.[1] A simple correlation shows no obvious relationship between the Leamer measure and growth.

The best-known formal empirical tests for the resource curse are found in the work of Sachs and Warner (1995a, 1995b, 1997, 1999, 2001), who employ natural resources exports as a share of GDP (gross domestic product) as their proxy. They consistently find a negative correlation with growth, much to the alarm of many resource-abundant countries.[2] Sachs and Warner suggest that this variable leads to counterintuitive results in some cases. Because of its substantial reexports of raw materials, Singapore, for example, appears very resource abundant. Because this gross measure is clearly not capturing the country's true factor endowments, Sachs and Warner replaced the values of Singapore and Trinidad and Tobago with net resource exports as a share of GDP. This measure, in fact, approximates Leamer's, and it is not clear why net values should be used only for these two cases. Numerous countries in Asia and Latin America have a large presence of export processing zones that would, using the gross measurer, overstate their abundance in manufacturing-related factors. This variable also shows substantial volatility over time, reflecting terms-of-trade movements, and hence the average for the period is probably a better measure than the initial period value that Sachs and Warner used in several of their papers.

Finally, in an effort using more disaggregated data, Stijns (2005) finds no correlation of fuel and mineral reserves on growth between 1970 and 1989. This confirms earlier work by Davis (1995), who found that mineral-dependent economies, defined by a high share of minerals in exports and GDP, did well relative to other countries across the 1970s and 1980s.

EXPORT CONCENTRATION AND GROWTH

Dependence on a single export, whether it is copper in Chile or potentially microchips in Costa Rica, can leave a country vulnerable to sharp declines in terms of trade. The presence of a single, very visible export may also give rise to a variety of political economy effects that are deleterious to growth. On the other hand, specialization is often associated with scale economies and hence higher productivity.

We employ two measures to capture different dimensions of concentration. First, we construct a Herfindahl index using export data disaggregated at the 4-digit level of the Standard Industrial Trade Classification (SITC). The index ranges from zero to one, and increases with concentration. This index is widely used in studies that focus on general indicators of economic concentration (for example, Antweiler and Trefler 2002).

Second, we employ the share of natural resource exports in total exports. This was used by Sachs and Vial (2001), again, as a measure of resource abundance, and was found to have a very robustly negative relationship to growth in a panel specification in differences. Again, we would argue that this measure has intrinsic interest, but as a specific measure of concentration of exports in one particular industry. While a simple correlation shows a negative relationship between this index and growth, it also shows a significant reranking of countries compared with the previous resource measures. Malawi, Nicaragua, Papua New Guinea, and Togo, among others, now appear as high-value cases, while Finland and Singapore fall among the lower-value cases.

ESTIMATION TECHNIQUES

Most of the work discussed above—and in fact much of the growth literature until recently—has been based on an estimation using per capita GDP growth as the dependent variable, and several independent variables—income per capita at the beginning of the period, a set of conditioning variables, and the trade value of interest. Moreover, most of these estimations have used cross-sectional data that lack any time dimension, although the drawbacks are well known.[3] As Levine and Renelt (1992) first pointed out in the growth context, cross-country growth regressions are sensitive to the variables included in the specification. Further, substantial bias may be induced by the correlation of unobserved country-specific factors and the variables of interest. Caselli, Esquivel, and Lefort (1996), for instance, pointed out that the difference in level of income with respect to the highest level of income in the sample of countries (that is, the level to which the other countries are converging) acts as a proxy for country-specific effects in cross-sectional regressions, and thus the resulting estimates are inconsistent. Reporting results closer to those in this chapter, Manzano and Rigobón (2007) found in a 1980–90 cross-section that Sachs-Warner's negative correlation of natural resources with growth disappears when they control for the initial ratio of foreign debt to GDP.

Cross-sectional regressions clearly suffer from endogeneity problems as well. In the growth context, Knight, Loayza, and Villanueva (1993) point out that, by construction, the initial level of income is correlated with the growth variable. However, the problem is much larger, as Caselli, Esquivel, and Lefort (1996) note, extending (as is often the case in macroeconomic studies) to the interdependence of virtually all of the relevant growth-related variables. Other papers on economic growth attempting to deal with both unobserved country-specific effects and endogenous explanatory variables include Easterly, Loayza, and Montiel (1997); Levine, Loayza, and Beck (2000); and Bond, Hoeffler, and Temple (2001).

Panel data (that is, the inclusion of data on many countries over time) offer a potential solution to the endogeneity problem through the use of lagged values as instruments for endogenous variables. The issue of unobserved country-specific effects can also be addressed, although the standard fixed or variable effects estimators are not consistent in the current context, where we implicitly include a lagged dependent variable—the initial level of GDP per capita. That is, regressions using panel data typically include a dummy variable for each country as independent variables, to capture the contribution of effects specific to each country on the dependent variable. However, in these estimations the lagged dependent variable is related to these dummy variables, biasing the coefficient estimates. Following Anderson and Hsiao (1982), Arellano and Bond (1991), and Caselli, Esquivel, and Lefort (1996) in the growth literature, we therefore estimate the relationship between the independent variables and growth in terms of the first difference over time. This process raises other econometric issues that we resolve as explained in the unabridged version of this chapter (Lederman and Maloney 2007).

ESTIMATION

The empirical strategy is to introduce the trade variable of interest first to a set of core conditioning variables and then to progressively add new variables, many now standard in the literature, to examine both robustness and suggestive channels of influence of the trade variable of interest. The basic conditioning set includes initial income of the period to capture standard convergence effects. Because we focus on trade structure and not openness, we include a policy-based index of openness provided by Sachs and Warner (1995a). Although the literature has been highly critical of virtually all such measures of openness (see, for example, Pritchett 1996 and Rodriguez and Rodrik 2000), to ensure consistency with the natural resource literature of Sachs and Warner, we use their measure. Nevertheless, it is worth pointing out that Wacziarg (2001) shows that the estimated effects of the trade-to-GDP ratio are virtually identical when the ratio is instrumented by the Sachs-Warner index as when it is instrumented by other policy indicators such as average tariffs and the non-tariff-barrier-coverage ratio.

The second conditioning set includes variables related to the accumulation of physical and human capital: the average ratio of investment to GDP and log of years of schooling of the adult population, which is the preferred measure of the stock of human capital (see, for example, Barro 2001). The third set adds growth in the terms of trade as a possible channel through which natural resource variables may affect growth. Finally, as a measure of macroeconomic stability of particular importance to the trade sector, we include the standard deviation of the real effective exchange rate over the period, calculated from monthly data. As numerous authors (see, for example, Servén 1998) suggest, macroeconomic volatility reduces investment and thus growth. However, other studies show that macroeconomic factors that are likely to be associated with real exchange rate volatility, such as episodes of high inflation, are related to both the level of investment and the rate of productivity growth (for example, Fischer 1993 and Bruno and Easterly 1998). This may also prove a channel through which our trade variables work. Time dummies are included in all of the regressions that rely on panel data.

The core data set is that of Heston and Summers (1991) updated to 2000. The estimation covers panels of five-year periods from 1980 to 1999 (one observation is lost to instruments). Summary statistics for all variables and the list of countries can be found in the full version of this chapter (Lederman and Maloney 2007). Table 2.1 (cross-sectional and panel results) reports in the first column the control variables used for the regression. Each of the subsequent columns reports the coefficient and significant level for the trade value indicated in the heading. For both sets of results (under the section labeled "Additional controls"), we combine the variables of interest along with the full conditioning set as tests of possible channels through which the principal variable of interest works. For instance, we add the export Herfindahl to the regression as a test of whether whatever effect resource abundance has on growth may work through export concentration.

In both the OLS (ordinary least squares) and panel exercises, the key conditioning variables either entered with the expected sign or were statistically insignificant (results available on request). For instance, in most specifications, initial GDP per capita enters negatively and significantly; the stock of human capital enters positively and significantly; and the Sachs-Warner measure of openness enters positively and significantly.

Table 2.1 Estimated Effect of Trade Structure on Growth, 1980–99

	Natural resource dependence						Export concentration						Intraindustry trade		
													Grubel-Lloyd index		
	Net NRX/labor force			NRX/GDP			Export Herfindahl			NRX/total exports			Cross-sectional data		
Variable		Sargan	Serial correlation		Sargan	Serial correlation		Sargan	Serial correlation		Sargan	Serial correlation		Sargan	Serial correlation
Cross-sectional data															
Basic conditioning	1.33	0.20	0.27	0.94***	0.48	0.49	–3.42	0.38	0.35	–0.12	0.17	0.34	2.37	0.47	0.42
+	(1.52)			(3.57)			(–1.18)			(–0.82)			(0.71)		
Capital accumulation	2.87*	0.39	0.53	0.68**	0.29	0.83	–11.40***	0.31	0.75	–0.57***	0.32	0.36	8.64**	0.35	0.80
+	(1.93)			(2.49)			(–3.04)			(–2.67)			(2.28)		
Growth of terms of trade	3.50**	0.45	0.48	0.65**	0.40	0.71	–9.43**	0.51	0.76	–0.36**	0.37	0.60	8.29**	0.50	0.92
+	(2.10)			(2.36)			(–2.48)			(–2.51)			(2.63)		
Macro stability	2.66*	0.50	0.56	0.69**	0.56	0.71	–8.79**	0.52	0.72	–0.34**	0.31	0.57	8.21**	0.54	0.85
	(1.83)			(2.62)			(–2.30)			(–2.08)			(2.63)		
Additional controls															
NRX/GDP							–10.32***	0.58	0.70				7.80**	0.49	0.81
							(–2.79)						(2.50)		
Leamer index							–9.70***	0.53	0.63				8.28**	0.62	0.94
							(–2.78)						(2.61)		
Export Herfindahl	3.05**	0.42	0.61	0.65**	0.35	0.62				–0.24	0.21	0.55	6.12*	0.42	0.81
	(2.09)			(2.11)						(–1.53)			(1.75)		
NRX/total exports							–8.92**	0.53	0.79				6.05**	0.41	0.74
							(–2.12)						(2.19)		

(Table continues on the following page)

Table 2.1 (continued)

	Natural resource dependence						Export concentration						Intraindustry trade		
													Grubel-Lloyd index		
	Net NRX/labor force			NRX/GDP			Export Herfindahl			NRX/total exports			Cross-sectional data		
Variable		Sargan	Serial correlation		Sargan	Serial correlation		Sargan	Serial correlation		Sargan	Serial correlation		Sargan	Serial correlation
Intraindustry trade	4.46**	0.33	0.71	0.64**	0.52	0.79	–8.93**	0.49	0.73	–0.21	0.29	0.77			
	(2.40)			(2.36)			(–2.02)			(–0.88)					
IIT + export Herfindahl	4.41**	0.32	0.66	0.62**	0.36	0.68				–0.18	0.28	0.80			
	(2.31)			(2.02)						(–0.85)					
Panel data (system estimates)															
Basic conditioning	1.33	0.20	0.27	0.94***	0.48	0.49	–4.75*	0.48	0.39	–0.29***	0.33	0.30	2.37	0.47	0.42
+	(1.52)			(3.57)			(–1.76)			(–2.67)			(0.71)		
Capital accumulation	2.87*	0.39	0.53	0.68**	0.29	0.83	–11.04***	0.36	0.72	–0.53***	0.26	0.34	8.64**	0.35	0.80
+	(1.93)			(2.49)			(–2.78)			(–4.27)			(2.28)		
Growth of terms of trade	3.50**	0.45	0.48	0.65**	0.40	0.71	–8.98**	0.52	0.70	–0.45***	0.34	0.50	8.29**	0.50	0.92
+	(2.10)			(2.36)			(–2.29)			(–3.51)			(2.63)		
Macro stability	2.66*	0.50	0.56	0.69**	0.56	0.71	–8.71**	0.51	0.71	–0.41***	0.34	0.48	8.21**	0.54	0.85
	(1.83)			(2.62)			(–2.20)			(–2.93)			(2.63)		

Additional controls												
NRX/GDP							−10.28***	0.50	0.70				7.80**	0.49	0.81
							(−2.70)						(2.50)		
Leamer index							−9.81**	0.47	0.63				8.28**	0.62	0.94
							(−2.18)						(2.61)		
Export Herfindahl	3.05**	0.42	0.61	0.65**	0.35	0.62				−0.36***	0.35	0.47	6.12*	0.42	0.81
	(2.09)			(2.11)						(−2.77)			(1.75)		
NRX/total exports							−7.84*	0.43	0.54				6.05**	0.41	0.74
							(−1.76)						(2.19)		
Intraindustry trade	4.46**	0.33	0.71	0.64**	0.52	0.79	−1.12	0.47	0.72	−0.35**	0.31	0.61			
	(2.40)			(2.36)			(−1.61)			(−2.20)					
IIT + export Herfindahl	4.41**	0.32	0.66	0.62**	0.36	0.68				−0.30*	0.35	0.58			
	(2.31)			(2.02)						(−1.94)					

Source: Authors' estimations.

Note: GDP = gross domestic product; IIT = intraindustry trade; NRX = natural resources exports. The dependent variable is the GDP per capita growth rate. The basic conditioning set includes the log of initial income of the period and a measure of openness (Sachs and Warner 1995a). Capital accumulation includes the average ratio of investment/GDP and the log of the years of schooling. Growth of terms of trade refers to the ratio of the export price index to the import price index over the period. Macroeconomic stability includes the standard deviation of the real exchange rate over the period. Number of countries = 65; number of observations = 143; *t* statistic in parentheses.

a. For Net NRX/labor force, NRX/GDP, and NRX/total exports, the coefficients are multiplied by 1,000.

b. For Export Herfindahl and the Grubel-Lloyd index, the coefficients are multiplied by 100.

* Significant at the 10 percent level. ** Significant at the 5 percent level. *** Significant at the 1 percent level.

FINDINGS

The estimates produced the following findings.

Resource Abundance Seems Not to Influence Growth

In the cross-section results, the Leamer measure of natural resource abundance is never significant until the introduction of a variable for intraindustry trade and the Herfindahl concentration index in the final exercise, when it shows a positive impact on growth at the 10 percent level. The panel results are dramatically different, suggesting the presence of the omitted variables and simultaneity biases discussed earlier. Net natural resource exports appear positively (although not quite significantly at the 10 percent level) related to growth with the core conditioning variables. However, including the capital accumulation variable increases the significance and magnitude somewhat, suggesting that high levels of natural resources could have some depressing effect on accumulation of human and physical capital. The terms-of-trade variable similarly suggests a depressing effect of volatility on growth and makes natural resource abundance significant at the 5 percent level. Macroeconomic stability seems to have a slight effect in the opposite direction.

But Investment, Terms of Trade, and Macroeconomic Stability Are Important

Taken together, capital accumulation, terms of trade, and macroeconomic stability appear to be channels through which resource abundance may negatively affect growth. Consistent with the cross-sectional results, a large increase in the significance of the natural resource export variable appears when the Herfindahl measure of export concentration is added, suggesting that resource-abundant countries may have more concentrated export structures. Thus, the question becomes why, after controlling for capital accumulation, terms of trade, macroeconomic stability, and export concentration, resource abundance has a positive impact on growth. One possibility is through higher rates of productivity growth, which would be consistent with the findings of Martin and Mitra (2001).

The results are broadly similar with the Sachs and Warner proxy (resource exports over GDP). Resources never appear significantly with any conditioning variables in the cross-section results. This is not attributable to the shifting of the sample period forward 10 years. When we replace Singapore's value with *net* exports, as they do, we again find Sachs and Warner's negative and significant impact of resources on GDP. Simply put, whatever the conceptual appeal of this measure, used in its unadjusted form in cross-section, it shows no impact on GDP.[4]

This conclusion changes in the panel regressions. Natural resource exports show a positive, significant (at the 1 percent level) relationship with growth, given the basic conditioning variables. Adding the capital accumulation variable makes their impact less positive and significant at the 10 percent level. This finding may suggest some stimulative impact of resource exports on physical and human capital accumulation. Controlling for terms-of-trade variations, macroeconomic stability, export concentration, and degree of intraindustry trade variables leads to no further changes, suggesting that these are not very important channels.

Reliance on Only a Few Exports Has Greater Negative Consequences for Growth

The cross-section and panel results are more consistent for both measures of export concentration. With the basic conditioning variables, the coefficient on the Herfindahl concentration index is of the same order of magnitude, and negative, in both regressions at the 10 percent level. Adding the capital accumulation variables makes the coefficient much more negative, so that the index of concentration is significant at the 1 percent level in both cases. In cross-section, the addition of new conditioning variables has a limited effect on the coefficient value or significance.

The panel findings, however, suggest a significant positive impact of export concentration on capital accumulation. There is some negative impact of terms-of-trade and macroeconomic stability of lower magnitude, suggesting an important channel through volatility as well. Among the additional controls, the introduction of natural resources exports divided by GDP makes the Herfindahl coefficient even more negative, suggesting that, in fact, natural resource abundance partly offsets the negative impact of concentration.

The natural-resources-exports-over-total-exports variable shows less similarity between the two estimation techniques. In cross-section, it is uniformly negative and appears insensitive to the addition of any of the controls or concentration measures. This would seem to suggest some intrinsic effect of a high natural resource concentration in exports that is not accounted for by any of the usual channels. Again, however, the panel results cast some doubt on this conclusion. The variable enters negatively and insignificantly with the basic conditioning variables. The introduction of capital accumulation, however, makes the coefficient strongly significant and negative, suggesting that, again, concentration has a positive effect on capital accumulation. The introduction of terms-of-trade volatility, again, has a modest effect of reducing, again, the size of the coefficient, suggesting a deleterious effect on growth. The influence of natural resource exports over exports weakens with the introduction of the additional controls. Introduction of the export Herfindahl makes the coefficient insignificant, suggesting that it is concentration, and not resources itself, that drives the results.

In sum, to the degree that there is any evidence of a negative impact of natural resources on growth, it is not happening through productivity growth as Sachs and Warner (1995b, 1999), among others, argue. Further, the only natural resource–related variable that enters with a significant and negative sign, natural resources as a fraction of exports, appears to be the result of its acting as a proxy for export concentration and not natural resources per se.

CONCLUSIONS AND POLICY IMPLICATIONS

This chapter suggests that trade variables related to natural resource abundance and export concentration do affect growth. But many of its findings are sharply at odds with some of the conventional wisdom.

In the case of natural resources, Sachs and Warner's assertion that resource abundance adversely affects growth is found not to be robust to a variety of measures of resource abundance or estimation technique. The measure with the strongest theoretical foundation, Leamer's net natural resource exports per worker, is slightly significant in one specification in the cross-section regressions, and strongly significant in the systems panel estimator, but always *positive*. This remains the case after controlling for several channels through which natural resources have been postulated to affect growth. Strikingly, broadly similar findings emerge using Sachs and Warner's measure of resource exports over GDP, once enforcing a consistent processing of the data: there is no evidence in cross-section of a negative impact of this variable on growth, and in the panel systems estimator, it always enters positively, if not always significantly. At the very least, we should abandon the stylized fact that natural resource abundance is somehow bad for growth and even perhaps consider a research agenda on the channels through which it may have a positive effect, possibly through inducing higher productivity growth.

Export concentration, measured both as a Herfindahl index and as natural resource exports as a share of exports, has a negative effect that is extremely robust in cross-section but less so in the panel regressions. The Herfindahl remains significant and negative with most control sets. However, the only specifications for which the resource export measure remains significant are poorly specified, and the result disappears when the Herfindahl measure of overall concentration is included. *Arguably, it is concentration per se, and not natural resources in particular, that is negatively correlated with growth.*

If indeed, there is no "resource curse," but there is a curse of export concentration, the implication is that policy makers should strive to provide a policy framework conducive to product and market diversification—but not necessarily one that promotes, through subsidies and incentives, diversification away from natural resource areas into manufactures.

NOTES

1. Assuming identical preferences, a country will show positive net exports of resource-intensive goods if its share of productivity-adjusted world endowments exceeds its share of world consumption. Usually, the net exports are then measured with respect to the quantity of other factors of production, such as the labor force. It is worth mentioning that the cited references show that the Heckscher-Ohlin model of factor endowments performs relatively well for natural resources net exports, but it performs less well for manufactures. The current debate in the trade literature revolves around the question of how the model might be amended (by considering, for example, technological differences across countries or economies of scale) to help predict better the observed patterns of net exports across countries. There is, however, no debate about the use of net exports as a proxy for revealed comparative advantage in this literature.
2. The other papers by Sachs and Warner (1997, 1999, 2001) contain the basic results of 1995b, at times using a slightly longer time span (1965–90 instead of 1970–89) and often including additional time-invariant explanatory variables such as dummies identifying tropical and landlocked countries, plus some additional social variables.

3. More recently, distinguished economists have raised serious concerns about the general practice of testing a plethora of hypotheses about economic growth by relying exclusively on cross-country growth regressions. See, for example, Solow (2001).
4. With the Sachs and Warner 1997 data, our sample of countries yields their results. Hence, the difference in findings is not caused by the sample of countries.

REFERENCES

Anderson, T. W., and Cheng Hsiao. 1982. "Formulation and Estimation of Dynamic Models Using Panel Data." *Journal of Econometrics* 18: 47–82.

Antweiler, Werner, and Daniel Trefler. 2002. "Increasing Returns and All That: A View from Trade." *American Economic Review* 92 (1): 93–119.

Arellano, Manuel, and Stephen Bond. 1991. "Some Tests of Specification for Panel Data: Montecarlo Evidence and an Application to Employment Equations." *Review of Economic Studies* 58 (2): 277–97.

Barro, Robert J. 2001. "Human Capital and Growth." *American Economic Review* 91 (2): 12–17.

Blomström, Magnus, and Ari Kokko. 2007. "From Natural Resources to High-Tech Production: The Evolution of Industrial Competitiveness in Sweden and Finland." In *Natural Resources: Neither Curse nor Destiny*, ed. Daniel Lederman and William F. Maloney, 213–56. Washington, DC: World Bank and Stanford University Press.

Bond, Stephen R., Anke Hoeffler, and Jonathan Temple. 2001. "GMM Estimation of Empirical Growth Models." CEPR Discussion Paper 3048, Centre for Economic Policy Research, London.

Bruno, Michael, and William Easterly. 1998. "Inflation Crises and Long-Run Growth." *Journal of Monetary Economics* 41 (1): 3–26.

Caselli, Francesco, Gerardo Esquivel, and Fernando Lefort. 1996. "Reopening the Convergence Debate: A New Look at the Cross-Country Growth Empirics." *Journal of Economic Growth* 1 (3): 363–89.

Cuddington, John T., Rodney Ludema, and Shamila A. Jayasuriya. 2007. "Prebisch-Singer Redux." In *Natural Resources: Neither Curse nor Destiny*, ed. Daniel Lederman and William F. Maloney, 103–40. Washington, DC: World Bank and Stanford University Press.

Davis, Graham. 1995. "Learning to Love the Dutch Disease: Evidence from Mineral Economies." *World Development* 23 (10): 1765–79.

Easterly, William, and Ross Levine. 2002. "Tropics, Germs, and Crops: How Endowments Influence Economic Development." NBER Working Paper 9106, National Bureau of Economic Research, Cambridge, MA.

Easterly, William, Norman Loayza, and Peter Montiel. 1997. "Has Latin America's Post-Reform Growth Been Disappointing?" *Journal of International Economics* 43: 287–311.

Estevadeordal, Antoni, and Alan M. Taylor. 2002. "A Century of Missing Trade?" *American Economic Review* 92 (1): 383–93.

Fischer, Stanley. 1993. "The Role of Macroeconomic Factors in Growth." *Journal of Monetary Economics* 32: 485–512.

Heston, Alan, and Robert Summers. 1991 "The Penn World Table (Mark 5): An Expanded Set of International Comparisons, 1950–1988." *Quarterly Journal of Economics* 106 (2): 327–68.

Irwin, Douglas. 2000. "How Did the United States Become a Net Exporter of Manufactured Goods?" NBER Working Paper 7638, National Bureau of Economic Research, Cambridge, MA.

Knight, Malcolm, Norman Loayza, and Delano Villanueva. 1993. "Testing the Neoclassical Theory of Economic Growth: A Panel Data Approach." *IMF Staff Papers* 40: 512–41.

Leamer, Edward. 1984. *Sources of International Comparative Advantage: Theory and Evidence.* Cambridge, MA: MIT Press.

Lederman, Daniel, and William F. Maloney, eds. 2007. *Natural Resources: Neither Curse nor Destiny.* Washington, DC: World Bank and Stanford University Press.

Levine, Ross, Norman Loayza, and Thorsten Beck. 2000. "Financial Intermediation and Growth: Causality and Causes." *Journal of Monetary Economics* 46: 31–77.

Levine, Ross, and David Renelt. 1992. "A Sensitivity Analysis of Cross-Country Growth Regressions." *American Economic Review* 82 (4): 942–63.

Manzano, Ozmel, and Roberto Rigobón. 2007. "Resource Curse or Debt Overhang?" In *Natural Resources: Neither Curse nor Destiny*, ed. Daniel Lederman and William F. Maloney, 41–70. Washington, DC: World Bank and Stanford University Press.

Martin, William, and Devashish Mitra. 2001. "Productivity Growth and Convergence in Agriculture and Manufacturing." *Economic Development and Cultural Change* 49 (2): 403–22.

Prebisch, Raúl. 1959. "Commercial Policy in the Underdeveloped Countries." *American Economic Review, Papers and Proceedings* 49 (2): 251–73.

Pritchett, Lant. 1996. "Measuring Outward Orientations in LDCs: Can It Be Done?" *Journal of Development Economics* 49 (2): 307–35.

Rodríguez, Francisco, and Dani Rodrik. 2000. "Trade Policy and Economic Growth: A Skeptic's Guide to the Cross-National Evidence." In *NBER Macroeconomics Annual 2000*, ed. Ben Bernanke and Kenneth Rogoff. Cambridge, MA: MIT Press.

Sachs, Jeffrey, and Joaquín Vial. 2001. "Can Latin America Compete?" In *The Latin American Competitiveness Report, 2001–2002*, ed. J. Vial and P. Cornelius, 10–29. Cambridge, MA: Center for International Development and World Economic Forum.

Sachs, Jeffrey, and Andrew Warner. 1995a. "Economic Reform and the Process of Global Integration." *Brookings Papers on Economic Activity*, 25th Anniversary Issue, Washington, DC: Brookings Institution, 1–118.

———. 1995b. "Natural Resource Abundance and Economic Growth." Revised. NBER Working Paper 5398, National Bureau of Economic Research, Cambridge, MA.

———. 1997. "Fundamental Sources of Long-Run Growth." *American Economic Review, Papers and Proceedings* 87 (2): 184–88.

———. 1999. "The Big Push, Natural Resource Booms and Growth." *Journal of Development Economics* 59: 43–76.

———. 2001. "Natural Resources and Economic Development: The Curse of Natural Resources." *European Economic Review* 45: 827–38.

Servén, Luis. 1998. "Macroeconomic Uncertainty and Private Investment in Developing Countries: An Empirical Investigation." Policy Research Working Paper 2035, World Bank, Washington, DC.

Solow, Robert. 2001. "Applying Growth Theory across Countries." *World Bank Economic Review* 15 (2): 283–89.

Stijns, Jean-Philippe. 2005. "Natural Resource Abundance and Economic Growth Revisited." *Resources Policy* 30 (2): 107–30.

Trefler, Daniel. 1995. "The Case of the Missing Trade and Other Mysteries." *American Economic Review* 85 (5): 1029–46.

Wacziarg, Romain. 2001. "Measuring the Dynamic Gains from Trade." *World Bank Economic Review* 15: 393–430.

Wright, Gavin, and Jesse Czelusta. 2007. "Resource-Based Growth Past and Present." In *Natural Resources: Neither Curse nor Destiny*, ed. Daniel Lederman and William Maloney, 183–211. Washington, DC: World Bank and Stanford University Press.

CHAPTER 3

EXPORT DIVERSIFICATION AND ECONOMIC GROWTH

Heiko Hesse

The process of economic development is one of structural transformation where countries move from producing "poor-country goods" to "rich-country goods." A precondition for this transformation is often the existence of an elastic demand for countries' exports in world markets so that countries are able to leverage global export markets without fearing negative terms-of-trade effects. In many developing countries, domestic demand is often very low, so exports remain one of the few channels that in the longer run significantly contribute to higher rates of per capita income growth in a country. Many countries that are commodity dependent or that exhibit a narrow export basket often suffer from export instability arising from inelastic and unstable global demand; thus, export diversification is one way to alleviate these particular constraints. Another issue relates to the competitiveness of a country's exports because globalization and accelerating cross-border trade expose countries' exports to global competition. To be successful in export diversification, countries' exports need to be globally competitive so that they can take advantage of leveraging world markets.

There are two underlying questions. Why do countries diversify their exports, and does diversification benefit countries' economic growth? The following reviews the existing literature and arguments for export diversification and provides an empirical analysis of the relationship of export diversification to growth. Similar to Lederman and Maloney (2007), I provide some robust empirical evidence of a positive effect of export diversification on per capita income growth. I also introduce some nonlinearity into the dynamic growth model, a novelty in this particular growth literature. I find that the effect of export diversification on growth is potentially nonlinear, with developing countries benefiting from diversifying their exports in contrast to the most advanced countries that perform better with export specialization.

THEORY, CONCEPTS, AND COUNTRY EXAMPLES

What are the theoretical reasons for believing that export diversification is conducive to higher per capita income growth? According to structural models of economic development, countries should diversify from primary exports into manufactured exports to achieve sustainable growth (Chenery 1979; Syrquin 1989). Vertical export diversification could, according to the Prebisch-Singer thesis, reduce declining terms of trade for commodity-dependent countries.

Export instability is another reason for seeking the benefits of export diversification, which is analogous to the portfolio effect in finance. Commodity products are often subject to volatile market prices, making countries dependent on exporting these commodities vulnerable to export instability. This could discourage necessary investments in the economy by risk-averse firms, increase macroeconomic uncertainty, and cause longer-term economic growth to suffer. Export diversification could therefore help to stabilize export earnings in the longer run (Ghosh and Ostry 1994; Bleaney and Greenaway 2001).

Endogenous growth models such as Matsuyama (1992) emphasize the importance of "learning by doing" in the manufacturing sector for sustained growth. Related to export diversification, there could be knowledge spillovers from new techniques of production, new management, or marketing practices that potentially benefit other industries (Amin Gutierrez de Pineres and Ferrantino 2000). Producing an expanding set of export products can be seen as a dynamic effect of export diversification on higher per capita income growth. Relatedly, Agosin (2007) develops a model of export diversification and growth where countries below the technological frontier widen their comparative advantage by imitating and adapting existing products.

Furthermore, models in the product cycle literature (Vernon 1966; Krugman 1979; Grossman and Helpman 1991) obtain diversity of export products by the North innovating and the South predominantly imitating and exporting the products from cheap labor countries.

The empirical literature on the link between export diversification and per capita income patterns is small. Al-Marhubi (2000), in a conventional cross-sectional country growth regression, adds various measures of export concentration to the basic growth equation and finds that export diversification promotes economic growth. These findings are robust to different model specifications. Also in a cross-sectional regression, Agosin (2007) finds that export diversification has a stronger effect on per capita income growth when a country's exports grow faster. Lederman and Maloney (2007), in a dynamic cross-country panel model, also find some evidence in support of diversification-led growth. Within-country studies by Amin Gutierrez de Pineres and Ferrantino (1997a, 1997b) as well as Herzer and Nowak-Lehmann D. (2006) examine the link between export diversification and economic growth in Chile, and their findings do suggest that Chile has benefited greatly from diversifying its export base.

In a seminal paper, based on domestic production and labor data, Imbs and Wacziarg (2003) investigate the relationship between domestic sectoral concentration and per capita income patterns across countries. They find a U-shaped pattern whereby countries in their early stages of development diversify production and specialize at higher income levels. This pattern is very robust across different definitions of their sectoral concentration variable and also across different model specifications. The turning point for countries that switch from domestic diversification to specialization is fairly robust at around $9,000 per capita. This means that most developing countries are actually in the diversifying stage over the course of their development path.

Following their empirical investigation, Imbs and Wacziarg (2003) develop some theoretical arguments for countries' incentives to diversify domestically and then specialize. Reasons for economic diversification include preference-based and portfolio arguments. Under certain assumptions, Engel effects imply that with increasing income levels economic agents demand a larger diversity of goods for consumption. Acemoglu and Zilibotti (1997) develop the portfolio argument, which holds that diversification is an endogenous process and that producers invest in a wide range of risky sectors, which leads to diversification.

The theoretical reasons for specialization relate both to the Ricardian theory of trade and to agglomeration effects. Decreasing transport costs lead to a reduction in the number of domestically produced products, thus promoting specialization (Dornbusch, Fischer, and Samuelson 1977).

At the same time, the existence of demand externalities makes it profitable for producers to cluster, which might lead to sectoral concentration.

This pattern of domestic diversification and specialization also holds for countries' exports, as shown by Cabellero and Cowan (2006) and Klinger and Lederman (2006), but the turning point kicks in at a higher GDP per capita level so only advanced economies typically benefit from concentrating their exports.

A new literature by Hausmann and Rodrik (2003), Hausmann, Hwang, and Rodrik (2006), and Hausmann and Klinger (2006) analyzes the benefits of export diversification and exports in general for economic growth, both empirically and theoretically. In their framework, economic growth is not driven by comparative advantage but by countries' diversification of their investments into new activities. An essential role is played by the entrepreneurial cost-discovery process. According to the model of Hausmann and Rodrik (2003), entrepreneurs face significant cost uncertainties in the production of new goods. If they succeed in developing new goods, the gains will be socialized (information spillovers), but the losses from failure end up being private. This leads to an under-provision of investments into new activities and a suboptimal level of innovation. The bottom line, according to Hausmann and Rodrik (2003), is that the government should play an important role in industrial growth and structural transformation by promoting entrepreneurship and creating the right incentives for entrepreneurs to invest in a new range of activities.

On a related topic, discoveries about foreign demand can be important to cost discoveries (Vettas 2000). Sometimes domestic producers do not know whether there will be enough foreign demand to justify producing and exporting an existing or a new good. Only when they start exporting the product, do foreign consumers become more aware of the product and its features, possibly triggering more foreign demand. Since other domestic producers of the same product observe its failure or success, imitation is an externality that could be conducive to higher growth. Agosin (2007) and Agosin and Bravo-Ortega (2007) illustrate these demand discoveries with exports of Chilean wines. Domestic production of Chilean wines goes back to the 17th century but only since the mid-1980s have some entrepreneurs introduced better foreign-production techniques to produce wines that appealed to the tastes of foreign consumers. The discovery of this new export opportunity has made wines one of the main export products in Chile.

Hausmann, Hwang, and Rodrik (2006) develop an indicator (*EXPY*) that measures the productivity level associated with a country's export basket. They find that countries that produce high-productivity goods enjoy faster growth than countries with lower-productivity goods. The authors develop a model based on the cost-discovery process that supports their empirical findings. The key is that the transfer of resources from lower-productivity to higher-productivity goods with the presence of elastic demand for these goods in export markets generates higher economic growth: countries are what they export.

As an example, consider figure 3.1, taken from Rodrik (2005), which graphs the income content of exports of some Asian and Latin American countries. It is striking that Argentina, Brazil, and Chile are at the bottom with the lowest level of quality of their export basket relative to their income. In comparison, Hong Kong (China), Mexico, and the Republic of Korea, with China close behind, have the highest income content of exports. Even though China has a lower level of income per

Figure 3.1 Latin America and East Asia: Income Content of Exports (*EXPY*)

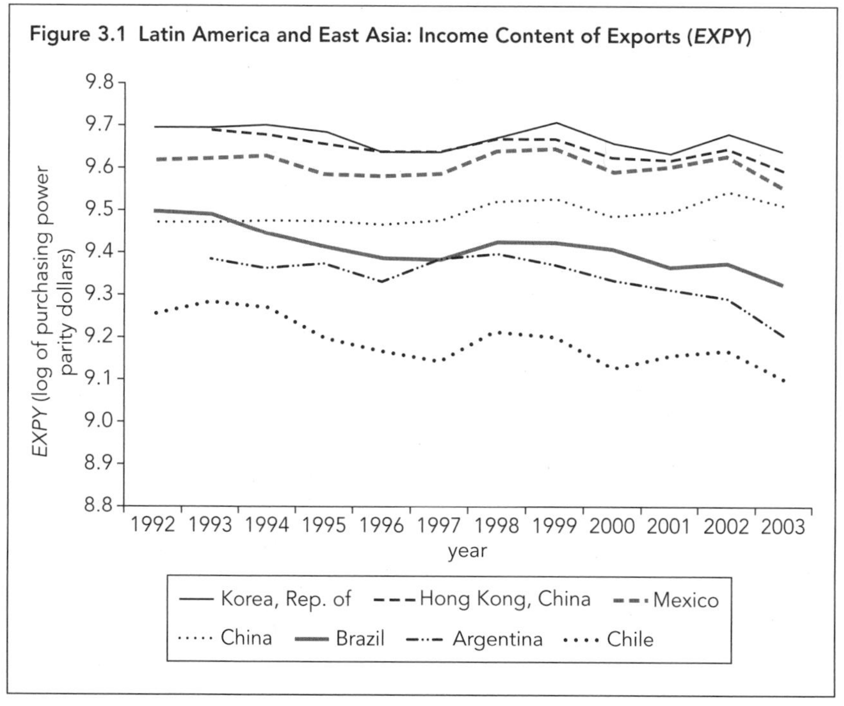

Source: Rodrik 2005.

capita than Argentina, Brazil, and Chile, its exports have a higher level of productivity. By diversifying their investments into higher productivity activities and goods, China is able to produce goods that do not correspond to their income level.

Hausmann and Klinger (2006) develop a model of structural transformation in the product space and empirically show that the speed of structural transformation depends on current export goods being located close to other goods of more sophistication and higher value. They find that the product space is very heterogeneous, and it is desirable for a country to have a high density of the product space near its productive capabilities. It is often the case in many developing countries that they have specialized in exporting certain goods but are not able to transfer those assets and skills to the production of more sophisticated goods. This might be another argument for export diversification because countries might be able to acquire skills and assets that could be relevant for goods in the nearby production space. In other words, there might be knowledge spillovers or learning by doing from export diversification (Amin Gutierrez de Pineres and Ferrantino 2000).

Another aspect is the role of innovation in export diversification. In principle, there is a distinction between inside-the-frontier (goods already produced elsewhere) and on-the-frontier innovations (patents). Klinger and Lederman (2006) investigate the relationship between innovation and export diversification and find that developing countries in the diversifying stage are mainly characterized by a higher frequency of inside-the-frontier discoveries. Conversely, along the line of the U-shaped-pattern finding of Imbs and Wazciarg (2003), more-advanced countries that are concentrating their exports are characterized by a decreasing level of inside-the-frontier discovery activities but substantially more on-the-frontier innovations. Figure 3.2 illustrates this pattern.

A new strand of literature investigates whether export growth is predominantly driven by growth at the extensive or intensive margin. Under extensive margin growth, countries export a wider set of products to existing or new geographical markets, whereas under intensive margin growth, an increase of existing products to current markets occurs. Hummels and Klenow (2005) and Pham and Martin (2007) in cross-sectional analyses find that most of the export growth is driven by growth at the extensive margin. This stands in contrast to Brenton and Newfarmer (2009, chapter 6 in this volume), whose results from panel data for 1995–2004 suggest that exporting larger quantities of existing products matters more than exporting

Figure 3.2 Diversification and Innovation

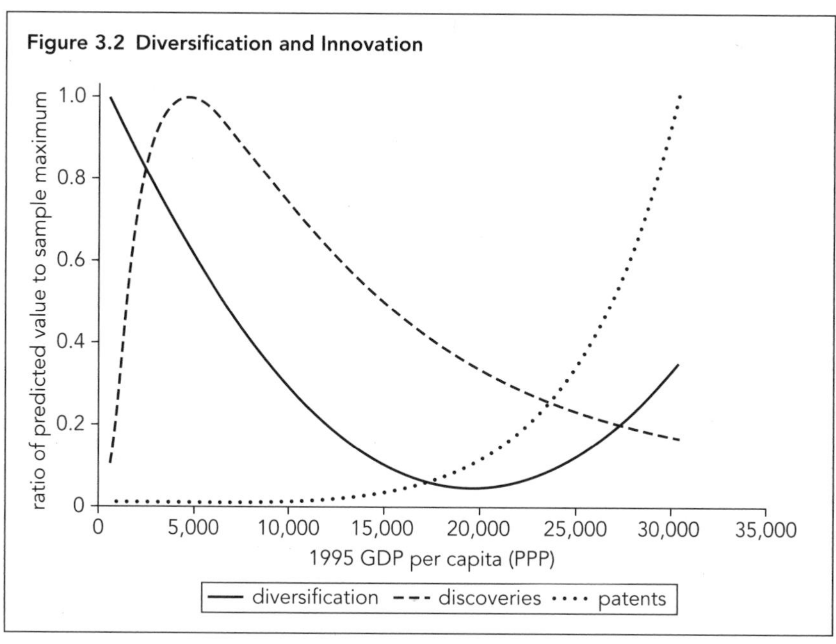

Source: Klinger and Lederman 2009, chapter 5 in this volume.

a wider set of products. They also find that exporting existing products to new geographical markets carries a higher weight in explaining export growth than discovery of new products. The conflicting findings could possibly result from different levels of disaggregation and types of regression models used (cross-sectional versus time series), so more work needs to be done for a better understanding of the contributions of extensive as well as intensive margin growth to countries' export performances.

It has often been argued that natural resource–based economies suffer from a "resource curse." Some of the reasons point toward historical declining terms of trade for primary commodities, the possible occurrence of Dutch-disease effects through an appreciating real exchange rate, or a lack of incentives within the commodity-based economy to diversify and industrialize. For instance, Sachs and Warner (2001) find a negative relationship between resource abundance and growth, while the results of Gylfason (2001) indicate an inverse relationship between resource intensity and education, which according to the author implies that natural resource–based economies might not have the incentives to invest heavily in human capital accumulation.

In recent years the perception of the resource curse has somewhat altered. Resource abundance could bring about technological progress and new knowledge (World Bank 2002), and some time series models do not find robust evidence for a resource curse (Lederman and Maloney 2007). Also, many advanced countries such as Australia, Canada, and the Scandinavian countries started out as resource-based economies but succeeded in diversifying their economies. Bonaglia and Fukasaku (2003) argue that resource-rich, low-income countries should diversify into resource-based manufacturing or processing of primary commodities instead of following the conventional path of low-skill manufacturing. For instance, both mining and forestry have developed into knowledge-intense sectors with high technological content in upstream as well as downstream activities. Similarly, the global growth of fresh food products has led to increasing vertical diversification (processing of those products) but also to horizontal diversification into closely related product groups such as cut flowers or specialty fresh vegetables for many low-income countries.

Following are a few country examples where export diversification and per capita income growth have been closely associated over some stage of their development path. Figure 3.3 shows the development of export concentration, measured by the Herfindahl index at the 4-digit level, and income per capita for Malaysia, Thailand, Chile, and Uganda during the period 1962–2000.

Both Malaysia and Thailand have seen a remarkable decline in export concentration over the past 40 years. Besides moving into manufacturing exports (such as clothing and electronics), the two countries also pursued the development of their resource-based sectors (palm oil and rubber in Malaysia and agriculture and fish in Thailand) into higher-value-added products.

Chile is often regarded as another successful example of a resource-based economy that diversified into new export activities. Many of the new export products—such as wine, salmon, fruits, and forestry products—are close to Chile's comparative advantage, especially its favorable agroecological environment, whereas manufacturing has been almost absent in Chile's export diversification (Agosin and Bravo-Ortega 2007).

Uganda is a case where export diversification has taken off only in recent years. It is landlocked and suffers from poor infrastructure connecting it to its coastal neighbors. Being adjacent to Lake Victoria, Uganda since the 1990s has developed a flourishing industry exporting fresh and processed

Figure 3.3 Evolution of Export Concentration and Real GDP per Capita, Selected Countries

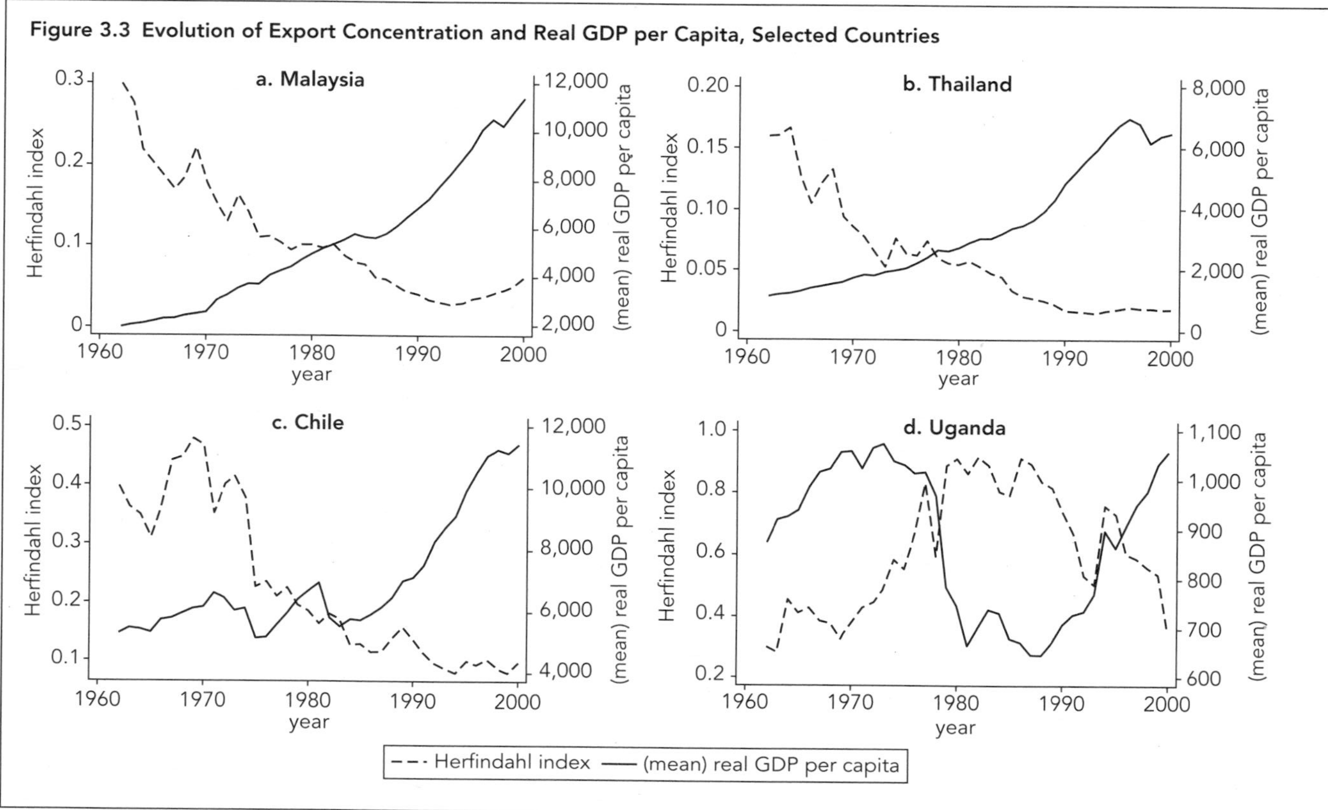

Source: Author's calculations, based on Feenstra and others 2005 and the Penn World Table (http://pwt.econ.upenn.edu/).

fish. It also heavily diversified into higher-value agricultural products such as cut flowers, fruits, and vegetables. One of the main determinants of Uganda's export success in these products lies in the sharp decline of freight rates and improvements in freight services so that these newly discovered export products could be airlifted out of Kampala. Uganda also benefited from spillovers across sectors in cold-storage systems (Bonaglia and Fukasaku 2003; Chandra, Boccardo, and Osorio 2007).

EMPIRICAL ANALYSIS

In this section, I estimate an augmented Solow growth model and investigate the relationship between export diversification and income per capita growth.

Solow Growth Model

The Solow growth framework provides an intuitive and theory-based strategy for testing the relationship between export diversification and GDP per capita growth. Rather than diving into the huge academic literature on cross-country regressions, which has often been criticized for its kitchen-sink approach by throwing in all kinds of possible explanatory factors of growth, I aim to keep the relevant explanatory variables small by relying on the predictions of the Solow growth model.

In the Solow growth model, a country's growth in output per worker is, among other things, a function of the initial output per worker, the savings rate, the initial level of technology, the rate of technological progress, the rate of depreciation, and the growth rate of the workforce. In the model, higher savings causes higher growth of output per worker, whereas an increasing growth rate of the labor force (adjusted for depreciation and technological progress) has the opposite effect on growth. In the augmented Solow growth model, a measure for human capital is added as an additional determinant of growth.

Results

Figure 3.4 presents a scatter plot of average export concentration (Herfindahl index) and cumulative GDP per capita growth over five-year

Figure 3.4 Export Concentration and GDP per Capita Growth, 1961–2000

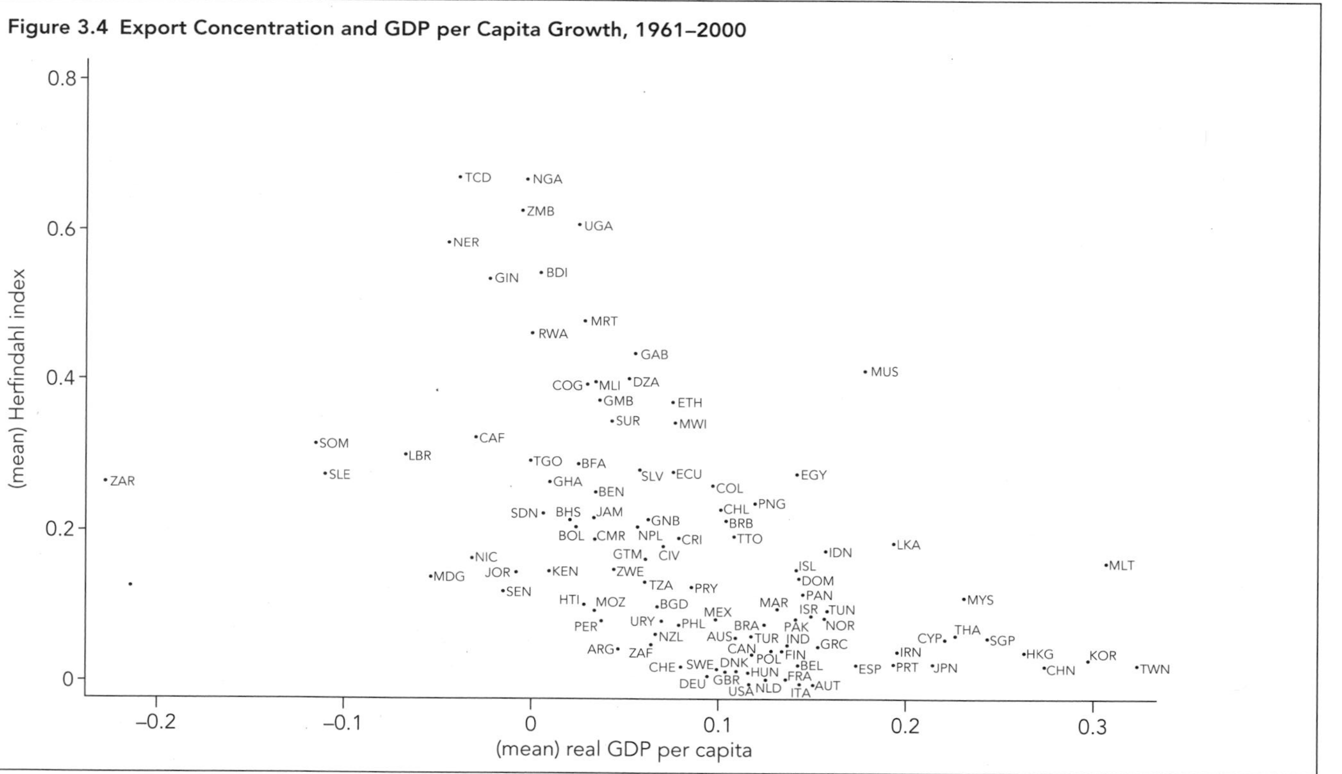

Source: Author's calculations, based on data from Feenstra and others (2005) and Penn World Table (http://pwt.econ.upenn.edu/).

(Note can be found on the following page)

Note : AFG = Afghanistan; ARG = Argentina; AUS = Australia; AUT = Austria; BDI = Burundi; BEL = Belgium; BEN = Benin; BFA = Burkina Faso; BGD = Bangladesh; BHS = The Bhamas; BOL = Bolivia; BRA = Brazil; BRB = Barbados; CAF = Central African Republic; CAN = Canada; CHE = Switzerland; CHL = Chile; CHN = China; CIV = Côte d'Ivoire; CMR = Cameroon; COG = Republic of Congo; COL = Colombia; CRI = Costa Rica; CYP = Cyprus; DEU = Germany; DNK = Denmark; DOM = Dominican Republic; DZA = Algeria; ECU = Ecuador; EGY = Arab Republic of Egypt; ESP = Spain; ETH = Ethiopia; FIN = Finland; FJI = Fiji; FRA = France; GAB = Gabon; GBR = United Kingdom; GHA = Ghana; GIN = Guinea; GMB = The Gambia; GNB = Guinea-Bissau; GRC = Greece; GTM = Guatemala; HKG = Hong Kong, China; HND = Honduras; HTI = Haiti; HUN = Hungary; IDN = Indonesia; IND = India; IRL = Ireland; ISL = Iceland; ISR = Israel; ITA = Italy; JAM = Jamaica; JOR = Jordan; JPN = Japan; KEN = Kenya; KOR = Republic of Korea; LBR = Liberia; LKA = Sri Lanka; MAR = Morocco; MDG = Madagascar; MEX = Mexico; MLI = Mali; MLT = Malta; MOZ = Mozambique; MRT = Mauritania; MUS = Mauritius; MWI = Malawi; MYS = Malaysia; NER = Niger; NGA = Nigeria; NIC = Nicaragua; NLD = Netherlands; NOR = Norway; NPL = Nepal; NZL = New Zealand; PAK = Pakistan; PAN = Panama; PER = Peru; PHL = Philippines; PNG = Papua New Guinea; POL = Poland; PRT = Portugal; PRY = Paraguay; RWA = Rwanda; SDN = Sudan; SEN = Senegal; SGP = Singapore; SLE = Sierra Leone; SLV = El Salvador; SOM = Somalia; SUR = Suriname; SWE = Sweden; TAI = Taiwan, China; TCD = Chad; TGO = Togo; THA = Thailand; TTO = Trinidad and Tobago; TUN = Tunisia; TUR = Turkey; TZA = Tanzania; UGA = Uganda; USA = United States; URY = Uruguay; ZAF = South Africa; ZAR = Democratic Republic of Congo; ZMB = Zambia; ZWE = Zimbabwe.

intervals for the sample period 1961–2000. There is some strong evidence of a negative correlation between the variables, with a correlation coefficient of over –0.51. As expected, many of the successful high-growing East Asian countries such as China, Korea, Malaysia, Taiwan (China), and Thailand are located in the lower right corner with relatively low levels of export concentration. Conversely, the figure indicates that many countries with poor growth performances in the past four decades have been sub-Saharan African countries with a very concentrated export sector.

Column 1 in table 3.1 presents the dynamic panel results for the augmented Solow model.[1] Investment has the predicted significantly positive effect on income per capita growth, whereas the population growth measure, adjusted by the rate of technological progress and depreciation, is significantly negatively influencing growth. Both initial income and schooling have the expected sign but are not significant in this model specification.[2]

There is some strong evidence from column 2 that export concentration is detrimental to GDP per capita growth, as expected and found in some previous studies such as Lederman and Maloney (2007). Countries that have diversified their exports in the past decades have on average enjoyed higher per capita income growth. This finding is very robust to the exclusion of developed countries from the sample (column 3), as well as to the inclusion of an openness variable that captures total trade relative to GDP (column 4).

In columns 5 and 6, I test for the presence of nonlinearity in the relationship between export concentration and GDP per capita growth. The squared term of export concentration is positively affecting growth, whereas the linear term is affecting growth negatively in column 5, even though the former is not statistically significant in this particular model specification. Similarly, the interaction between export concentration and log income is significantly positive in contrast to the strong negative impact of the linear term on income per capita growth in column 6. Overall, there is some evidence from these dynamic panel regressions that the effect of export concentration is potentially nonlinear, with poorer countries benefiting from diversifying their exports in contrast to richer countries that perform better with export specialization.[3] It is very interesting to find this pattern in the cross-country dynamic growth regressions, which is also supportive of Imbs and Wacziarg (2003).

CONCLUSION

Overall, the evidence is strong that export concentration has been detrimental to the economic growth performance of developing countries in the past decades. This empirical model did not investigate the specific channels through which export concentration affects per capita growth. As discussed, one reason could be the reduction of declining terms of trade, especially for commodity-dependent countries. Another reason, put forward by Hausmann and Rodrik (2003), relates to the cost-discovery process faced by entrepreneurs and the valuable contribution government policies can make in alleviating ensuing problems of coordination and information externalities. This can result in a diversification of investments into a new range of activities and higher levels of growth.

Table 3.1 Estimation of Augmented Solow Growth Model by System GMM

Variable	(1)	(2)	(3)	(4)	(5)	(6)
Initial GDP per capita	–0.029	–0.053	–0.074	–0.077	–0.067	–0.068
	(0.471)	(0.191)	(0.100)	(0.022)**	(0.082)*	(0.064)*
Schooling	0.019	0.035	0.063	0.064	0.054	0.032
	(0.534)	(0.202)	(0.039)**	(0.014)**	(0.064)*	(0.303)
Population growth	–0.346	–0.292	–0.299	–0.315	–0.255	–0.233
	(0.052)*	(0.059)*	(0.089)*	(0.017)**	(0.104)	(0.133)
Investment	0.008	0.006	0.007	0.004	0.005	0.007
	(0.022)**	(0.007)***	(0.020)**	(0.011)**	(0.017)**	(0.003)***
Export concentration		–0.27	–0.304	–0.297	–0.482	–1.474
		(0.002)***	(0.003)***	(0.001)***	(0.084)*	(0.029)**
Openness				0.001		
				(0.066)*		
Export concentration^2					0.275	
					(0.403)	

Export concentration*						0.161
GDP per capita						(0.068)*
Constant	–0.736	–0.361	–0.158	–0.298	–0.143	–0.075
	(0.037)**	(0.244)	(0.691)	(0.268)	(0.704)	(0.800)
Observations	648	629	455	629	629	629
Number of countries	99	96	71	96	96	96
Time period	1965–2000	1965–2000	1965–2000	1965–2000	1965–2000	1965–2000
Hansen test	0.530	0.834	0.991	0.995	0.992	0.994
AB-test for AR(2) in differences	0.214	0.397	0.311	0.440	0.419	

Source: Author's calculations.

Note: The dependent variable is real GDP per capita growth. All estimations include time dummy variables for each period and allow for robust standard errors. Oil-exporting and Eastern European countries are excluded, as are developed countries in column 3. GMM = generalized method of moments. Robust p values are in parentheses.

* Significant at the 10 percent level. ** Significant at the 5 percent level. *** Significant at the 1 percent level.

ANNEX: ECONOMETRIC METHODOLOGY AND DATA

I estimate a dynamic panel model of growth rather than conventional cross-sectional country growth regressions. The cross-sectional regressions suffer from various pitfalls that have been extensively discussed in the literature. First, they do not account for the fact that most variables are endogenously determined. For example, by construction, the initial level of income is correlated with the dependent growth variable (Knight, Loayza, and Villanueva 1993). According to Caselli, Esquivel, and Lefort (1996), most macroeconomic variables are interdependent in the cross-sectional regressions, leading to a misspecified model. Second, cross-sectional country growth regressions suffer from an omitted variable bias because they cannot capture unobserved time-invariant country-specific factors such as the initial level of technology. Third, a lot of valuable information is lost by aggregating the information from the sample because dynamic relationships cannot be analyzed over time.

I use an empirical strategy that has been frequently used in the growth literature (see, for example, Caselli, Esquivel, and Lefort 1996; Levine, Loayza, and Beck 2000; Bond, Hoeffler, and Temple 2001; Hoeffler 2002; and Lederman and Maloney 2007). I estimate dynamic panel growth models based on the GMM (generalized method of moments) estimator developed by Arellano and Bond (1991). The GMM estimator overcomes the problems of the OLS (ordinary least squares) estimator from the conventional cross-sectional regressions mentioned above. Taking first-differences of the regression equation removes the unobserved time-invariant country-specific effects, such as the unobserved initial level of technology, so there is no omitted variable bias across time-invariant factors. Also, there is no problem of endogeneity within the explanatory variables because lagged values of these explanatory variables can be used as instruments. Finally, the dynamic panel estimation allows for multiple time series observations so valuable information is not lost—in contrast to the conventional cross-country regressions.

Two types of GMM estimators have been frequently used for growth regressions. The first-difference GMM estimator, developed by Arellano and Bond (1991), uses first-differenced equations with suitable lagged levels as instruments. The system GMM estimator, developed by Arellano and Bover (1995) and Blundell and Bond (1998), uses, in addition, equations in levels with lagged first-differences as instruments.

Bond, Hoeffler, and Temple (2001) and Hoeffler (2002) argue and show that the system GMM estimator is more suited to estimating growth equations than is the first-differenced GMM estimator. Many explanatory variables, such as output, are highly persistent, so their lagged levels might be only very weak instruments for the first-differenced equations. In this situation, the first-differenced GMM estimator potentially suffers from a downward bias (Blundell and Bond 1998), so the additional set of first-differenced instruments and equations in levels makes the system GMM estimator more efficient by overcoming the weak instrument problem in the first-differenced GMM estimator. To investigate the relationship between export diversification and economic growth, I therefore use the system GMM estimator throughout, similar to Lederman and Maloney (2007) in their study.

I estimate a general growth equation of the following form:

$$\Delta y_{i,t} = \alpha y_{i,t-1} + x'_{i,t} + \beta + \gamma_t + \eta_i + v_{i,t},$$

where $\Delta y_{i,t}$ denotes the log difference of per capita income in period t, $y_{i,t-1}$ is the log initial income, $x_{i,t}$ is a vector of potential determinants of growth, γ_t captures samplewide time effects, η_i are the unobserved time-invariant country-specific effects, and $v_{i,t}$ is the residual error component.

The data set covers up to 99 countries and data from 1961–2000, with Eastern European and oil-exporting countries excluded. As common in the dynamic panel growth literature, the data are averaged across smaller time periods to avoid most of the short-run business cycle effects that might distort the growth estimations. In general, the time series is averaged over five-year periods: 1961–1965, 1966–1970, and so forth, giving a time dimension of eight periods.

As usual in the academic literature (for example, Bond, Hoeffler, and Temple 2001; and Hoeffler 2002), per capita income growth is used as a proxy for growth in output per worker, and population growth is used as a proxy for labor force growth in the regression analysis.

In the basic augmented Solow growth regression, the dependent variable is growth of real GDP per capita, adjusted for purchasing power parity, over five-year intervals. Further components of the Solow model are the log of initial income of the period and savings rate that are proxied by the average investment share of real GDP over each five-year period. It has been common in the literature (see, for example, Mankiw, Romer, and Weil 1992; Caselli, Esquivel, and Lefort 1996; or Hoeffler 2002) to assume constant rates of technological progress depreciation across countries, which sum to 0.05. Logs are taken of the sum of the population growth variable (which is also averaged over each five-year period) and 0.05. In the Solow model, this variable is predicted to be negatively associated with per capita GDP growth. Also, to account for differences in human capital, the log of years of schooling variable by Barro and Lee (2000) is included in the panel estimations. They collected comprehensive data on educational attainment for a large set of countries in five-year intervals.

The main variable of interest that is added to the augmented Solow growth regressions, export diversification, is calculated from the Feenstra and others (2005) data set on bilateral trade flows from 1962 to 2000. It is based on the 4-digit Standard International Trade Classification, revision 2, and recently has been frequently used in trade studies since it is very comprehensive in scope and is not missing observations as in the usual U.N. Comtrade (Commodity Trade Statistics Database) data set. As far as I know, the Feenstra and others (2005) data set has not been used before for such a growth exercise; for example, Lederman and Maloney (2007) calculate their measure from the Comtrade data. Specifically, for each country and year, the Herfindahl index is calculated from the disaggregated export data, and the index is averaged, this time over four-year periods beginning with 1962–1965, and ending with 1996–2000.[4] Because the Herfindahl index is a measure of export concentration, I expect it to be negatively related to GDP per capita growth.

A small caveat on using the Herfindahl index as a measure of export concentration is in order. Many previous studies do not mention that the Herfindahl index does not capture all exports of an economy, such as services, and therefore it can be seen only as an imperfect proxy for the level of export diversification in any given country. A problem is that export data for different sectors are subject to different levels of disaggregation (Imbs and Wacziarg 2003). In general, manufacturing data are available in a more disaggregated form than export data on services, which makes it difficult to combine different export sectors into one coherent Herfindahl index. But I believe that my measure for export concentration is well suited to draw some reasonable inferences on the cross-country patterns of export concentration and per capita income growth.[5]

By including export concentration unconditionally into the growth regressions, I implicitly assume that the relationship between export concentration and GDP per capita growth is linear. In other words, the effect of export concentration on per capita income growth is the same regardless of the level of income. As discussed earlier, Imbs and Wacziarg (2003) in a seminal paper have found a U-shaped pattern of sectoral domestic concentration and per capita income across countries. Countries in their early stages of development diversify production and specialize at higher income levels.

These patterns also hold for countries' exports, as shown by Cabellero and Cowan (2006) and Klinger and Lederman (2006) in a regression of the Herfindahl index on per capita income and its squared term. I too obtain the same results for my sample. Given the nonlinearity of the relationship between export concentration and growth, I introduce some interactions terms of export concentration into the growth regressions, a novelty in this particular literature. Specifically, I include the squared term of export concentration, as well as the interaction of log income and export concentration, to test for a U-shaped pattern. The finding of a U-shaped pattern would mean that not all countries would benefit from diversifying their exports.

Finally, to test the robustness of the export concentration variable, I individually include additional control variables in the regressions such as a measure for openness as well as measures for agriculture, manufacturing, and services all relative to GDP. Table 3A.1 provides an overview of the variable descriptions and their sources. Furthermore, I change the sample periods as well as the sample of countries included to test the sensitivity of the export concentration variable.

As mentioned earlier, most macroeconomic variables are interdependent in the conventional cross-sectional regressions, and the GMM estimation helps to overcome these problems of endogeneity. I adopt a relatively conservative strategy and assume in the augmented Solow model that both the investment and the population growth variables are endogenously determined and that initial income as well as the schooling measure are predetermined.[6] Similarly, I assume that all variables added to the augmented Solow model such as export concentration are also endogenously determined. As instruments in the system GMM estimation, I use lagged levels and differences up to t-4 and also test the sensitivity of these assumptions. The assumption that export concentration is endogenously determined is sensible since exports are a main component of per capita income.

Robustness Test

Table 3A.2 provides some further sensitivity tests. The modification of the time period in columns 1 and 2 does not change the main finding that, in general, export concentration is detrimental to economic growth.[7] Columns 3–5 individually add further control variables such as agriculture, manufacturing, and services all relative to GDP to the basic model, and the previous findings do not change.

Table 3A.1 Variable Definitions and Sources

Variable	Description	Source
Real GDP per capita growth	Adjusted for purchasing power parity, based on the chain index and calculated over five-year intervals	Penn World Table (PWT) 6.1
Schooling	Natural log of years of schooling	Barro and Lee (2000)
Population growth	Natural logs of the sum of the population growth variable (averaged over five-year intervals) and 0.05, which proxies for the rate of technological progress and depreciation	World Bank World Development Indicators (WDI) database
Investment	Investment share of real GDP per capita	PWT 6.1
Export concentration	Herfindahl index, which is the sum of squared export shares scaled by 10,000 for each country and year, based on the 4-digit SITC, revision 2, classification. The average over five-year intervals is taken.	Feenstra and others (2005) and author's construction
Openness	Exports plus imports divided by real GDP per capita in 2000 constant prices. The average over five-year intervals is taken.	PWT 6.1
Agriculture/GDP ratio	Value added of agriculture in constant 2000 US$ as a share of GDP. The average over five-year intervals is taken.	WDI database
Manufacturing/GDP ratio	Value added of manufacturing in constant 2000 US$ as a share of GDP. The average over five-year intervals is taken.	WDI database
Services/GDP ratio	Value added of services in constant 2000 US$ as a share of GDP. The average over five-year intervals is taken.	WDI database

Source: Author.

Table 3A.2 Additional Estimation of Augmented Solow Growth Model by System GMM

Variable	(1)	(2)	(3)	(4)	(5)
Initial income	–0.035	0.014	–0.06	–0.071	–0.1
	(0.305)	(0.652)	(0.222)	(0.055)*	(0.027)**
Schooling	0.034	0.012	0.054	0.026	0.05
	(0.213)	(0.675)	(0.113)	(0.383)	(0.063)*
Population growth	–0.271	–0.165	–0.392	–0.252	–0.478
	(0.073)*	(0.226)	(0.027)**	(0.161)	(0.002)***
Investment	0.006	0.005	0.007	0.007	0.007
	(0.006)***	(0.011)**	(0.006)***	(0.006)***	(0.005)***
Export concentration	–0.226	–0.167	–0.165	–0.284	–0.207
	(0.010)**	(0.065)*	(0.087)*	(0.008)***	(0.044)**
Agriculture/GDP ratio			0.001		
			(0.524)		
Manufacturing/GDP ratio				0.002	
				(0.213)	
Services/GDP ratio					0.002
					(0.237)

(Table continues on the following page)

Table 3A.2 (continued)

Variable	(1)	(2)	(3)	(4)	(5)
Constant	–0.457	–0.538	–0.646	–0.135	–0.636
	(0.174)	(0.164)	(0.062)*	(0.666)	(0.051)*
Observations	555	464	562	493	562
Number of countries	96	96	94	94	94
Time period	1975–2000	1980–2000	1965–2000	1965–2000	1965–2000
Hansen test	0.822	0.583	0.983	0.997	0.989
AB-test for AR(2) in differences	0.380	0.219	0.428	0.114	0.421

Source: Author's calculations.

Notes: Dependent variable is real GDP per capita growth. Robust p values are in parentheses. All estimations include time dummy variables for each period and allow for robust standard errors. Oil-exporting and Eastern European countries are excluded.

* Significant at the 10 percent level. ** Significant at the 5 percent level. *** Significant at the 1 percent level.

I did not empirically investigate the specific channels through which export concentration affects per capita growth. The addition of possible channels to the growth regressions and measurement of their effects on export diversification by looking at the change of the coefficient size of the export diversification variable did not seem the right way, because this is often a very fragile exercise and frequently depends on the underlying assumptions in the dynamic panel model as well as the type of regression model adopted.

NOTES

My thanks go to Roberto Zagha as well as Jessica Boccardo, Steve Bond, Vandana Chandra, William Cline, Uri Dadush, Marcel Fafchamps, Anke Hoeffler, Leonardo Iacovone, Tehmina Khan, David Lederman, Eduardo Ley, Bill Maloney, Yuwi Manachotphong, Peter Neary, Martha Denisse Pierola, Mike Spence, and Francis Teal. I also thank participants at a World Bank conference on export diversification and a Commission on Growth and Development Workshop on Global Trends and Challenges held at Yale University. This chapter was prepared for the Commission on Growth and Development while the author worked at the World Bank and for the commission. The views expressed in this chapter are those of the author and do not necessarily represent those of the International Monetary Fund (IMF) or IMF policy. Any mistake or omission is solely my own responsibility.

1. All system generalized method of moments (GMM) panel estimations include time dummy variables for each period, allow for standard errors that are asymptotically robust to heteroskedasticity, and exclude Eastern European and oil-exporting countries.
2. The Hansen test does not show any problems with the instruments, and there are also no second-order autocorrelation problems in the model.
3. I obtain very similar results for the nonlinearity regressions when using ordinary least squares or fixed effects.
4. The Herfindahl index is the sum of squared export shares scaled by 10,000 for each country and year. It ranges from 0 to 1, and higher values constitute a more concentrated export structure.
5. The Herfindahl index includes items from the following broad sectors: food and live animals; beverages and tobacco; crude materials; mineral fuels, lubricants, and related materials; animal and vegetable oils, fats, and waxes; chemicals and related products; manufactured goods chiefly classified by material; machinery and transport equipment; miscellaneous manufactured articles; and commodities and transactions not classified elsewhere.
6. By "endogenous," I mean that, for example, investment is correlated with past and current shocks to per capita GDP growth but not with future shocks. In contrast, the assumption that initial income is predetermined implies that it is correlated with

shocks to per capita income growth in the preceding five-year periods but not in the current and future periods. Hoeffler (2002) also assumes that initial income is predetermined. I also test for the sensitivity of the underlying assumptions.

7. Technically, this statement is not fully correct because initial income is included in the dynamic panel model, so I effectively estimate a levels equation. In other words, I capture the effect of export concentration on the per capita GDP level rather than the growth rate. I also estimated a preliminary growth model that excludes initial income but uses the lagged growth rate with some further model modifications. The estimated model provides some evidence that export concentration is also negatively related to the per capita GDP growth rate. For this, the Herfindahl variable must be stationary, and preliminary tests confirm that it is. Therefore, I continue to relate the explanatory variables to the per capita income growth rate in the main text, similar to most of the academic literature, even though this is not fully technically correct. Also, figure 3.3 showed a strong negative correlation between the Herfindahl and per capita income growth, supporting my reasoning. See Bond, Leblebicioglu, and Schiantarelli (2004) for further information in a very similar context.

REFERENCES

Acemoglu, D., and F. Zilibotti. 1997. "Was Prometheus Unbound by Chance? Risk, Diversification and Growth." *Journal of Political Economy* 105 (4): 709–51.

Agosin, M. R. 2007. "Export Diversification and Growth in Emerging Economies." Working Paper 233. Departamento de Economía, Universidad de Chile, Santiago.

Agosin, M. R., and C. Bravo-Ortega. 2007. "The Emergence of New Successful Export Activities in Chile." Latin American Research Network, Inter-American Development Bank, Washington, DC.

Al-Marhubi, F. 2000. "Export Diversification and Growth: An Empirical Investigation." *Applied Economics Letters* 7: 559–62.

Amin Gutierrez de Pineres, S., and M. J. Ferrantino. 1997a. "Export Diversification and Structural Change: Some Comparisons for Latin America." http://ssrn.com/abstract=36231.

———. 1997b. "Export Diversification and Structural Dynamics in the Growth Process: The Case of Chile." *Journal of Development Economics* 52: 35–91.

———. 2000. *Export Dynamics and Economic Growth in Latin America*. Burlington, VT: Ashgate Publishing Ltd.

Arellano, M., and S. R. Bond. 1991. "Some Tests of Specification for Panel Data: Monte Carlo Evidence and an Application to Employment Equations." *Review of Economic Studies* 58 (2): 277–97.

Arellano, M., and O. Bover. 1995. "Another Look at the Instrumental-Variable Estimation of Error Component Models." *Journal of Econometrics* 68 (1): 29–52.

Barro, R. J., and J. W. Lee. 2000. "International Data on Educational Attainment: Updates and Implications." Working Paper 42. Center for International Development, Harvard University, Cambridge, MA.

Bleaney, M., and D. Greenaway. 2001. "The Impact of Terms of Trade and Real Exchange Volatility on Investment and Growth in Sub-Saharan Africa." *Journal of Development Economics* 65: 491–500.

Blundell, R., and S. R. Bond. 1998. "Initial Conditions and Moment Restrictions in Dynamic Panel Data Model." *Journal of Econometrics* 87: 115–43.

Bonaglia, F., and K. Fukasaku. 2003. "Export Diversification in Low-Income Countries: An International Challenge after Doha." Working Paper 209. Organisation for Economic Co-operation and Development, Paris.

Bond, S. R., A. Hoeffler, and J. Temple. 2001. "GMM Estimation of Empirical Growth Models." CEPR Discussion Paper Series 3048. Centre for Economic Policy Research, London.

Bond, S. R., A. Leblebicioglu, and F. Schiantarelli. 2004. "Capital Accumulation and Growth: A New Look at the Empirical Evidence." Working Paper 8. Nuffield College, Oxford University, Oxford, U.K.

Brenton, Paul, and Richard Newfarmer. 2009. "Watching More than the Discovery Channel to Diversity Exports." In *Breaking Into New Markets: Emerging Lessons for Export Diversification*, ed. Richard Newfarmer, William Shaw, and Peter Walkenhorst, 111–24. Washington, DC: World Bank.

Cabellero, R. J., and K. Cowan. 2006. "Financial Integration without the Volatility." Massachusetts Institute of Technology, Cambridge, MA.

Caselli, F., G. Esquivel, and F. Lefort. 1996. "Reopening the Convergence Debate: A New Look at Cross-Country Growth Empirics." *Journal of Economic Growth* 1 (3): 363–89.

Chandra, V., J. Boccardo, and I. Osorio. 2007. "Export Diversification and Competitiveness in Developing Countries." World Bank, Washington, DC.

Chenery, H. 1979. *Structural Change and Development Policy*. New York: Oxford University Press.

Dornbusch, R., S. Fischer, and P. Samuelson. 1977. "Comparative Advantage, Trade and Payments in a Ricardian Model with a Continuum of Goods." *American Economic Review* 67: 823–39.

Feenstra, R., R. Lipsey, H. Deng, A. C. Ma, and H. Mo. 2005. "World Trade Flows: 1962–2000." Working Paper 11040. National Bureau of Economic Research, Cambridge, MA.

Ghosh, A. R., and J. Ostry. 1994. "Export Instability and the External Balance in Developing Countries." *IMF Staff Papers* 41: 214–35.

Grossman, G., and E. Helpman. 1991. *Innovation and Growth in the Global Economy*. Cambridge, MA: MIT Press.

Gylfason, T. 2001. "Natural Resources, Education, and Economic Development." *European Economic Review* 45 (4–6): 847–59.

Hausmann, R., J. Hwang, and D. Rodrik. 2006. "What You Export Matters." Working paper. Center for International Development, Harvard University, Cambridge, MA.

Hausmann, R., and B. Klinger. 2006. "Structural Transformation and Patterns of Comparative Advantage in the Product Space." Working Paper 128. Center for International Development, Harvard University, Cambridge, MA.

Hausmann, R., and D. Rodrik. 2003. "Economic Development as Self-Discovery." *Journal of Development Economics* 72: 603–33.

Herzer, D., and F. Nowak-Lehmann D. 2006. "What Does Export Diversification Do for Growth? An Econometric Analysis." *Applied Economics* 38: 1825–38.

Hoeffler, A. E. 2002. "The Augmented Solow Model and the African Growth Debate." *Oxford Bulletin of Economics and Statistics* 64 (2): 135–58.

Hummels, D., and P. J. Klenow. 2005. "The Variety and Quality of a Nation's Exports." *American Economic Review* 95 (3): 704–23.

Imbs, J., and R. Wacziarg. 2003. "Stages of Diversification." *American Economic Review* 93 (1): 63–86.

Klinger, B., and D. Lederman. 2006. "Diversification, Innovation, and Imitation inside the Global Technological Frontier." Research Policy Working Paper 3872. World Bank, Washington, DC.

———. 2009. "Diversification, Innovation, and Imitation of the Global Technological Frontier." In *Breaking Into New Markets: Emerging Lessons for Export Diversification*, ed. Richard Newfarmer, William Shaw, and Peter Walkenhorst, 101–10. Washington, DC: World Bank.

Knight, M., N. Loayza, and D. Villanueva. 1993. "Testing the Neoclassical Theory of Economic Growth: A Panel Data Approach." *IMF Staff Papers* 40: 512–41.

Krugman, P. 1979. "A Model of Innovation, Technology Transfer and the World Distribution of Income." *Journal of Political Economy* 87: 253–66.

Lederman, D., and W. F. Maloney. 2007. "Trade Structure and Growth." In *Natural Resources: Neither Curse nor Destiny*, ed. Daniel Lederman and William F. Maloney, 15–39. Washington DC: World Bank and Stanford University Press.

Levine, R., N. Loayza, and T. Beck. 2000. "Financial Intermediation and Growth: Causality and Causes." *Journal of Monetary Economics* 46: 31–77.

Mankiw, G. N., D. Romer, and D. N. Weil. 1992. "A Contribution to the Empirics of Economic Growth." *Quarterly Journal of Economics* 107: 407–37.

Matsuyama, K. 1992. "Agricultural Productivity, Comparative Advantage, and Economic Growth." *Journal of Economic Theory* 58: 317–34.

Pham, C., and W. Martin. 2007. "Extensive and Intensive Margin Growth and Developing Country Exports." World Bank, Washington, DC.

Rodrik, D. 2005. "Policies for Economic Diversification." *CEPAL Review* 87: 7–23.

Sachs, J., and A. Warner. 2001. "The Curse of Natural Resources." *European Economic Review* 45 (4–6): 827–38.

Syrquin, M. 1989. "Patterns of Structural Change." In *Handbook of Economic Development*, ed. H. Chenery and T. N. Srinavasan. Amsterdam: Elsevier Science Publishers.

Vernon, R. 1966. "International Investment and International Trade in the Product Cycle." *Quarterly Journal of Economics* 80: 190–207.

Vettas, N. 2000. "Investment Dynamics in Markets with Endogenous Demands." *Journal of Industrial Economics* 48 (2): 189–203.

World Bank. 2002. *From Natural Resources to the Knowledge Economy: Trade and Job Quality.* Washington, DC: World Bank.

CHAPTER 4

EXPOSURE TO EXTERNAL SHOCKS AND THE GEOGRAPHICAL DIVERSIFICATION OF EXPORTS

Marc Bacchetta, Marion Jansen, Carolina Lennon, and Roberta Piermartini

While openness to trade can generate substantial economic benefits, openness can also increase an economy's vulnerability to external shocks that reduce welfare. The literature analyzing economies' exposure to external shocks through trade has so far focused on product-specific price shocks; it is argued that terms-of-trade variability is higher if export products are highly concentrated, particularly if those products are characterized by high price volatility (such as commodities or oil). Thus, export diversification can reduce output volatility by reducing the price variability of the basket of goods a country exports.

By contrast, little attention has been paid to the role of country-specific shocks (affecting trading partners) that do not have an effect on world prices, perhaps because exporters were expected to be easily able to redirect production from one trading partner to another. Recent contributions to the theoretical trade literature, however, emphasize the existence of fixed costs related to entry into new markets. The redirection of exports is therefore likely to be costly and to take time. The main goal of this chapter is to show that exporters are exposed to country-specific shocks that affect trading partners and that geographical diversification is one of the determinants of the degree of risk this exposure entails for the economy of exporting countries.

In empirical work, exposure to external shocks has often been taken into account by including terms-of-trade variation into regressions determining economic performance. Terms-of-trade volatility reflects price variations in the bundle of exported goods, where the weights of individual goods within the basket are, in principle, kept constant. Terms-of-trade volatility is likely to be affected by both product-specific shocks and country-specific shocks, but the variable does not allow a distinction to be made between the relevance of country- and product-specific shocks for countries' exposure to external volatility through trade. The variable also does not take into account the effect shocks may have on quantities exported.

Drawing on portfolio theory, we construct a measure for exporters' exposure to country-specific shocks in trading partners. This measure takes into account the volatility of demand in export markets and the degree to which the cycles of different trading partners are correlated. We construct this variable using bilateral trade data for a group of 180 countries over a period from 1962 to 2004.[1] Using panel regressions, we find that this measure consistently has a positive and significant impact on the volatility of exporters' gross domestic product (GDP). We also find that the correlation between trading partners' cycles is important in determining countries' volatility and that geographical diversification of exports affects the extent to which countries are exposed to external country-specific shocks.

This chapter first discusses the relevant literature and then introduces the variable we use to measure exposure to country-specific shocks and discusses other variables relevant for our analysis. The results of the empirical analysis are then presented.

LITERATURE OVERVIEW

Open economies are subject to external shocks that can increase the volatility of output, with potentially serious implications. Ramey and Ramey (1995) have shown that countries with higher output volatility tend to grow more slowly, and Aizenman and Marion (1999) have found that higher volatility reduces private investment. There is also evidence that the adverse effects of declines in output are felt most strongly by the poorest households, which lack the resources to smooth consumption. As shown in figure 4.1, output volatility is considerably

Figure 4.1 Output Volatility by Income Group, 1965–2006

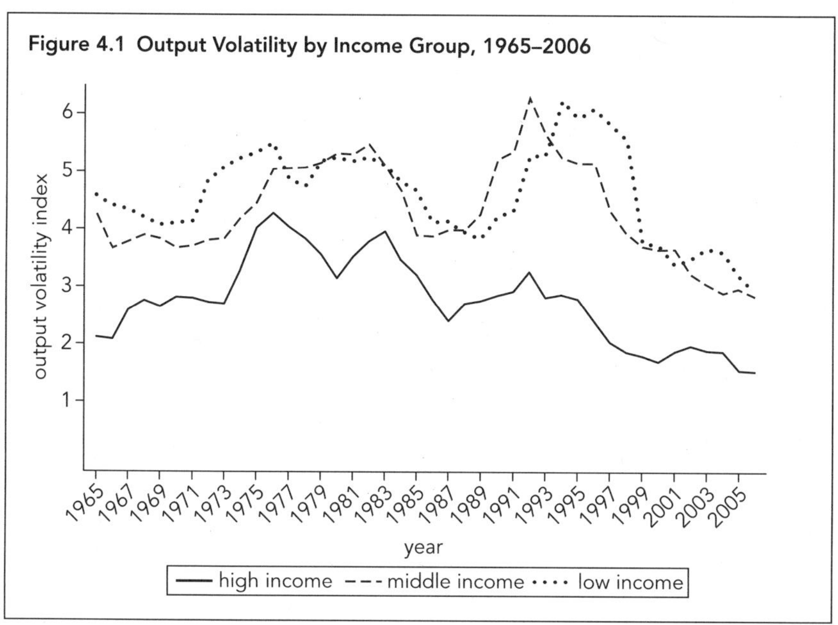

Source: Authors' calculations using GDP data from World Development Indicators database.

higher for low-income countries than for high-income countries. Interestingly, while output volatility in low-income countries has fluctuated considerably over the past 40 years, its level was lower in 2004 than it was in the 1960s.

The sources of output volatility are not well understood and may include terms-of-trade shocks, domestic policy mismanagement, thin financial markets, and institutional and political factors (for example, democracy may be associated with less variable output than autocracy) (Malik and Temple 2006). These explanations are clearly not mutually exclusive and may interact in various ways. Empirical research on the causes of macroeconomic volatility in developing countries has used three main approaches.[2] The first approach is to estimate the contribution of various types of shocks using a vector autoregression (VAR) model in a panel setting. The second is to make the same estimation using quantitative, stochastic, dynamic, multisector equilibrium models calibrated on developing economies. The third is to regress directly the volatility of growth on various explanatory variables.

Several recent papers using a panel VAR approach find that external factors make only a minor contribution to output volatility.[3] Ahmed (2003) finds that short-term fluctuations in output, inflation, and the real exchange rate in six Latin American countries are driven less by external shocks (changes in the terms of trade, foreign output, and U.S. real interest rate) than by domestic economic disturbances. Raddatz (2007) finds that external shocks can explain only a small fraction of the output variance of a typical low-income country; internal factors play the main role. And Broda (2004) finds that terms-of-trade shocks accounted for a relatively small share of real GDP volatility in a sample of non-oil-exporting countries from 1973 to 1996.

These results contrast with those of several other studies that use quantitative, stochastic, dynamic, multisector equilibrium models calibrated to represent a typical African economy to show that terms-of-trade shocks and the degree of openness explain an important part of the variation in output volatility. Kose (2002) finds that roughly 88 percent of aggregate output fluctuations can be explained by world price shocks. His results reinforce the results of earlier work by Mendoza (1995) and Kose and Riezman (2001).

A third category of papers attempts to explain growth volatility by regressing the volatility of growth on various explanatory variables, and with a few exceptions, their results suggest that terms-of-trade volatility, the degree of openness, or both contribute to higher volatility in developing countries. Easterly, Islam, and Stiglitz (2001) find that openness exposes a country to greater growth volatility but that this effect is significantly attenuated in richer countries with deeper financial systems. Cavallo (2007) finds that the net effect of trade openness on output volatility is stabilizing (exposure to trade raises output volatility through the terms-of-trade channel but reduces volatility generated by external finance). Calderon, Loayza, and Schmidt-Hebbel (2005) find that trade openness has only a small impact on volatility and then only in low-income countries. They also find that trade openness reduces the volatility effect of terms-of-trade shocks, while it increases the volatility effect of the growth rate of trade partners. Di Giovanni and Levchenko (forthcoming) find that trade openness contributes to output volatility, because sectors that are more open to international trade are more volatile and because higher overall trade openness is accompanied by increased specialization (these effects are found to dominate the effect that more-open sectors are less correlated with the rest of the home economy, which tends to reduce the impact of openness on volatility).

Hausmann and Gavin (1996) find that, in addition to economic policy, external shocks, involving both terms of trade and capital flows, are an important determinant of macroeconomic volatility in Latin America. By contrast, Rodrik (2001) finds that the volatility of capital flows, but not of terms of trade, is significantly related to the volatility of the gross national product in Latin America and the Caribbean. Using a Bayesian approach, Malik and Temple (2006) find that terms-of-trade volatility has explanatory power for output volatility in poor countries, regardless of the choice of conditioning variables. Easterly and Kraay (2000) and Jansen (2004) find that openness and terms-of-trade volatility contribute significantly to output volatility in small states, with Easterly and Kraay attributing the relationship to openness, and Jansen (along with Malik and Temple 2006) emphasizing the role of export concentration.[4]

This chapter contributes to the existing literature by introducing measures for geographical diversification into regressions explaining income volatility. The process has two steps. First, we develop a new variable that captures a country's exposure to external risk through trade. This variable measures the risk arising from the volatility of the trading partners. The underlying idea is that the economic performance in importing countries is likely to affect the economic volatility of their trading partners. Countries whose main export markets are very volatile are, therefore, more likely to "import" volatility from their trading partners and to be more exposed to external fluctuations. In addition, the correlation between the business cycles of trading partners is likely to matter. This chapter is therefore close to Calderon, Loayza, and Schmidt-Hebbel (2005), who also look at the variations in partner countries' GDP. One major difference is that our work takes the covariance between partner countries' GDP changes into account.

Second, we show that geographical diversification can help reduce countries' exposure to external shocks. This second idea resonates with the work of Brenton and Newfarmer (2009, chapter 6 in this volume), who show that expanding sales in existing products in existing markets (growth at the intensive margin) has greater weight in export growth than does diversification into new products and new geographic markets (growth at the extensive margin), but that growth into new geographic markets appears to be more important than discovery of new export products in explaining export growth. In this chapter, we argue that for a given level of risk exposure, having a larger number of trading partners will make it easier to adjust to shocks, for instance, by shifting exports from one partner hit by a negative shock to another partner with a healthier economy.

MEASURING EXPOSURE TO EXTERNAL SHOCKS

Openness exposes countries to different types of external shocks. The relevant economic literature analyzing economies' exposure to external shocks through trade has so far focused on price shocks, that is, shocks to the prices of imported or exported goods. Those shocks have typically been measured by variability in the terms of trade and have often been associated with product-specific shocks. It has been argued that countries whose export products are highly concentrated experience higher variability in their terms of trade; that appears to be particularly the case when a country's exports are concentrated in products characterized by high price volatility (Love 1983; Hausmann and Gavin 1996).

In this chapter, we argue that country-specific shocks in partner countries may also be important and that they may affect others directly, even if they do not affect world prices. Recent theoretical literature has highlighted the existence of fixed costs of exporting and has argued that these costs may be country specific (Melitz 2003). This phenomenon may imply that exporters cannot easily redirect their exports from partner countries hit by a negative demand shock to other countries where demand is strong. In particular, it may be difficult to redirect exports from an existing partner to a new trading partner.

Demand shocks in partner countries may, as a consequence, affect the quantity and price of exports and, in particular, may imply that export prices differ across partner countries. The importance of price-to-market behavior, whereby producers in one country set different prices for their product depending on the country in which it is sold, has indeed been stressed in the literature (Knetter 1993).

The aim of this chapter is to analyze whether country-specific shocks matter in addition to product-specific shocks. This is a relevant policy question because it is necessary to know the source of volatility to design policies to shield the economy from shocks. In particular, the geographical diversification of exports is likely to be more appropriate to buffer against country-specific shocks, whereas product diversification may help to smooth output in the face of product-specific shocks.

Singling Out Exposure to Country-Specific External Shocks

Shocks in export demand are likely to be linked to and even driven by income shocks in trading partners. Increases in the trading partners' GDP are likely to increase the demand for imports, and decreases in partners' GDP are likely to lower their demand for imports. GDP volatility in partner countries is therefore likely to be a good proxy for export demand volatility.

Countries' exposure to demand shocks in partner countries is likely to be higher, the higher the GDP volatility in those partner countries. But a country's degree of exposure is also likely to depend on whether GDP changes move in the same or in opposite directions in different partner countries. In the latter case, demand changes in one country can balance out demand changes in other countries, reducing the exposure to partner country shocks in the exporting country.

The exposure to risk through economic integration with partner countries is therefore likely to depend on three factors: the geographical diversification of exports, the volatility of markets that are served, and the correlation between the fluctuations in different partner countries.

All this is taken into account in the following measure based on the risk of the portfolio asset used in portfolio theory. We call this variable exposure to country-specific shocks (ECSS), and it is calculated as follows:

$$ECSS_i = \sum_j \left(\frac{x_{i,j}}{X_i}\right)^2 \operatorname{var} GDPgrowth_j + \sum_j \sum_z \frac{x_{i,j}}{X_i}\frac{x_{i,z}}{X_i} \operatorname{cov}(GDPgrowth_j, GDPgrowth_z),$$

where the first item on the right-hand side reflects the risk associated with variances in partner countries' GDP and the second item reflects the risk associated with the covariance of partner countries' GDP variation. Variances and covariances are weighted by the importance of individual partner countries in country *i*'s export basket. We calculated variances and covariances over periods of five and ten years. Most of our regressions use the five-year variables, but we use the ten-year variables for robustness checks.

It can be shown that in an equally weighted export basket, $ECSS_i$ = (1/n)(average variance) + (1 − 1/n)(average covariance), implying that the contribution of variance terms goes to zero and the contribution of the covariance term goes to "average covariance" as the number of trading partners becomes very large.

Figure 4.2 reflects how the five-year ECSS behaved, on average, for our sample of countries over the period 1966–2004. For most of that period, the contribution of partner countries' variance has been more important than the contribution of partner countries' covariance. Interestingly, covariances went up and were significantly higher than variances in the 1970s and early 1980s, two periods marked by oil crises. The two peaks in the covariance contribution could indicate that energy shocks affect large numbers of countries in the same way, reflecting a situation of global contagion.

The behavior of the ECSS differs across countries depending on the volatility of their trading partners. A shock in one trading partner may affect the variance component of the total portfolio risk for a country if the trading partner has enough weight in the country's total exports. If other partners are hit by the same shock, or if the shock in one trading partner affects others, then the covariance component may also increase.

Figure 4.2 Average Level of Exposure to Country-Specific Shocks, 1966–2004

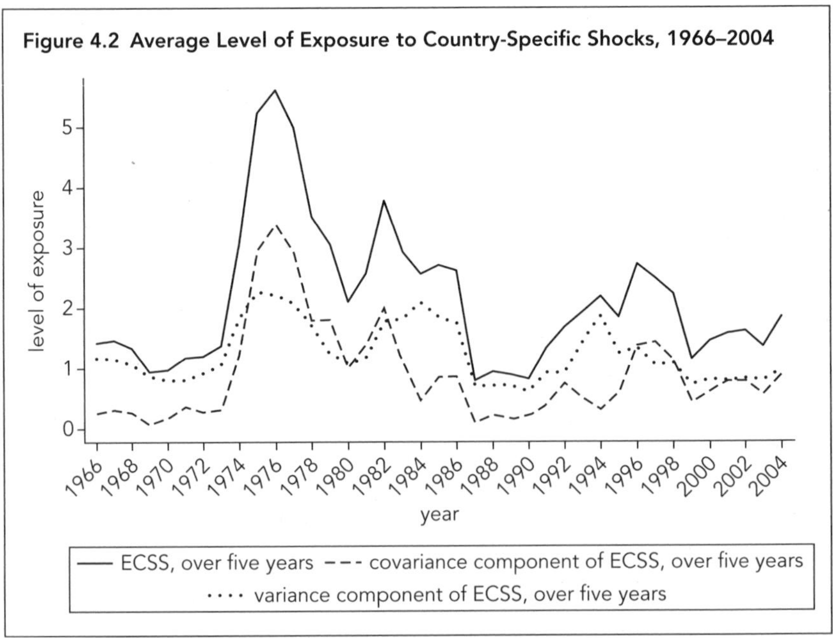

Source: Authors' calculations using GDP data from the World Bank World Development Indicators database and trade data from U.N. Comtrade (Commodity Trade Statistics Database).

Note: ECSS = exposure to country-specific shocks.

The effect of country-specific shocks on individual trading partners' ECSS is illustrated in figure 4.3, which depicts the behavior of the ECSS in Singapore and Brazil and highlights two location-specific shocks: the Asian financial crisis in 1997 and the Argentine financial crisis in 2001.

Figure 4.3 Exposure to Country-Specific Shocks for Singapore and Brazil, 1966–2004

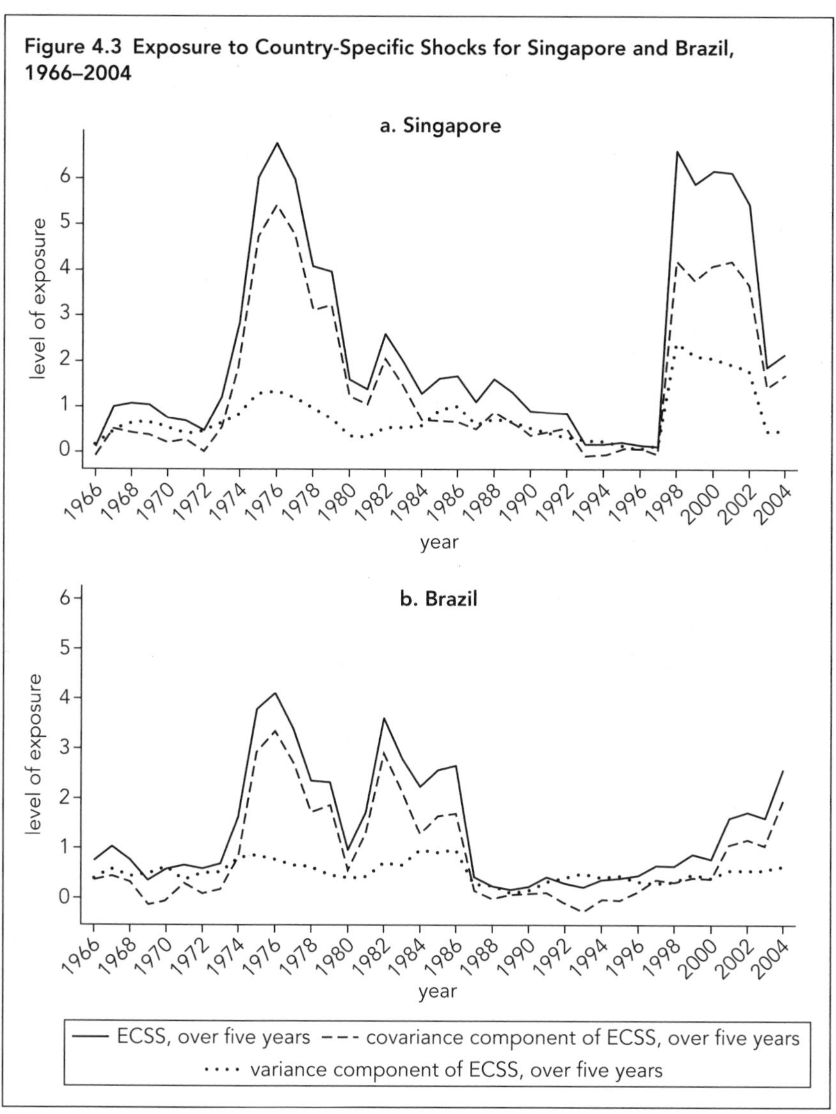

Source: Authors' calculations using GDP data from World Development Indicators database and trade data from U.N. Comtrade.

Note: ECSS = exposure to country-specific shocks.

The figure shows that the Asian crisis had a strong impact on Singapore's portfolio covariance (which indicates a certain level of regional concentration of Singapore's exports). In contrast, Brazil's ECSS was strongly affected not by the Asian crisis but by the Argentine crisis in 2001. Interestingly, the Asian crisis hardly affected the average global ECSS, as illustrated in figure 4.2.

Terms-of-Trade Volatility and Product-Specific External Shocks

Ideally, we would like to build a measure for exposure to product-specific shocks along the same lines as the ECSS variable. But to do so, we would need information on global prices for all export goods over our sample period, and that information is not available.[5] One measure that comes close to what we have in mind is the volatility of the terms of trade (the relationship between export and import prices, where the prices of individual products are weighted by the importance of each product in the export or import basket). A frequently used measure is the so-called "barter terms of trade" from the World Bank's World Development Indicators database.[6] The "net barter terms of trade" are calculated as the ratio of the index of export prices to the corresponding index of import prices measured relative to the base year 2000.[7] This measure is available only from 1980 onward. In compiling net barter or commodity terms of trade, export and import prices are often based on unit value indexes of merchandise exports and imports.[8] Prices may therefore end up being country specific and not necessarily reflective of world prices. Country-specific shocks in partner countries may therefore also affect this variable. Figure 4.4 illustrates that terms-of-trade volatility has been significantly lower in high-income countries than in middle- and low-income countries over the past two decades.

Diversification of Exports

The definition of the ECSS suggests that countries that spread their exports over a larger set of export partners will import less volatility, at least to the extent that the economic volatility of their export partners is not too highly correlated. Because countries cannot do much about the volatility of their export partners but can affect the geographical diversification of their exports, we are interested in the possible role of geographical diversification as a determinant of income volatility. In particular

Figure 4.4 Terms-of-Trade Volatility by Income Group, 1985–2005

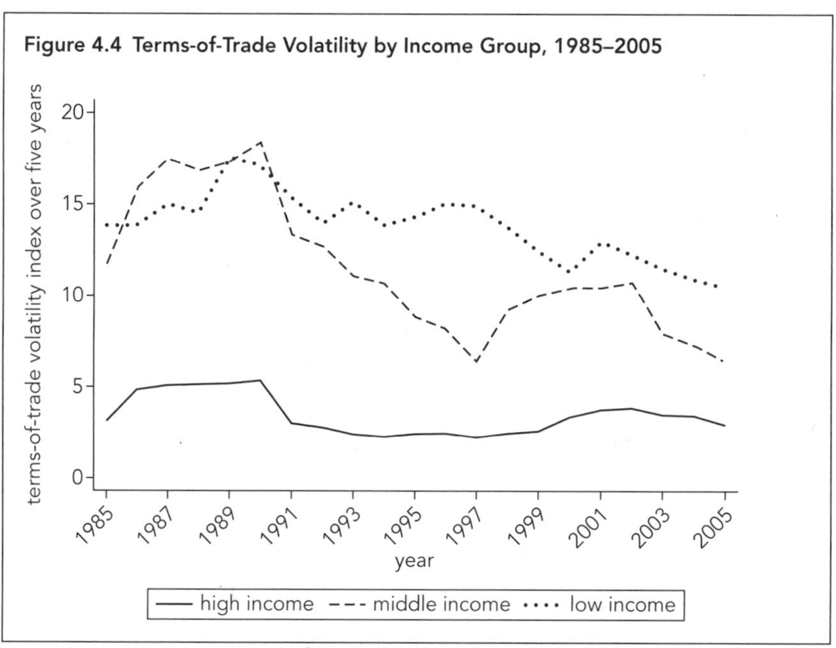

Source: Authors' calculations using terms-of-trade data from World Development Indicators database.

we are interested in the role of the number of partner countries, for we assume that the country-fixed cost of entering a market needs to be overcome only once and does not depend on quantities exported. We build our variables using a data set that includes 3-digit SITC trade data for a group of 180 countries for the period from 1962 to 2004.

Figure 4.5 shows, for high-, middle-, and low-income countries, the evolution of the geographical and product diversification by the number of partners and by the number of traded products over the period 1960–2004. In all three country groups, the increase in the number of trading partners was more significant than the increase in the number of products. In high-income countries, the number of exported products remained, on average, quite stable over time, while the number of trading partners increased by over 50 percent. Product exports in high-income countries are more diversified than they are in middle-income countries and more diversified in middle-income countries than they are in low-income countries. But when it comes to the number of partners, the difference between middle-income countries and low-income

Figure 4.5 Geographical and Product Diversification by Income Group, 1962–2004

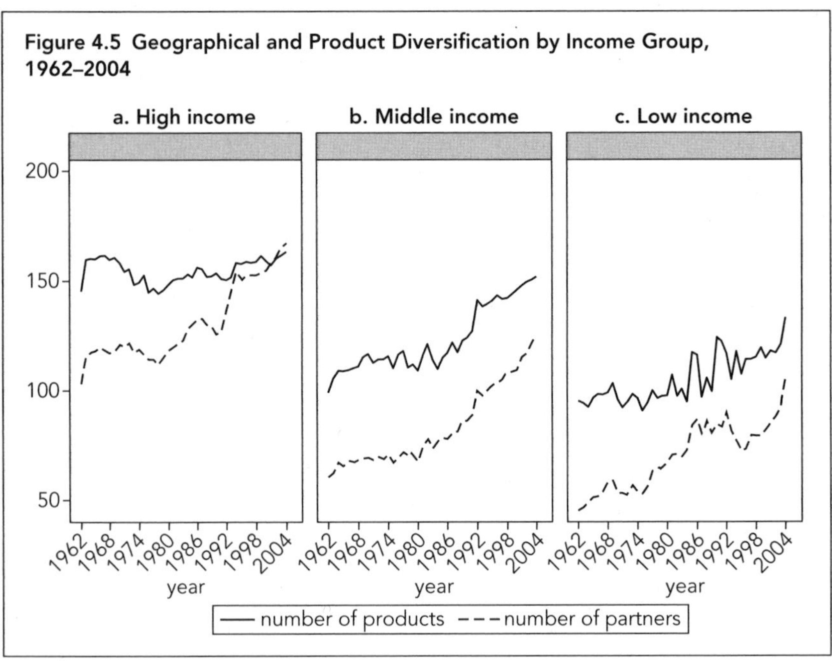

Source: Authors' calculations using U.N. Comtrade.

countries is less important. There were even years in the 1980s in which low-income countries had more trading partners than did middle-income countries.

Export Diversification and Exposure to External Shocks

Table 4.1 reflects the evolution of all the variables discussed so far over the four decades of our sample and for low-, middle-, and high-income countries. It also reflects how the ECSS and its components evolved over the same period. As noted earlier, the ECSS and the covariance of GDP changes were highest in the 1970s and early 1980s, a period marked by two oil shocks that triggered high volatility across the world. In the 1990s, variance within individual countries reached levels similar to those in the 1960s, but the covariance among countries was higher, maybe reflecting increased levels of global integration.

In particular, data for the ECSS variable show that during the 1960s and 1970s, low-income countries exhibited the highest exposure to external

Table 4.1 Summary Statistics by Income Group, 1963–2002

Variable	Income	1963–72	1973–82	1983–92	1993–2002
Exposure to country-specific shocks	High	0.82	4.08	1.11	1.45
	Middle	1.27	4.81	1.46	2.94
	Low	2.22	5.73	1.28	2.31
Variance	High	0.57	1.60	0.81	0.51
	Middle	1.19	2.44	1.10	1.34
	Low	1.90	3.77	0.77	1.28
Covariance	High	0.25	2.48	0.30	0.93
	Middle	0.08	2.38	0.35	1.59
	Low	0.33	1.96	0.51	1.03
Number of products	High	152	143	150	153
	Middle	108	109	116	139
	Low	91	91	97	108
Number of partners	High	109	109	121	144
	Middle	64	67	77	100
	Low	48	55	68	73
Terms-of-trade barter	High			4.21	3.21
	Middle			15.42	9.52
	Low			16.10	14.20

Source: Authors' calculations using GDP and terms-of trade data from World Development Indicators database and trade data from U.N. Comtrade.

shock, but since then, the middle-income countries presented the highest exposure to external shocks. With respect to the evolution of export diversification, the difference between high-, middle-, and low-income countries is more pronounced in the case of products than in the case of partners. For the terms-of-trade variable, data are available only for the last two decades in the study. Terms-of-trade volatility in both decades is much lower in high-income countries than in middle- and low-income countries. Middle-income countries have been more successful in reducing terms-of-trade volatility than low-income countries, which is in line with the evolution of terms of trade depicted in figure 4.4.

GEOGRAPHICAL DIVERSIFICATION, PRODUCT DIVERSIFICATION, AND THE EXPOSURE TO EXTERNAL SHOCKS

The definition of the ECSS indicates that it depends on exporters' number of trading partners, the weight of individual trading partners in the exporting country's portfolio, the volatility of trading partners' economies, and the correlation between the economic cycles of trading partners. To obtain an idea of how dependent the ECSS is, on average, on geographical diversification, we run the following regression.

$$ECSS_{it} = \beta_0 + \beta_1 geodiv_{i,t} * worldvolatility_t + \beta_2 geodiv^2_{i,t} * worldvolatility + \beta_3(CONTROL) + u_{it}.$$

We proxy economic volatility in trading partners by world volatility and conjecture that, for any given level of world volatility, geographical diversification helps to decrease exposure to risk. In particular, we assume that the relationship between geographical diversification and the ECSS is not linear. That is, we expect that the potential to reduce risk decreases, the higher a country's level of geographical diversification. We use two different measures for diversification in our regressions: the number of partner countries and the Herfindahl index (a measure of geographical export concentration, which is larger, the more exports are concentrated in few countries). We expect β_1 to be negative when using the number of partners measure and positive when using the Herfindahl index. In both cases we expect β_2 to have the opposite sign of β_1. Our findings for our overlapping periods reflect these expectations (table 4.2).

It is interesting to compare the turning points of the nonlinear relationships for the two types of regressions. When using the number of partners, the minimum of the predicted functions lies around 126 partners. High-income countries tend to have more than 126 partners, while low- and middle-income countries tend to have fewer. The latter would therefore, according to our results, benefit from increasing their number of trading partners. Using the Herfindahl index, the turning point lies at a concentration level of 0.96, implying that all countries—low, middle, and high income—can still achieve lower levels of exposure to external risk by further reducing the concentration of their exports.

To assess the role of country- and product-specific external shocks as a determinant of domestic volatility, we run the following regression using our panel data set:

$$GDPvol_{it} = \beta_0 + \beta_1 TOTvol_{i,t} + \beta_2 ECSS_{i,t} + \beta_3(CONTROL) + u_{it},$$

where *GDPvol* is the GDP volatility, $TOTvol_{i,t}$ is the volatility of the barter terms of trade for country *i* at time *t*, $ECSS_{i,t}$ is the main variable of

Table 4.2 Explaining Exposure to External Country-Specific Shocks

	Panel fixed effects			
Explanatory variable	**1**	**2**	**3**	**4**
Number of partners × world volatility	–0.039***	–0.041***		
	[0.010]	*[0.010]*		
Number of partners squared × world volatility	0.000***	0.000***		
	[0.000]	*[0.000]*		
Herfindahl index × world volatility			11.842***	11.810***
			[3.329]	*[3.329]*
Herfindahl index squared × world volatility			–6.141*	–6.114*
			[3.568]	*[3.568]*
Openness		–1.028*		–0.553
		[0.617]		*[0.602]*
Country fixed effects	Yes	Yes	Yes	Yes
Time fixed effects	Yes	Yes	Yes	Yes
Observations	1,770	1,770	1,770	1,770
Number of id_reporter	104	104	104	104
R^2: within	0.07	0.07	0.08	0.08
Rho	0.23	0.26	0.27	0.27

Source: Authors' calculations.

Note: Standard errors are in brackets.

*** Significant at the 1 percent level. ** Significant at the 5 percent level. * Significant at the 10 percent level.

interest—the variable denoting the overall risk of country-specific shocks—and is a vector of control variables: openness, GDP per capita, and population. The error term is $u_{i,t}$.[9] Because of restrictions in the availability of terms-of-trade data, regressions use data from 1985 onward.

Columns 1 to 3 of table 4.3 report the results of the estimation of the equation above for a panel of five-year averages and overlapping periods. The results show that countries' GDP volatility is positively affected by both terms-of-trade volatility and the exposure to country-specific shocks. Openness is consistently associated with higher volatility. In particular, the results in column 3 indicate that if a country spreads its exports increasingly over partners with different business cycles and, say, moves from the 75th percentile in the covariance component of the ECSS variable to the 25th percentile, its GDP volatility falls by 0.44 point. If a country increases the share of its exports destined to countries with low volatility and moves, for instance, from the 75th percentile to the 25th percentile in the variance component of the ECSS variable, it can reduce its GDP volatility by 0.02 point. This result implies that the correlation between trading partners' cycles is more important in explaining exporters' GDP volatility than the size of cycles in individual trading partners.

Table 4.3 GDP Volatility and Exposure to Risk (five-year averages)

	Full sample				Restricted sample[a]
	Overlapping periods			Nonoverlapping periods	
Explanatory variable	**1**	**2**	**3**	**4**	**5**
Terms-of-trade (barter) volatility	0.028***	0.028***	0.027***	0.036	0.040**
	[0.009]	*[0.009]*	*[0.009]*	*[0.026]*	*[0.017]*
Exposure to country-specific shocks		0.039*		0.220**	0.199**
		[0.022]		*[0.107]*	*[0.095]*
Covariance			0.570***		
			[0.080]		
Variance			0.037*		
			[0.022]		
Openness	1.859***	1.885***	1.928***	1.901	1.782
	[0.562]	*[0.562]*	*[0.554]*	*[1.576]*	*[1.146]*
GDP per capita	0	0	0	0	0
	[0.000]	*[0.000]*	*[0.000]*	*[0.000]*	*[0.000]*
Population	0	0	0	0	0
	[0.000]	*[0.000]*	*[0.000]*	*[0.000]*	*[0.000]*
Country fixed effects		Yes	Yes	Yes	Yes
Time fixed effects		Yes	Yes	Yes	Yes
Observations	1,770	1,770	1,770	334	256
Number of id_reporter	104	104	104	104	71
R-sq: within	0.05	0.05	0.08	0.07	0.08
Rho	0.55	0.55	0.56	0.53	0.44

Source: Authors' calculations.

Note: Standard errors are in brackets. Regressions in columns 1 to 3 used the panel fixed-effect estimation method with both country and time fixed effects. The same regressions were run as pooled regressions with country and time dummies, and the results were robust to this change in specification.

a. The sample includes only countries represented in the sample of Calderon, Loayza, and Schmidt-Hebbel (2005).

*** Significant at the 1 percent level. ** Significant at the 5 percent level. * Significant at the 10 percent level.

As a robustness check, we run the same regressions with nonoverlapping data. The results are reported in column 4 of table 4.3. Our ECSS variable remains significant with the expected sign, but terms-of-trade volatility becomes insignificant. This finding is surprising, as terms-of-trade volatility has been found to be significant in previous empirical literature, including in the paper by Calderon, Loayza, and Schmidt-Hebbel (2005), where the specification of the empirical model is similar to ours. To understand why we obtain results different from those of Calderon, Loayza, and Schmidt-Hebbel, we run our regression using the same sample of countries used in their paper. The results of this regression are reported in column 5 and show that terms-of-trade volatility is significant for that sample.

CONCLUSIONS

Openness exposes countries to different types of external shocks. The relevant economic literature analyzing economies' exposure to external shocks through trade has so far focused on price shocks, that is, shocks to the prices of imported or exported goods. Those shocks are typically measured by terms-of-trade variability and are associated with product-specific shocks. In particular, it has been argued that terms-of-trade variability is higher if the number of export products is relatively low and if exports are concentrated in products characterized by a high price volatility (such as commodities or oil).

In this chapter, we argue that country-specific shocks in partner countries may also be important and that they may affect others directly, even if they do not affect world prices. Recent theoretical literature has highlighted the existence of fixed costs of exporting and has argued that those costs may be country specific (Melitz 2003). This may imply that exporters cannot easily redirect their exports from partner countries hit by a negative demand shock to other countries where demand is strong. In particular, it may be difficult to redirect exports from an existing partner to a new trading partner. Demand shocks in partner countries may, as a consequence, affect the quantity and price of exports and, through this bias, affect the economy of the exporting country.

To test our hypothesis empirically, we drew on portfolio theory and constructed a measure for exporters' exposure to country-specific shocks of trading partners. This measure takes into account the volatility of demand in export markets and the degree to which the cycles of different trading partners are correlated. Using a data set of 180 countries over a period from 1985 to 2004 and controlling for terms-of-trade volatility, our panel regressions confirmed that our variable consistently has a positive and significant impact on exporters' GDP volatility. In other words, exposure to demand shocks abroad affects a country's income volatility. In particular, we found that the correlation between trading partners' cycles was an important factor in determining the volatility of individual countries.

In this chapter, we also examined what determines a country's degree of exposure to external, country-specific shocks. We found that for given levels of external (world) volatility, geographical diversification helps to buffer external shocks and thus reduces transmission of external volatility to the exporting economy. Yet the relationship between exposure to shocks and geographical diversification is nonlinear, indicating that the "beneficial" effect of diversification becomes smaller, the more diversified a country.

NOTES

This chapter reflects the opinions of the authors and cannot be attributed to the World Trade Organization (WTO) Secretariat or WTO members.

1. In most of our regressions, we consider only the period from 1985 onward because our terms-of-trade variable is available only from 1980 onward.
2. While most of these researchers restrict their attention to developing countries, a few studies (indicated below) cover both developed and developing countries.
3. This work is in the line of Deaton and Miller (1996) and Hoffmaister, Roldos, and Wickham (1998), who have used VAR to estimate the impact of terms-of-trade shocks on different macroeconomic variables and found that terms-of-trade shocks account for only a small fraction of output volatility in African countries.
4. Baxter and Kouparitsas (2000) decompose terms-of-trade volatility into what they term a "goods price effect" (difference in product composition) and a "country price effect (cross-country differences in the price of a particular class of goods). They show that their decomposition is not unique and find substantial variation across countries in the relative contribution of the two effects.
5. The World Bank produced such information but only until 1991 and only for three categories of goods: nonfuel commodities, fuels, and manufacturing goods (Baxter and Kouparitsas 2000).
6. This measure is used, for instance, in Broda (2004) and Elbadawi and Hegre (2004).

7. These calculations are based on data from the United Nations Conference on Trade and Development and the International Monetary Fund.
8. For national accounting purposes, when the increases in the value of export and import are to be separated into a price and a volume component, export and import price indices include the price of both merchandise and services.
9. We do not include dummies for oil-exporting countries or transitional economies, because all our regressions control for country fixed effects.

REFERENCES

Ahmed, Shaghil. 2003. "Sources of Macroeconomic Fluctuations in Latin America and Implications for Choice of Exchange Rate Regime." *Journal of Development Economics* 72: 181–202.

Aizenman, Joshua, and Nancy Marion. 1999. "Volatility and Investment: Interpreting Evidence from Developing Countries." *Economica* 66 (262): 157–79.

Baxter, Marianne, and Michael A. Kouparitsas. 2000. "What Can Account for Fluctuations in the Terms of Trade." Working Paper 2000–25. Federal Reserve Bank of Chicago.

Brenton, Paul, and Richard Newfarmer. 2009. "Watching More than the Discovery Channel to Diversity Exports." In *Breaking Into New Markets: Emerging Lessons for Export Diversification*, ed. Richard Newfarmer, William Shaw, and Peter Walkenhorst, 111–24. Washington, DC: World Bank.

Broda, Christian. 2004. "Terms of Trade and Exchange Rate Regimes in Developing Countries." *Journal of International Economics* 63 (1): 31–58.

Calderon, Cesar, Norman Loayza, and Klaus Schmidt-Hebbel. 2005. "Does Openness Imply Greater Exposure?" Policy Research Working Paper 3733. World Bank, Washington, DC.

Cavallo, Eduardo. 2007. *Output Volatility and Openness to Trade: A Reassessment.* Washington, DC: Inter-American Development Bank.

Deaton, Angus, and Ron Miller. 1996. "International Commodity Prices, Macroeconomic Performance and Politics in Sub-Saharan Africa." *Journal of African Economies* 5 (Suppl.): 99–191.

Di Giovanni, Julian, and Andrei Levchenko. Forthcoming. "Trade Openness and Volatility." *Review of Economics and Statistics.*

Easterly, William, Roumeen Islam, and Joseph Stiglitz. 2001. "Shaken and Stirred: Explaining Growth Volatility." In *World Bank Conference on Development Economics, 2000*, ed. Boris Pleskovic and Nicholas Stern, 191–212. Washington, DC: World Bank.

Easterly, William, and Aart Kraay. 2000. "Small States, Small Problems? Income, Growth, and Volatility in Small States." *World Development* 28 (11): 2013–27.

Elbadawi, Ibrahim, and Havard Hegre. 2004. "Globalization, Economic Shocks and Armed Conflict." Paper presented at the Conference on Globalization, Territoriality, and Conflict, January 16–18, San Diego, Calif.

Hausmann, Ricardo, and Michael Gavin. 1996. "Securing Stability and Growth in a Shock Prone Region: The Policy Challenge for Latin America." Working Paper 315. Inter-American Development Bank, Washington, DC.

Hoffmaister, Alexander W., Jorge E. Roldos, and Peter Wickham. 1998. "Macroeconomic Fluctuations in Sub-Saharan Africa." *IMF Staff Papers* 45 (1): 132–60.

Jansen, Marion. 2004. "Income Volatility in Small and Developing Economies: Export Concentration Matters." Discussion Paper 3. World Trade Organization, Geneva.

Knetter, M. M. 1993. "International Comparisons of Price-to-Market Behavior." *American Economic Review* 83: 473–86.

Kose, M. A. 2002. "Explaining Business Cycles in Small Open Economies: How Much Do World Prices Matter?" *Journal of International Economics* 56 (2): 299–327.

Kose, M. A., and Raymond Riezman. 2001. "Trade Shocks and Macroeconomic Fluctuations in Africa." *Journal of Development Economics* 65 (1): 55–80.

Love, James. 1983. "Concentration, Diversification and Earnings Instability: Some Evidence on Developing Countries' Exports of Manufacturing or Primary Products." *World Development* 11 (9): 787–93.

Malik, Adeel, and Jonathan Temple. 2006. "The Geography of Output Volatility." Discussion Paper 5516. Centre for Economic Policy Research, London.

Melitz, Marc J. 2003. "The Impact of Trade on Intra-Industry Reallocations and Aggregate Industry Productivity." *Econometrica* 71 (6): 1695–725.

Mendoza, E. G. 1995. "The Terms of Trade, the Real Exchange Rate and Economic Fluctuations." *International Economic Review* 36: 101–37.

Raddatz, Claudio. 2007. "Are External Shocks Responsible for the Instability of Output in Low-Income Countries?" *Journal of Development Economics* 84 (1): 155–87.

Ramey, G., and V. A. Ramey. 1995. "Cross-Country Evidence on the Link between Volatility and Growth." *American Economic Review* 85 (5): 1138–51.

Rodrik, Dani. 2001. "Why Is There So Much Economic Insecurity in Latin America?" *CEPAL Review* 73: 7–31.

CHAPTER 5

DIVERSIFICATION, INNOVATION, AND IMITATION OF THE GLOBAL TECHNOLOGICAL FRONTIER

Bailey Klinger and Daniel Lederman

Recent research by Imbs and Wacziarg (2003) showed that economic development in lower- and middle-income countries is associated with increasing diversification rather than with specialization. This chapter studies one aspect of economic diversification, namely, the production of new export products. These are not new in the sense of novel inventions new to the world, but rather are existing export products that are new to a particular country's productive structure, because they had not been exported from there before. Discovering that a product can be profitably produced in a particular country where it has never been produced before—an "inside-the-frontier innovation"—creates valuable social knowledge (Hausmann and Rodrik 2003). Firms that imitate the first mover derive benefits from such discoveries, yet they pay nothing for it. That is, imitation raises the social returns relative to the private returns and is clearly desirable from a social viewpoint. However, imitation also means that first movers cannot appropriate all the value created by their investments in discovery, because this type of innovation cannot be protected by the intellectual property rights regimes used to spur on-the-frontier innovation. Because entrepreneurs cannot appropriate all of the value they create, they underinvest in the experimentation necessary to discover new export opportunities, and consequently the process of productive diversification and private sector development stagnates.

However interesting this theory is, the market failure hypothesis warrants investigation. We develop a measurement of discovery activity using disaggregated product-level export data available for a large sample of countries and provide an empirical test to identify the existence of market failures affecting discovery.

A FRAMEWORK FOR DISCOVERY AND IMITATION

The frequency of discoveries in a country depends on the returns from discovering a new export and the first mover's ability to appropriate those returns; that ability is determined in part by barriers to entry. If barriers to entry are costly, then there will be fewer imitators to capture the value spilling over from the first mover's demonstration of the viability of the new export. However, if barriers to entry are light, then imitators will be able to copy the pioneer's discovery, giving first movers less of an incentive to experiment, thus lowering the frequency of discovery.

Entry barriers also affect the first mover's profitability directly. If the costs of establishing a new venture and contracting employees are high, then the returns to the first mover are lower, no matter what proportion of those benefits the first mover is able to appropriate. For this reason, returns to discovery also depend directly on barriers to entry, with higher barriers implying lower returns.

In this framework, a rise in returns unambiguously increases incentives for discovery. A rise in barriers to entry has an ambiguous relationship with discovery, however, for it implies lower returns to the first mover, but also a greater ability to appropriate those returns because of lower imitation. Thus, if the potential for imitation reduces incentives for discovery, then the effect of higher returns on export discoveries would be *greater* in countries with *higher* barriers to entry. Conversely, the effect of higher returns on export discoveries would be *smaller* in countries with *lower* barriers to entry. This, then, is our test of the market failure hypothesis: how does the relationship between increases in the returns to discovery and the frequency of observed discovery vary with barriers to entry?

DATA AND METHODOLOGY

To test this hypothesis, we develop a measure of inside-the-frontier innovation based on export data, because highly disaggregated data on production are unavailable for most countries. The problem with using export data seems obvious: a product emerging as a new export may have been produced domestically for some time and therefore would not represent a true inside-the-frontier innovation. However, exporting a particular good for the first time, even if it was already produced domestically, is itself an entrepreneurial act that requires discovery and can be imitated (Ibeh 2003). In other words, the act of exporting is itself a discovery worth investigating. Furthermore, the increasing importance of trade and foreign markets for developing countries, most of which are pursuing an export-led development strategy, means that discovering new products is primarily a search for new exports.

Worldwide export data are drawn from United Nations Comtrade (Commodity Trade Statistics Database) under the Harmonized Commodity Description and Coding System (HS), available beginning in the early 1990s for most countries at the 6-digit level of disaggregation (approximately 5,000 products). These data have been used widely to analyze export dynamism and growth, as well as geographic patterns in export growth, but until now they have not been used to study the emergence of new exports.

To identify a discovery, we require three periods: an initial period used to confirm that the good was never before exported (1994–96); a window during which time the discovery can emerge (1997–2002); and then a final period when the discovery is confirmed to be an established export (exported for at least $10,000 in both 2002 and 2003). Given the short time frame of available data, only a cross-sectional measure of discovery flows is possible. After eliminating microstates and countries missing more than two consecutive years of export data during the 1994–2003 window, we are left with a sample of 73 countries representing all regions and levels of development, and we identify 3,089 cases of discovery during 1997–2002.[1]

RESULTS

We expect episodes of discovery to depend on the level of development. At low levels of income, discovery involves the production of goods that have been invented elsewhere but that are new to the country or firm (inside-the-frontier innovation). As countries become richer, they approach the global technological frontier, and discovery involves the creation of products new to the world. Thus, discovery activity is likely to be more frequent at lower levels of development when countries are further from the global technological frontier and to decline as incomes approach high-income levels.

Export data indicate that diversification tends to rise with income until a relatively high level of income is reached and then to decline as economies become more specialized.[2] Comparing data on export discoveries (defined as described above) with on-the-frontier innovation (patent counts defined as in Lederman and Saenz 2005), we find that the frequency of discovery initially rises with per capita income, reaching a maximum in the neighborhood of $4,000 GDP per capita (table 5.1 and figure 5.1). Beyond that point, inside-the-frontier innovation is replaced by on-the-frontier innovation, which increases exponentially with GDP per capita. This relationship between distance to the frontier, the nature of innovation, and the stages of productive diversification reveals that we must control for the level of development (in quadratic form) when testing the model of innovation and imitation.

What other important influences on the frequency of discoveries should be considered in testing our model? One possibility is that discoveries are concentrated in certain industries, so that episodes of discovery are driven by changes in factor endowments associated with the process of development. For example, discoveries in poor countries could be concentrated in labor-intensive goods, and as growth occurs and factor endowments change, discoveries would be concentrated in capital-intensive goods.

However, data on the sectoral distribution of discoveries provide little support for this view. While the number of discoveries in labor-intensive goods does peak at a slightly lower income level ($3,626 per capita) than in capital-intensive goods ($4,546 per capita), nearly all types of goods reach their maximum discovery frequency in the range of $3,600 to $4,900 per capita GDP and then decline, with no commodity group peaking beyond $7,000 per capita (figure 5.2). This evidence suggests that

Table 5.1 The Changing Nature of Innovation

Variable	Off the frontier: discoveries	On the frontier: patents
ln (GDP per capita)	8.667	–16.237
	(6.53)***	(2.96)***
ln (GDP per capita)	–0.514	1.059
	(6.67)***	(3.43)***
Constant	–32.289	65.872
	(5.71)***	(2.74)***
Number of observations	73	68

Source: Authors' calculations.

Note: Estimated using negative binomial estimators. *Z* statistics in parentheses.

*** Significant at the 1 percent level.

Figure 5.1 Diversification and Innovation

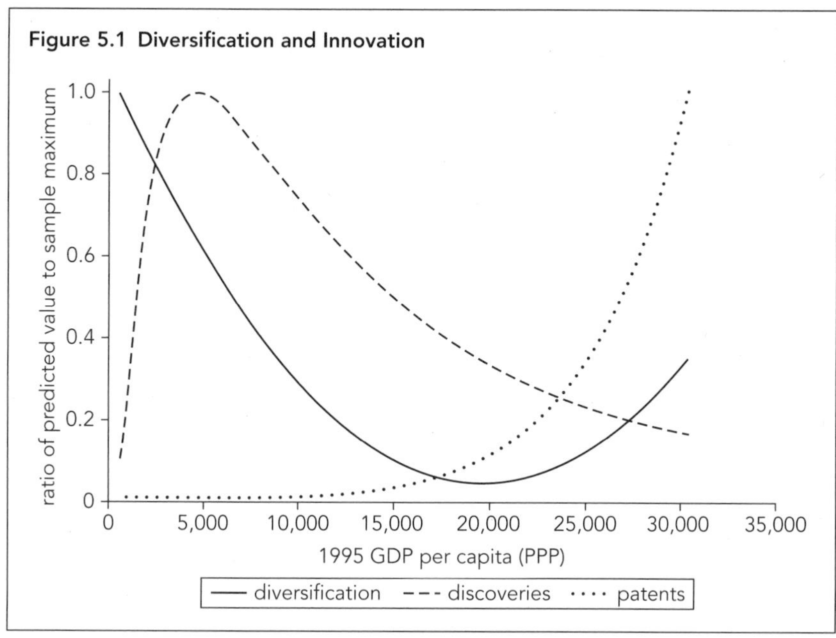

Source: Authors' calculations.

although discovery might be part and parcel of the process of productive diversification, it does not seem to be a by-product of shifting comparative advantage.

Finally, the size of the economy may affect the frequency of discoveries. Countries with larger populations are likely to have a larger pool of entrepreneurs, leading to more experiments and a higher frequency of discovery. It is also possible that a larger pool of imitators, although increasing the social value of discovery, would reduce incentives for entrepreneurs to experiment, resulting in a lower frequency of discovery. However, scale variables such as total population, working-age population, and number of person-years of education in the country were not found to be statistically significant in any test of the model discussed in the following paragraphs.[3]

TESTING THE MODEL

As described earlier, our model tests for the presence of market failures in the process of discovery by examining how the relationship between the

Figure 5.2 Discovery and GDP by Leamer Commodity Groups

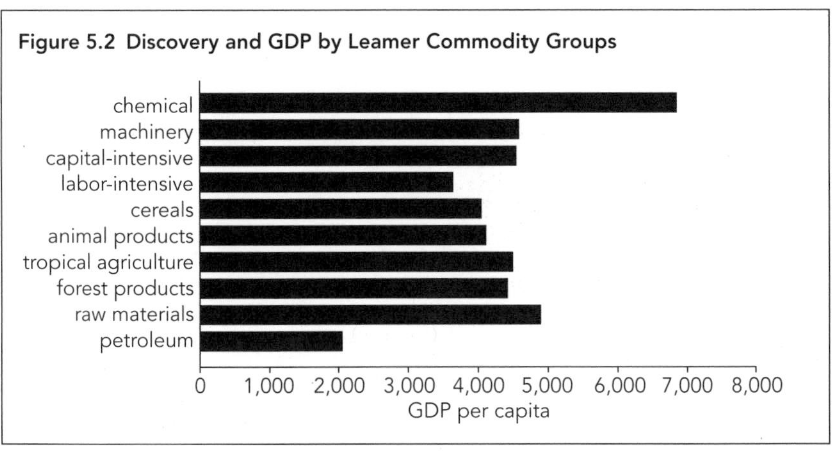

Source: Authors' calculations based on Leamer (1984).

frequency of discovery and the returns to discovery changes with barriers to entry. Barriers to entry are measured by an index constructed from objective measures of the costs and delays in starting a new business, enforcing contracts, and hiring employees (reported in the World Bank's *Doing Business* database for 2004).[4] The indicators for registering a new business would be most appropriate if discovery is undertaken by new entrepreneurs, whereas the measures of labor-market rigidities would be most appropriate if discovery is the work of existing firms. It is not clear which is the case, and this could also vary by country and by industry. Moreover, all these regulatory measures are highly collinear. A composite index of these variables is consequently the most appropriate measure, which we construct using principal components analysis.[5]

Our measure of exogenous returns to export discoveries is the annual growth of exports of the commodity export basket, excluding export goods identified as discoveries, minus the annual growth rate of nonexport GDP. The growth of nonexport GDP is netted out of our measure so that it more directly captures the returns to exports, as compared with production of goods and services for domestic consumption, which are not captured in the merchandise trade data used to identify export discoveries. This measure of export returns was calculated separately for each of 10 commodity categories.

Three other modifications to the model and testing procedure are required to control for the influences on the frequency of discoveries that were discussed above. First, it is possible that entry barriers have a differential impact on the frequency of discoveries across industries.

Therefore, our analysis conducted at the country–commodity group level examines the relationship between the number of discoveries in a particular country commodity group and export growth in that country commodity group, as well as how that relationship changes with barriers to entry across countries. Second, the frequency of discoveries is in part determined by income level, so GDP per capita and GDP per capita squared are included as independent variables. Third, discovery may be affected by factor endowments, so we include a measure of historical net exports per capita in that particular commodity group (Leamer 1984). Fourth, to control for differences across commodity groups and the different number of products composing each commodity cluster, we include dummy variables for each commodity group. Finally, we control for historical discoveries by country commodity group using export data at a higher level of aggregation.[6] This measure is available for a longer time period but identifies only broad, sectoral-level discoveries rather than disaggregated product-level discoveries.

We thus have a model where the number of discoveries, for each country commodity group, depends on per capita income, historical discoveries, factor endowments, entry barriers, and dummy variables for each commodity group and country. Estimating this model shows that the number of discoveries is positively related to GDP per capita (with the expected U-shaped relationship) and to the number of historical discoveries, but not to factor endowments. Further, export growth has a positive and significant effect on the frequency of export discoveries, but the magnitude of this effect rises with barriers to entry.[7] This result is consistent with our hypothesis that barriers to entry encourage discovery by reducing the impact of imitators on the returns to discovery. Further estimations suggest that the relationship between barriers to entry and discovery is subject to a threshold effect (differing depending on the level of barriers to entry). For countries with low barriers to entry, the marginal impact of higher returns to exports on the number of discoveries is negligible. But for countries with mid- to high-level entry barriers, this effect becomes much larger and statistically significant.

CONCLUSIONS AND POLICY IMPLICATIONS

Recent research has highlighted the importance of diversification for developing countries, a process that may be hindered by spillovers in the discovery of new products for export. We find that discovery has a larger response to increased profitability in countries with higher barriers to entry, indicating that imitation of first movers may be leading to fewer cases of inside-the-frontier discoveries than otherwise would occur. Imitation may occur because other firms gain information on production costs that are not predictable ex ante (Hausmann and Rodrik 2003), learn the characteristics of foreign demand (Vettas 2002), free ride on investments to cultivate foreign demand (Bhagwati 1968; Mayer 1984), learn the redesigns needed to meet foreign safety standards, or through some other unidentified channel.

Regardless of the particular channel, this finding suggests that public support for experimentation in new sectors and activities may be warranted. Increasing barriers to entry is not an advisable way to increase discovery, however. Indeed, imitation is the channel through which the returns of inside-the-frontier innovation are socialized. Moreover, such barriers are directly related to lower levels of private sector development (World Bank 2005) and, according to Hausmann and Rodrik's (2003) model, would lead to underspecialization of the economy, since widespread imitation leads to the efficient focusing of resources in the most profitable sectors. Imitation of profitable new export sectors increases economic efficiency and therefore should be encouraged rather than hindered. Furthermore, supporting new production with barriers to entry protects beneficiaries from market discipline, an action that would be repeating the errors of import-substituting industrialization policies by not allowing the market to eventually "pick the winners."

Support mechanisms that do not build up inefficient barriers insulating firms from competition and that instead balance government and market failures represent a more productive way forward. Such policies are not completely new. From Lesotho's Pioneer Industries Bill of 1967 to China's National New Product Program of 1988, various mechanisms focused specifically on new products have already been deployed. Evaluating the results of such programs would provide an even better test of the market failure hypothesis and represents a promising avenue for future research.

NOTES

This chapter is extracted from World Bank Policy Research Working Paper 3872, where further details can be found. The authors are grateful for the valuable feedback provided by Caroline Freund, Andrés Rodríguez-Clare, Guillermo Perry, William F. Maloney, Ricardo Hausmann, Dani Rodrik, Ana-María Oviedo, and Jim Lahey. The authors are responsible for all remaining errors. This research was funded by the Office of the Chief Economist for Latin America and the Caribbean. All comments are welcome and should be sent to dlederman@worldbank.org and bailey_ klinger@ksgphd.harvard.edu.

1. The sample composition can be found in the appendix to the larger paper (Klinger and Lederman 2006). A few products appear as export discoveries because customs begins to report goods separately that were previously included in a "not elsewhere specified" group. We eliminate 19 significant outliers that are likely cases of reclassification (the methodology and products affected are given in the same appendix).
2. See Imbs and Wacziarg (2003) for an analysis based on domestic production and labor data. The same result is reviewed for export data in a paper by Cadot, Carrère, and Strauss-Kahn (2007).
3. Nor were measures of financial system development, initial exports, institutional quality, or infrastructure statistically significant.
4. These data, available only for 2003, are the best measures available of entry barriers. It is unlikely that the regulatory regime changed significantly during the sample period.
5. The quality of the data corresponding to the variable on the costs of starting a new business across countries is notoriously weak. Our results are similar if that factor is excluded from the composite index.
6. The aggregation is taken from SITC Revision 1 at the 3-digit level.
7. Barriers to entry are not found to have a direct impact on discovery frequency, indicating that barriers only affect discovery either through their impact on export profitability or through the interaction with exports.

REFERENCES

Bhagwati, J. 1968. "The Theory and Practice of Commercial Policy: Departures from Unified Exchange Rates." *Special Papers in International Economics*. New Jersey: Princeton University Press.

Cadot, O., C. Carrère, and V. Strauss-Kahn. 2007. "Export Diversification: What's Behind the Hump?" CEPR Discussion Paper DP6590. Center for Economic Policy Research, London.

Hausmann, R., and D. Rodrik. 2003. "Economic Development as Self-Discovery." *Journal of Development Economics* 72: 603–33.

Ibeh, Kevin I. N. 2003. "Toward a Contingency Framework of Export Entrepreneurship: Conceptualizations and Empirical Evidence." *Small Business Economics* 20: 49–68.

Imbs, J., and R. Wacziarg. 2003. "Stages of Diversification." *American Economic Review* 93 (1): 63–86.

Klinger, Bailey, and Daniel Lederman. 2004. "Discovery and Development: An Empirical Exploration of 'New' Products." Policy Research Working Paper 3450, World Bank, Washington, DC.

———. 2006. "Diversification, Innovation, and Imitation inside the Global Technological Frontier." Policy Research Working Paper 3872. World Bank, Washington, DC.

Leamer, Edward E. 1984. *Sources of Comparative Advantage: Theory and Evidence*. Cambridge MA: MIT Press.

Lederman, Daniel, and Laura Saenz. 2005. "Innovation around the World, 1960–2000." Policy Research Working Paper 3774, World Bank, Washington, DC.

Mayer, Wolfgang. 1984. "The Infant-Export Industry Argument." *Canadian Journal of Economics* 17 (2): 249–69.

Vettas, Nikolaos. 2002. "Investment Dynamics in Markets with Endogenous Demand." *Journal of Industrial Economics* 48 (2): 189–203.

World Bank. 2004. *Doing Business in 2004: Understanding Regulation.* Washington, DC: World Bank.

———. 2005. *World Development Report 2005: A Better Investment Climate for Everyone*. Washington, DC: World Bank and Oxford University Press.

CHAPTER 6

WATCHING MORE THAN THE DISCOVERY CHANNEL TO DIVERSIFY EXPORTS

Paul Brenton and Richard Newfarmer

In seeking to accelerate export diversification, much of the focus in the past has been on increasing the number of products that are exported. Hausmann and Rodrik (2003) continue in this vein and focus on the "discovery process" of exporting, contending that firms in developing economies tend to underinvest in discovery because would-be first movers into export markets fear their initially high returns would be eroded by subsequent new entry, and they thus underinvest in searching for new export activities. A policy corollary is that governments can usefully deploy industrial policies to stimulate discovery and hence diversification.

Klinger and Lederman (2004) create a model to test the hypothesis that the threat of imitation inhibits the rate of "discovery." They proxy barriers to entry by using the average time it takes to register a formal firm (from the World Bank's *Doing Business* surveys), and find that indeed barriers to entry are associated with increased discovery and diversification. From this they deduce that some type of subsidy to the discovery process is warranted.

While discovery of new export products may be important to the process of export growth, one must look at the whole export product cycle. For example, what are the obstacles to sustaining new product exports? Brenton, Pierola and von Uexküll (2009, chapter 7 in this volume) show that lower-income developing countries do fairly well in generating new product exports ("births"), but that a high proportion do not survive to maturity ("deaths"). This finding suggests that activity during the acceleration phase of the export product might be as important as the discovery phase.

Policy that is focused solely on the discovery phase may miss other important opportunities for driving export growth. Hence, it is necessary to understand the contribution of various sources of export growth in developing countries before drawing strong policy conclusions regarding one particular element of the growth process. To this end, this chapter asks the question, Are countries with rapidly growing exports performing well because they are intensifying existing exports to existing markets or because they are bringing new products to market or because they are extending the reach of existing products to markets in third countries? After reviewing the export performance of a wide group of developing countries during the period 1995–2004, the chapter explores the importance of, and the potential for, the growth of existing exports to new markets.

OLD-GROWTH EXPORTS VERSUS NEW-GROWTH EXPORTS

Over time, the growth of exports can be divided into the expansion of existing products to old markets (the intensive margin) and the expansion of existing and new products to new geographic markets, as well as the expansion of new products to old markets (the extensive margin). This study builds upon previous analyses of the role of the intensive and extensive margins in export growth (such as those by Evenett and Venables 2002, Besedes and Prusa 2007, and Zahler 2007) by using data for a broader set of developing-country exports to a wider group of importers and for a more detailed commodity breakdown.

Our examination of the growth of exports from 99 developing countries to 102 developed- and developing-country markets over 1995–2004, accounting for 87 percent of imports from the developing-country exporters, shows the preponderance of growth at the intensive margin.[1] For a list of the countries in the study, see annex 6A. For the 99 exporters as a whole, the intensive margin accounted for 80 percent of the contribution to total export growth, while the extensive margin contributed only 20 percent (figure 6.1).

Within the intensive margin, existing export flows that experienced an increase (equivalent to 105 percent of total export growth) were slightly offset by those export flows that fell (20 percent of total export growth) or disappeared (4 percent of total export growth). Within the

Figure 6.1 Decomposition of Export Growth for 99 Developing Countries, 1995–2004

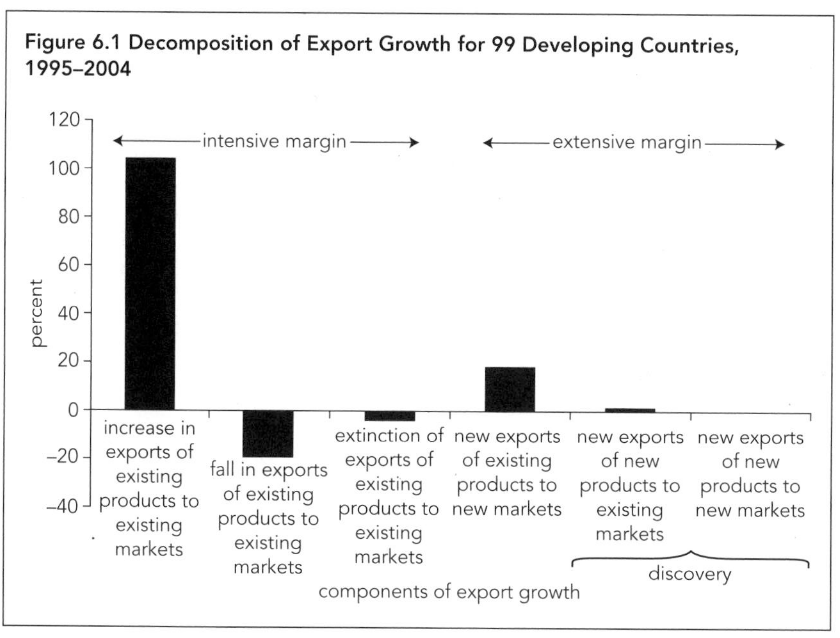

Source: Authors' calculations based on U.N. Comtrade (Commodity Trade Statistics Database).

Note: Each bar equals the change in exports for the category divided by the change in total exports.

extensive margin, the export of existing products to new markets accounted for about 18 percent of total export growth, while the export of new products accounted for only 1 percent of growth.

These conclusions largely hold for each of the geographic regions. In all geographic regions, the intensification of existing export flows makes the largest contribution to export growth, in most regions offset only slightly by the decline or extinction of existing flows (table 6.1). The decline and extinction of existing export products are somewhat more important in sub-Saharan Africa, which is also the only region where the extensive margin made a larger contribution to export growth than the intensive margin. In none of the regions was the export of new products a significant source of export growth between 1995 and 2004. These results are also consistent across income groups, where export growth is dominated by the intensive margin. (We also repeated the exercise for an earlier period to determine if the results were consistent, and they were; see annex 6B.)

Table 6.1 Contribution of the Intensive and Extensive Margins to Export Growth, by Region (percent)

	Intensive margin			Extensive margin			Total = 100%	
Region	Increase in exports of existing products to existing markets	Fall in exports of existing products to existing markets	Extinction of exports of existing products to existing markets	New exports of existing products to new markets	New exports of new products to existing markets	New exports of new products to new markets	Intensive	Extensive
Africa	106.9	–37.7	–25.9	46.1	10.2	0.4	43.3	56.7
Middle East and North Africa	92.1	–16.9	–7.6	30.1	2.4	0.0	67.6	32.4
Europe and Central Asia	89.8	–14.7	–7.3	29.8	2.4	0.0	67.8	32.2
Latin America and the Caribbean	105.7	–21.9	–8.6	23.1	1.6	0.0	75.3	24.7
South Asia	104.3	–21.6	–5.0	20.8	1.5	0.0	77.7	22.3
East Asia and Pacific	106.7	–19.3	–1.7	13.8	0.5	0.0	85.7	14.3

Source: Authors' calculations based on U.N. Comrade.

EXPLOITING THE EXTENSIVE MARGIN

Countries that are already producing in many markets and have highly diversified export portfolios obviously have less potential to increase exports at the extensive margin and therefore a broader base for the intensive margin to propel growth. However, countries with a less-developed productive base have, as Besedes and Prusa (2007) suggest, enormous opportunities to further exploit the extensive margin for growth.

One way to measure that geographic potential for a specific country is to look at the products it exports, compare that to the number of countries importing those products around the world, and then measure the share of geographic markets the country actually reaches. This we call the *index of export market penetration.*[2] For the given range of products that a country exports, the index will be higher for countries that service a large proportion of the number of national markets around the world that import that product. Countries that export only to a small number of the overseas markets that import the products that the country exports will have a low value on the index.

Indeed, by this measure, countries with higher per capita incomes tend to have more success in exploiting the available markets for the goods that they export. This is illustrated in figure 6.2, which shows a positive correlation between the log of the index of export market penetration and the log of GDP (gross domestic product) per capita (table 6.2). Further, the positive

Figure 6.2 Export Market Penetration and per Capita Income

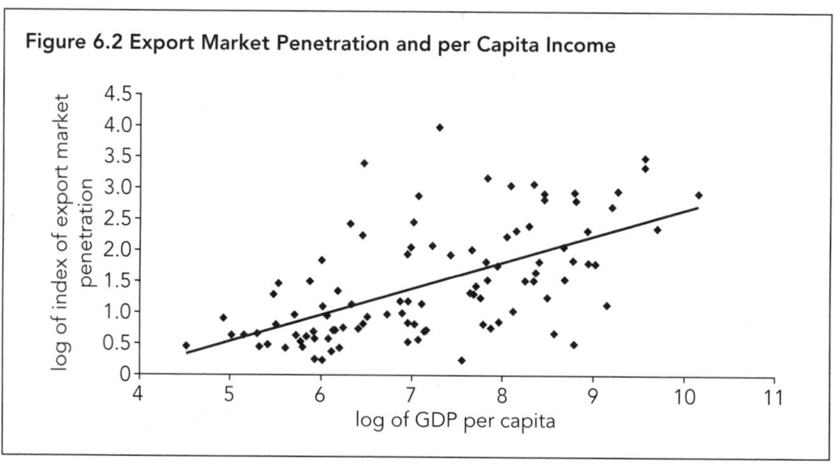

Source: Authors' calculations.

and significant relationship between export market penetration and GDP per capita remains after controlling for economic size (log of GDP).[3]

Example: Albania Reaches Fewer Markets than Does the Czech Republic

A specific example helps in understanding the large differences in export market penetration between countries of different income levels. Albania, with a per capita income of $2,400 in 2004, exported 955 products, about one-third of the number exported by the Czech Republic, with a per capita income of $10,500 (column 2 of table 6.3). These 955 products generated 2,050 bilateral export flows for Albania. In contrast, the Czech Republic's 2,863 exported products generated over 50,000 bilateral flows. Thus, the number of bilateral export flows for Albania was only 4 percent of that for the Czech Republic (column 3 of table 6.3), even though the number of potential flows for Albania is around 35 percent of that of the Czech Republic (column 4). Thus, Albania is

Table 6.2 Regression Results for Dependent Variable Log of Index of Export Market Penetration

Log of GDP per capita	0.42	0.09
	(0.06)	(0.04)
Log of GDP		0.38
		(0.03)
Adjusted R^2	0.35	0.77

Source: Authors' calculations.

Note: Standard errors are in parentheses.

Table 6.3 Export Market Penetration for Albania and the Czech Republic, 2004

Country	Number of products exported	Actual number of export relationships	Potential number of export relationships	Export market penetration
Albania	955	2,050	90,350	2.27
Czech Republic	2,863	50,187	258,904	19.38
Ratio	0.35	0.04	0.35	

Source: Authors' calculations based on U.N. Comtrade.

currently exploiting just 2 percent of the potential bilateral flows for the products that it exports, while the Czech Republic is exploiting almost 20 percent of its available export opportunities (column 5).[4]

What could explain why countries such as Albania exhibit a much lower number of bilateral trade flows for their export products than countries with higher levels of income per capita? Here the recently developed model of trade with heterogeneous firms (Melitz 2003) is useful in highlighting critical parameters that can limit the number of trade flows. In the Melitz model, there is a distribution of firms within a country with differing productivities and hence differing marginal costs. Exporters must incur the fixed costs of entering markets (both the domestic and overseas markets) and variable trade costs (such as transportation and tariffs).

For every market in the world, including the domestic market, local firms face a cutoff condition that is defined as the highest marginal cost at which firms can enter the market. Because sales to the domestic market do not incur trade costs, the domestic cutoff marginal cost, conditioned by domestic demand, will determine the number of firms that enter the local market. Exporters need not necessarily serve the local market since local demand may not exist or be sufficient. However, in activities with scale economies, producing for the domestic market may enable firms to expand output to an extent that reduces marginal costs below the threshold to export to overseas markets. Hence, policies that raise the fixed costs of entry into the local market and the marginal costs of selling domestically can affect the number of firms and the potential number of exporters. This points to the importance of the overall incentive regime governing investment, the business climate, labor regulations, and the costs of key inputs. The latter will be determined by the trade regime and the efficiency of ports and customs for firms dependent on imported inputs, as well as by the provision of backbone services such as telecommunications, energy, water, and finance.

Bilateral exports will be stimulated by a fall in the fixed costs of entering overseas markets and by a decline in trade costs. Fixed costs are likely to emanate from the costs of obtaining market information, marketing in overseas markets, and producing to the standards of that market. Trade costs will arise from the costs of clearing customs and ports in the exporting and importing countries, transport costs, tariffs and other restrictions on market access, and the costs of conformity assessment for the overseas market.

In a world in which firms differ in their productivities, trade costs allow low-productivity firms that sell only to the domestic market to survive. Thus, a fall in trade costs induces a reallocation of resources within sectors away from low-productivity firms that exit the industry toward the most productive nonexporting firms that are now able to expand through exporting and to existing high-productivity exporters that can increase overseas sales further. As a result, industry productivity expands and incomes rise (Bernard and others 2003).

Possible Market Interventions to Boost the Rapid-Growth Phase

In this context, are there market imperfections that might justify government intervention in the rapid-growth phase, much as Hausmann and Rodrik posit exist in the discovery phase? Indeed it is possible to hypothesize several.

- Factor market imperfections: Costs of capital may prevent sufficient expansion of supply from reaching new export markets, and labor market regulations may prevent flexible deployment of labor.
- Informational asymmetries: Costs of gathering information about opportunities in new export markets may be high because few firms in a developing country export to that new market relative to competing suppliers from other countries.
- Imperfection in domestic services markets: Costs of key input services—telecommunications, transportation, and finance—are often high, in many instances because of policy barriers to entry (state monopolies prevent entry, for example).
- Transportation imperfections: Costs of transport to third markets may be high because the low quantity of total exports from a given developing country deprives exporters of scale economies in transport. Similarly, cartel arrangements in shipping drive up prices—and more so to developing countries (World Bank 2002).

Other imperfections could undoubtedly be identified. The point is that given the importance of the intensive margin, any strategy for using exports to grow would be remiss if it focused only on the discovery channel.

CONCLUSIONS: POLICIES AND OPEN QUESTIONS

Because of the importance of existing exports in the overall growth performance of a country's exports, policies that focus excessively on the discovery phase—to the exclusion of attention to existing products—are bound to miss opportunities to propel growth. Moreover, in the search for new markets, exploring the obstacles to penetrating new geographic markets is arguably as worthy of a priori policy attention as is exploring obstacles to discovery of new product exports.

How can policies remedy the types of market failures that may impede expansion into third markets? In many cases, these constraints to competitiveness require specific interventions and institutions. Supply-side constraints may impede firms from satisfying demands in existing markets—and typically infrastructure reliability and cost are crucial among these. Moreover, weak performance in the index of export market penetration, as shown in this study, underscores the importance of export promotion agencies—and even the need for economic officers in foreign embassies—in overcoming informational asymmetries that impede the search for third markets. Investment promotion regimes, standards bodies, and customs agencies are likely to be important to support innovation and clustering. Finally, diagnosis of underperformance in all these areas should result in policy initiatives to overcome obstacles. To be effective, experience suggests that these initiatives should be brought together within a strategy for competitiveness rather than as a series of ad hoc interventions.

This chapter opens up other interesting questions of research on diversification. At the intensive margin, have successful countries performed well because, during the mature stage of a product, they have invested in raising quality and introducing differentiation that allows them to exploit the intensive margin? At what stage in the export cycle did firms choose to seek new geographic markets—at a point when growth in existing markets began to slow, or in an earlier acceleration phase? Also, the findings on product deaths merit closer scrutiny and might be amenable to policy remedies. Why do low-income countries with apparent success in the discovery phase of the export cycle experience a greater rate of premature product demise? A recent article (Besedes and Prusa 2006) argues that sustaining growth in the first two to four years is crucial to moving into the acceleration phase. All of this suggests that watching more than the discovery channel might lead to a more comprehensive policy vision.

ANNEX 6A: COUNTRY COVERAGE

Table 6A.1 Developing-Country Exporters, by Income Level

Low income	Lower middle income	Upper middle income	High income
Bangladesh	Albania	Argentina	Korea, Rep. of
Benin	Algeria	Chile	Singapore
Burkina Faso	Angola	Costa Rica	Slovenia
Burundi	Armenia	Croatia	Taiwan, China
Cambodia	Azerbaijan	Czech Republic	
Central African Republic	Bolivia	Equatorial Guinea	
Chad	Brazil	Estonia	
Ethiopia	Bulgaria	Gabon	
Gambia, The	Cameroon	Hungary	
Ghana	Cape Verde	Latvia	
Guinea	China	Lithuania	
Guinea Bissau	Colombia	Malaysia	
India	Dominican Republic	Mauritius	
Kenya	Ecuador	Mexico	
Kyrgyz Republic	Egypt, Arab Rep. of	Panama	
Lao PDR	El Salvador	Poland	
Madagascar	Georgia	Romania	
Malawi	Guatemala	Slovak Republic	
Mali	Guyana	South Africa	
Mauritania	Honduras	Trinidad	
Mongolia	Indonesia	Turkey	
Mozambique	Jamaica	Uruguay	
Nepal	Jordan	Venezuela, R. B. de	
Niger	Kazakhstan		
Nigeria	Morocco		
Pakistan	Nicaragua		
Rwanda	Paraguay		
São Tomé and Principe	Peru		
Senegal	Philippines		
Sierra Leone	Sri Lanka		
Sudan	Thailand		
Tajikistan	Tunisia		
Tanzania	Turkmenistan		
Togo	Ukraine		
Uganda			
Uzbekistan			
Vietnam			
Zambia			

Source: World Bank data.

Table 6A.2 Importing Countries and Economies

Algeria
Argentina
Australia
Austria

Bahrain
Bangladesh
Barbados
Belgium
Bolivia
Brazil
Burkina Faso
Burundi

Cameroon
Canada
Chile
China
Colombia
Costa Rica
Croatia
Cyprus
Czech Republic

Denmark
Dominica

Ecuador
Egypt, Arab Rep. of
El Salvador
Estonia

Finland
France

Gambia, The
Germany
Greece
Guatemala

Honduras
Hong Kong, China
Hungary

Iceland
India
Indonesia
Ireland
Israel
Italy

Japan
Jordan

Kazakhstan
Kenya
Korea, Rep. of
Kyrgyz Republic

Latvia
Lithuania
Luxembourg

Macao, China
Macedonia
Madagascar
Malawi
Malaysia
Maldives
Malta
Mauritius
Mexico
Moldova
Morocco

Netherlands
New Zealand
Nicaragua
Norway

Oman

Pakistan
Paraguay
Peru
Philippines
Poland
Portugal

Qatar

Romania

Saudi Arabia
Seychelles
Singapore
Slovak Republic
Slovenia
South Africa
Spain
St. Kitts and Nevis
St. Lucia
St. Vincent and the Grenadines
Sudan
Sweden
Switzerland

Taiwan, China
Tanzania
Thailand
Togo
Trinidad and Tobago
Tunisia
Turkey

Uganda
United Kingdom
United States
Uruguay

Venezuela, R. B. de

Zambia
Zimbabwe

Source: World Bank data.

ANNEX 6B: DECOMPOSITION OF EXPORT GROWTH OVER A DIFFERENT TIME PERIOD

To help assess the robustness of the results discussed above, we applied the decomposition of exports to a different period. We want to maintain the same developing-country exporters, but moving to an earlier growth period reduces the number of import-reporting countries. To maintain a large sample, we chose the period 1993–2002, for which there are 78 reporting importers.

Figure 6B.1 shows that the broad conclusions from the main analysis are replicated in this different growth period. The main driver of export growth for the developing countries in the sample was the increase in exports of existing products to existing markets. Growth at the intensive margin again dominates growth at the extensive margin. Within the latter, it is exports of existing products to new markets that is most important. Products that were not exported in 1993 but that were exported in 2002 did not contribute significantly to export growth.

Figure 6B.1 Decomposition of Export Growth of 99 Developing Countries: 1993–2002

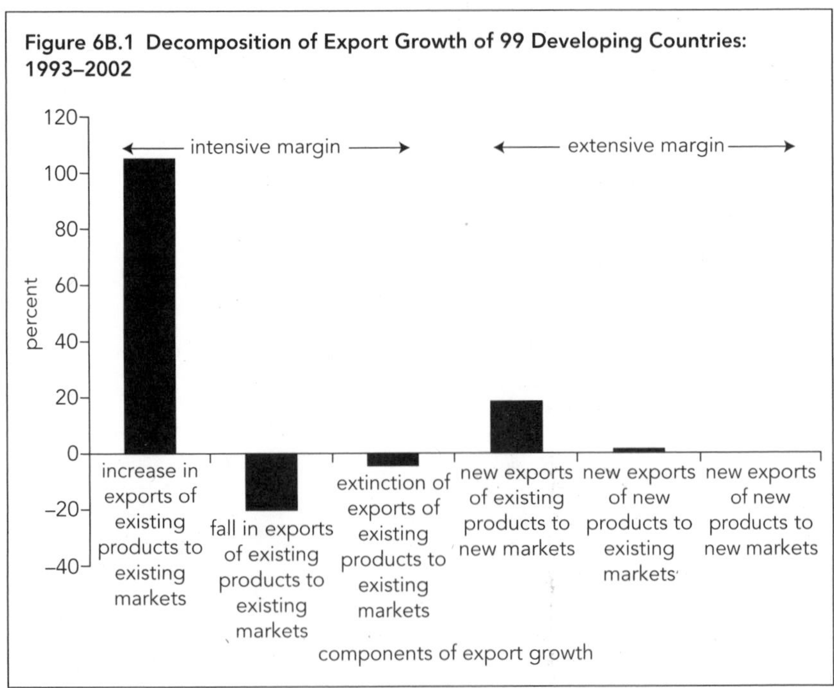

Source: Authors' calculations based on U.N. Comtrade.

NOTES

1. Small island economies, Middle East oil exporters, and a number of other countries, typically African countries in conflict, were excluded. There are 3,078 products, after removing gas, crude petroleum, and 34 specific steel products for which there is clearly a problem of data consistency over time. The data are import data reported for the Standard International Trade Classification (SITC) from partner countries in U.N. Comtrade (Commodity Trade Statistics Database). Data reported for the SITC are used rather than data reported for the Harmonized System, because the former has more countries for the 10-year period analyzed (102 versus 95) and because the latter has been subject to two revisions that may have introduced inconsistencies, despite efforts to establish a consistent time series. The numbers discussed here are essentially trade-weighted averages of the various components of export growth. The conclusions are not sensitive to the inclusion or exclusion of China (the country with the greatest weight in the sample).
2. This index is defined as the ratio of the actual number of bilateral trade flows to potential bilateral trade flows. Formally, for exporter j, for whom I_{ij} is the set of products (i) in which positive exports are observed, we define $Y_{ijk} = 1$ for $X_{ijk} > 0$, else $Y_{ijk} = 0$; and $Z_{ik} = 1$ for $M_{ik} > 0$, else $Z_{ik} = 0$, where X_{ijk} is the value of exports of product i from exporter j to importer k, and M_{ik} is the value of imports of product i by importer k. Then our index of export market penetration is given by $IEMP_j = \sum_{i \in I_{ij}} \sum_k Y_{ijk} \Big/ \sum_{i \in I_{ij}} \sum_k Z_{ik}$.
3. Note that the relationship between export market penetration and relative income is robust to different thresholds of exports (we also run these regressions for an index of export market penetration for exports that exceed $10,000 and also for exports in excess of $1 million).
4. Again, conclusions remain with the different thresholds for exports, as discussed in the previous footnote.

REFERENCES

Bernard, A., J. Eaton, B. Jensen, and S. Kortum. 2003. "Plants and Productivity in International Trade." *American Economic Review* 93: 1268–90.

Besedes, Tibor, and Thomas Prusa. 2006. "Ins, Outs, and the Duration of Trade." *Canadian Journal of Economics* 39 (1): 266–95.

———. 2007. "The Role of Extensive and Intensive Margins and Export Growth." Working Paper 13628, National Bureau of Economic Research, Cambridge, MA.

Brenton, Paul, Martha Denisse Pierola, and Erik von Uexküll. 2009. "The Life and Death of Trade Flows: Understanding the Survival Rates of Developing-Country Exporters." In *Breaking Into New Markets: Emerging Lessons for Export Diversification*, ed. Richard Newfarmer, William Shaw, and Peter Walkenhorst, 127–44. Washington, DC: World Bank.

Evenett, Simon, and Anthony Venables. 2002. "Export Growth in Developing Countries: Market Entry and Bilateral Trade Flows." Working paper, University of St. Gallen, Berne.

Hausmann, Ricardo, and Dani Rodrik. 2003. "Economic Development as Self-Discovery." *Journal of Development Economics* 72: 603–33.

Klinger, Bailey, and Daniel Lederman. 2004. "Discovery and Development: An Empirical Exploration of 'New' Products." Policy Research Working Paper 3450, World Bank, Washington, DC.

Melitz, Marc. 2003. "The Impact of Trade on Intra-Industry Reallocations and Aggregate Industry Productivity." *Econometrica* 71: 1695–725.

World Bank. 2002. *Global Economic Prospects.* Washington, DC: World Bank.

Zahler, A. 2007. "Decomposing World Export Growth and the Relevance of New Destinations." Working paper, Center for International Development, Harvard University, Cambridge, MA.

PART II

POLICIES: LESSONS FROM EXPERIENCE

Chapters 7–14 focus on selected aspects of diversification and policy experiences in promoting diversification.

CHAPTER 7

THE LIFE AND DEATH OF TRADE FLOWS: UNDERSTANDING THE SURVIVAL RATES OF DEVELOPING-COUNTRY EXPORTERS

Paul Brenton, Martha Denisse Pierola, and Erik von Uexküll

One of the distinguishing patterns in export diversification concerns the life and death of trade flows.[1] Countries with rapidly diversifying export portfolios seem to outperform countries that are diversifying more slowly—not in the number of new export flows that emerge, but rather in the survival rates of these new flows once they are introduced. Can low-income countries adopt policies that improve the chances of survival of new export flows and thereby boost exports?

To answer this question, this chapter first provides data on the frequency with which trade in specific partner country and product categories fails to occur (represented by zeroes in bilateral trade matrices). We then look to past writings for insights explaining the survival or death of new export flows. This work suggests that initially small flows tend to have a lower chance of survival than flows that are larger initially. To dig deeper, we build on an initial analysis of the duration of U.S. import flows by Besedes and Prusa (2006) and investigate the survival rates of detailed product flows from a broader sample of 44 exporting countries over the period 1985 to 2006. This is complemented with a small case study for Ecuador that utilizes firm-level data and investigates firm entry into exporting and subsequent survival. This review allows us to hone in on key factors that explain variations in the probability of survival of export flows and, in a final section, draw some policy implications.

THE FREQUENCY OF ZEROES IN BILATERAL TRADE MATRICES

Recent studies have noted the preponderance of zeros in bilateral trade flow statistics. For example, Baldwin and Harrigan (2007) find that of the potential export flows of the United States (defined by the matrix of the 8,880 goods with positive exports at the 10-digit level of the U.S. trade classification and the 100 largest import markets), 70 percent of the entries are zero. In other words, relatively few countries are importing the goods that the United States exports. The incidence of these zeros is found to be positively correlated with distance and negatively related to the size of the import market. Brenton and Newfarmer (2007) construct an index of export market penetration that captures the extent to which a country is selling its exports to the countries that import these products. The index takes a value of 100 if a country serves all of the markets that consume products of the type the country is exporting, and is lower to the extent that these consuming countries do not buy the exporting country's products. The 2004 median value of this index for 99 developing-country exporters is 3.6 percent (so 96.4 percent of potential bilateral export flows are zero). They also find that values of the index are positively correlated with GDP per capita: higher-income countries tend to exploit a larger number of the available trade flow opportunities.

The preponderance of bilateral trade zeroes in part reflects the frequency of exit. Besedes and Prusa (2006) find that a large proportion of U.S. bilateral import flows at a detailed product level are short-lived, with a median duration of between two and four years. Alvarez (2002) finds that of the more than 1,900 firms reporting export activity in a survey of Chilean manufacturing firms over 1990–96, only 20 percent reported exporting in every year of the sample.

TRADE THEORY, ZEROES IN BILATERAL TRADE MATRICES, AND ENTRY AND EXIT IN TRADE MARKETS

The large number of bilateral trade flows that are equal to zero focuses attention on the conditions that encourage the initiation of trade flows (entry into the market) and the disappearance of flows (exit). Recent trade theory has devoted considerable analysis to the determinants of entry, but less has been written on exit. One important insight: it is difficult to reconcile the frequency of zeroes in bilateral trade matrices with traditional explanations of international trade.[2] Models of international trade that incorporate the costs involved in entering and sustaining exporting, including those related to obtaining information, have had more success in elaborating the conditions that govern the sustainability of export flows.

Exporting Firms' Lack of Information on Costs

Uncertainty about the fixed costs of exporting may result in firms with relatively low productivity entering a market, only later to discover that they are unable to survive. Indeed, firms may deliberately enter export markets to discover the exact nature of these costs and withdraw if they are unexpectedly high. In this case initial entry is likely to take place on a small scale and exit is likely to be prevalent. Short-term entry may reflect the search processes that are necessary to match suppliers and buyers in the overseas market. "Sometimes their product isn't right for the market, or the country they chose was not a good fit, or their approach or agents are not right," one export consultant said (Rauch 1996). By contrast, when information on the costs of exporting is available or can be obtained at little cost, then entry is likely to be on a larger scale, and exit after a short period should be less prevalent. Such information is likely to be easier to obtain the greater the presence of exporters of other products to the particular overseas market and the greater the overall experience in exporting the specific product.

Buyers Lack of Information on Exporters

Rauch and Watson (2003) emphasize that buyers in developed-country markets incur search costs in finding developing-country suppliers and may be uncertain about the supplier's ability to deliver large orders to the buyer's specifications. The buyer may obtain information about the capacity of the supplier by starting with small orders that generate no profits but that reveal whether the establishment of a longer-term relationship, which may require costly investments in training the supplier, is likely to succeed. The model suggests that the higher the search cost and the lower the probability that the supplier will be able to meet the buyer's requirements, the more likely buyers in importing countries are to start a relationship with an exporter with small orders. The model also predicts that export flows that begin with large orders will tend to have longer duration. That is because buyers tend to initiate large orders with suppliers that have lower production costs and are less likely to look for an alternative supplier.

The Implications of Contract Enforcement

Araujo and Ornelas (2007) focus on the importance of credibility in an environment of weak contract enforcement. Potential exporters look for partnerships with distributors in overseas markets, but where the institutional environment is weak, some distributors with little concern for the future will behave opportunistically and default. Distributors can improve their access to exporters by establishing a reputation for reliability, and export flows will increase over time (and exporters' costs decline) as exporters become better aware of the trustworthiness of the distributor. The probability of exit from exporting declines the longer the partnership with a distributor continues. Improvement in the institutions for contract enforcement has a direct and positive effect on exports by reducing uncertainty and improving the expected return of the exporter.

Search Costs and Policy Consistency

Edwards (2007) shows that search costs tend to bias exporters to continue existing relationships. In addition, firms with established relationships are likely to be less sensitive to changes in the relative prices of different suppliers than are firms and distributors that are still looking for a satisfactory partner. This finding suggests that inappropriate trade policies, even if reversed, can have long-run adverse impacts. For example, preferential import liberalization may lock in trade diversion (resulting from information costs) even after a subsequent multilateral reduction of tariffs has removed tariff preferences.

Product Quality

Imperfect information and contract enforcement are likely to be of greater significance for buyers searching among suppliers providing products of different quality.[3] In other words, the matching of exporters and buyers tends to be easier for standard and homogeneous products. Much of the discussion concerning export diversification in developing countries centers on how to increase exports of differentiated products, especially manufactures, and reduce the importance of homogeneous products, particularly commodities. Rauch (1999) presents tentative evidence that search costs are higher; matching is more difficult; and proximity, common language, and colonial links are more important for differentiated products than for homogeneous products that are traded on organized international exchanges. Quality considerations underline the importance of institutions governing metrology, testing, and conformity assessment, where weak facilities in developing countries increase uncertainty and may entail additional costs in sending products to more-developed countries for assessments of quality and conformity with private or public standards.

EMPIRICAL SUPPORT FOR THEORIES EXPLAINING THE PREVALENCE OF ZEROES IN BILATERAL TRADE MATRICES

To investigate conditions governing the sustainability of trade flows, we adopt a simple model that builds on the theoretical insights discussed above. This model assumes that firms differ in productivity; that entry costs to exporting are fixed and are related to the costs of obtaining information; and that differences in quality among similar export products mean that only firms that can produce goods of sufficiently high quality are able to export to distant markets. This model has two important implications. First, bilateral trade zeroes will be more frequent the larger the distance between markets; because trade costs rise with distance, firms with lower productivity will not find it profitable to serve more distance markets. Second, bilateral trade zeroes will be less frequent the larger the importing country: as the size of the foreign market increases, the ability of lower-productivity firms to incur the fixed costs of exporting will improve. To investigate whether export survival is more difficult for exporters from developing countries than for those from high-income countries, we test these hypotheses using cross-country bilateral trade data at a detailed product level. We complement this with an analysis of entry and exit into exporting at the firm level using a survey of Ecuadoran manufacturers.

Data Sets Employed

We track the sustainability of export flows by observing the evolution of bilateral trade flows at a detailed product level over time: a positive trade flow followed by a zero entry indicates exit from exporting. Two data sets are used. The first involves reports by importing countries (import data are generally viewed as more reliable than export data, particularly when measuring developing countries' exports) at a detailed commodity classification that is consistent over time, so that changes in trade flows cannot be attributed to changes in classification. Taking into consideration the maximum number of importers available, at the most detailed commodity level, with consistent data for a 21-year period, our data set involves 44 exporters to 56 importers for 1,271 product categories at the Standard International Trade Classification 5-digit level.[4] We exclude very small values and treat an export occurrence in excess of $1,000 as a flow, but we do test the sensitivity of our conclusions to flow size.[5] The analysis is expressed in terms of the *hazard rate*, or the probability that a positive export flow in one period is followed by zero exports in the next (the hazard rate is defined in annex 7C).

We also investigate an alternative source of information at the firm level. The data set used for this analysis is from the continuous manufacturers survey carried out by the National Institute of Statistics of Ecuador. The survey covers 2,771 firms from 1993 to 2003, of whom 805 were exporters at some point. The sectors included in the sample accurately represent the main manufacturing sectors in the Ecuadoran economy, including food and beverages, textiles, apparel, wood, rubber and plastic, paper, and automobiles.

Description of Survival Rates

Both data sets reveal that the probability that an export flow will disappear declines the longer the duration of the export flow. Figure 7.1 shows the estimated survival rates of export flows at 1, 5, 10, and 20 years for each exporting country, ordered by per capita income. For low-income countries, hazard rates are particularly high in the first years of the duration of a trade flow. For Malawi, just 35 percent of flows survive beyond a year. For Taiwan, China, and the Republic of Korea, around 60 percent of trade flows survive for more than a year. The survival rate at 10 years is around 30 percent for Taiwan, China, and Korea and around 15 percent for the low-income countries in Africa. Figure 7.2 confirms a positive correlation between export survival and per capita income in the exporting country. Export flows from low-income countries have a lower probability

Figure 7.1 Survival Rates of Export Flows, Selected Countries, 1985–2005

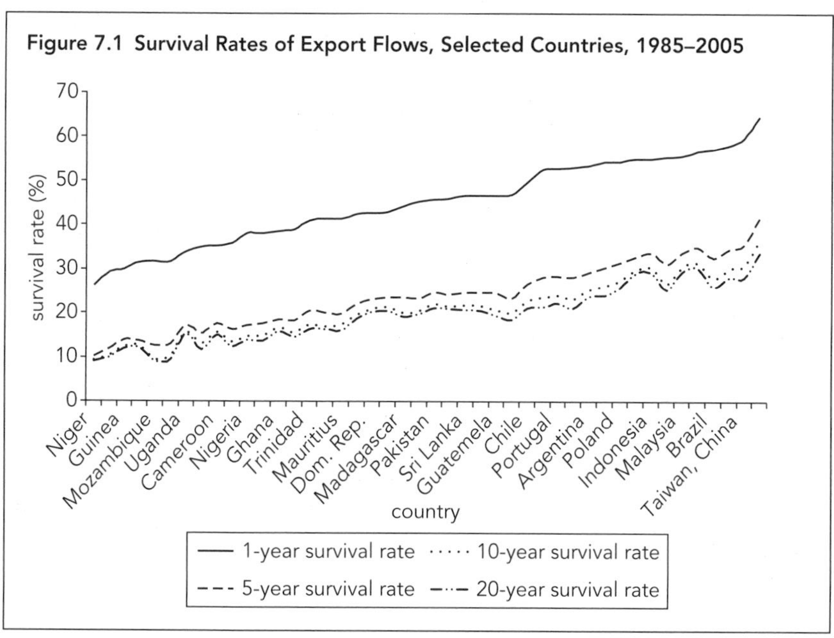

Source: Authors' calculations.

Figure 7.2 Ten-Year Survival Rates of Export Flows, 2004

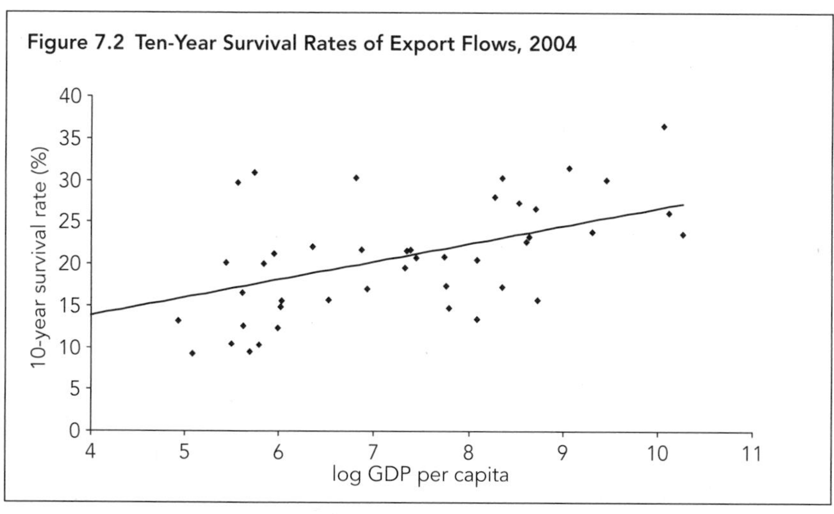

Source: Authors' calculations, based on World Development Indicators database.

of survival than flows from higher-income countries. Limiting the sample to trade flows above $50,000 (to reduce the likelihood of misclassification and to exclude observations attributable solely to the reexport of imported goods[6]) tells the same story: hazard rates are lower the longer the duration of the export flow, and survival rates and country income are positively correlated.

The data from Ecuador's manufacturing survey confirm the prevalence of export spells of short duration (figure 7.3). Of the 1,014 episodes of exporting during the sample period, 27 percent survived for just one year. Less than half of the episodes of exporting lasted more than four years. Firms that export for longer periods have a much lower hazard rate than firms with less export experience.

Investigation of Factors Affecting Export Survival

We now proceed to investigate factors that may explain differences in hazard rates. In particular, we explore why export flows in low-income countries have substantially higher hazard rates than those for higher-income countries.

Figure 7.3 Survival Rates for Ecuadoran Exporters

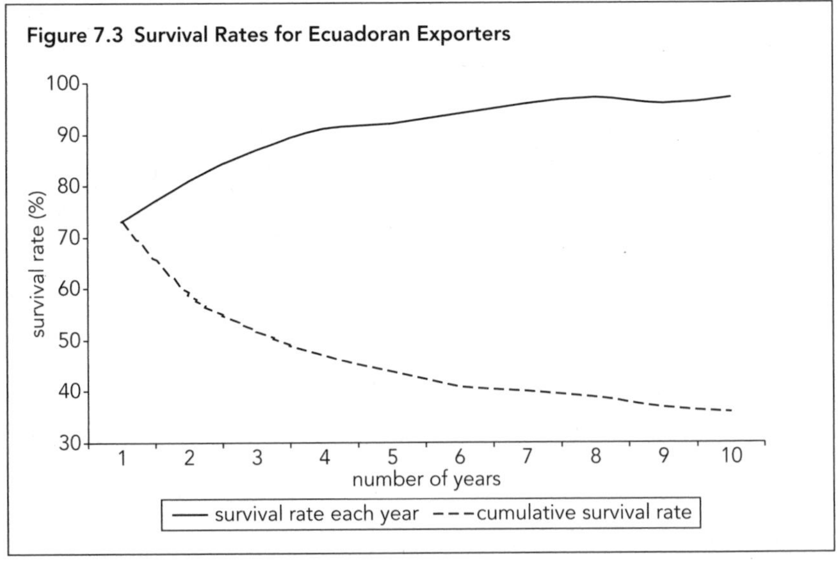

Source: Authors' calculations.

The independent variables that influence hazard ratios are

- the initial value of exports;
- distance as an indicator of trade costs;
- country variables that influence the cost of searching (proximity, common language, colonial ties);
- the total value of exports of the product, to capture experience with exporting a product;
- the size of the overall bilateral export flow, to capture knowledge of the particular import market; and
- the size of total imports of a product (there are likely to be a larger number of buyers in bigger markets, increasing the chance of the exporter supplier finding a suitable match).

We also include a number of policy variables, such as

- a measure of the variability of the bilateral exchange rate around the time that the flow is initiated;
- a measure of the deviation of the bilateral exchange rate in the year of entry from the period average, as a crude proxy for exchange rate misalignment; and
- measures of tariffs and trade preferences (the average tariff at the five-digit level over the available observations, a measure of the change in tariffs before and after 2000, and the presence of a preferential agreement between the two countries).[7]

Finally, we experiment with dummy variables for trade between poor countries and other countries in the sample to assess whether, after controlling for the variables above, exporters from low-income countries still face higher hazard rates.

The results reported in annex 6B show the impact of a one-unit change in an independent variable on the ratio of the estimated hazard function to base hazard function. The key issue is whether the value of the coefficient is significantly greater than 1 (meaning the variable increases the hazard) or less than 1 (meaning the variable reduces the hazard). For example, a coefficient of 1.1 would mean that a one-unit increase in the independent variable increases the hazard by 10 percent in any period t.[8] Care has to be taken when comparing the relative magnitudes of estimated coefficients because interpretation depends upon the definition of the variable.

The analysis of cross-country bilateral trade flows strongly supports the prediction that the larger the initial export flow the lower the hazard rate. The results also show that the hazard rate increases with distance. Similarly, the data from the Ecuadoran survey show a very strong positive impact of the size of the initial export on the firm's export survival rate. We also found a strong correlation between the size of the firm (in total sales) and the size of exports upon entry into exporting. This last finding suggests that relatively large firms are more likely to succeed in exporting than smaller firms.

Variables included to proxy information, search costs, and ease of matching all influence the hazard ratio significantly. Trading with a neighbor, common language, and colonial ties all reduce the hazard rate significantly. It is interesting that the size of overall exports of a product reduces the hazard, as does the size of the overall bilateral trade flow. Hence, increases in exports of existing products can help to reduce the hazard rate of exporters entering new markets. The size of the import market for a particular product is also a significant determinant of the hazard rate, but the size of the impact appears to be less important than the size of exports of the product and the magnitude of bilateral trade.

Without controlling for the other variables, the parameters on the dummy variables for rich to poor, poor to poor, and poor to rich country trade relationships are all significantly greater than one, suggesting that exports from poor countries and exports to poor countries face a higher hazard rate than exports between rich countries. However, once we control for initial size of exports, distance, and the proxies for information and search costs, the size of the parameters on these dummies declines substantially, indicating that most of the difference in hazard ratios between rich and poor countries can be explained by variables in the model.

The exchange rate terms, especially the term designed to capture variability, substantially increase the hazard rate. The tariff variables, although statistically significant, are very close to unity, while the preferential trade variable suggests that preferential access to an overseas market reduces the hazard faced by exporters.

These results appear to be robust to the, albeit crude, treatment of left censoring and when the sample is restricted to larger trade flows.[9] In this exercise, we include multiple episodes of exporting for the same product exporter-importer flow. To check the robustness of our results to the presence of these multiple spells, we also estimate the model including just one randomly selected episode of exporting for each product exporter-importer combination. This does not change the results in any substantive way.[10]

Treating these multiple spells more effectively is a challenge for our future work. Currently we treat all export episodes in the same way.

However, subsequent entries into exporting may not be independent of previous failed attempts. If information spills over, then firms may learn from the failures of others. We also need to allow for the possibility of cross-product and cross-market spillovers. An exporter of a particular product may learn from the export success or failure of other similar products. An exporter to a particular market may learn from experience in another similar or neighboring market.

CONCLUSIONS AND POLICY IMPLICATIONS

Successful export growth and diversification require not only entry into exporting but survival and subsequent growth. Our analysis confirms the conclusions of Besedes and Prusa (2006) that introducing new export flows appears to be less of a problem for developing countries than sustaining them over time. Survival rates are considerably lower for export flows of short duration, especially in the first five years of the life of a flow for developing countries. Our analysis suggests that the size of the initial export flow and measures relating to information and search costs, together with exchange rate volatility, are important factors explaining differences in hazard rates of export flows.

The importance of the initial size of exports is consistent with work by Brenton and von Uexküll (2007), who find that technical assistance targeted at specific export products tends to be more effective, in terms of the subsequent growth of exports, for larger export flows. The high hazard rate for initially small flows suggests caution in public policy interventions that are aimed specifically at exporters that start small. Reasoning along similar lines to Rauch (2007), we find that broad institutional changes favoring small firms relative to large firms in an economy are likely to have a relatively small impact on trade relative to reforms that favor entry of large firms.

The high hazard rate for initially small export flows also indicates that governments, through their export promotion agencies and trade consulates around the world, should pay particular attention to supporting new exports from their countries in new markets. Active engagement with exporters may well identify policy obstacles that, if removed, would increase the survival rate of exports.

Our analysis also suggests that the size of total exports of a product and the overall level of trade between two countries are important to the survival of new entrants in a market. Hence, the expansion of exports of existing products is important in allowing for future export growth and diversification.

Finally, policy measures that create a bias for or against exports of existing key products may affect the fate of prospective exports. On the negative side, for example, an export tax on a raw material or intermediate export, designed to support exports of the finished product, may actually act to constrain export diversification by limiting the flow of information from overseas markets and the experience of exporting. Similarly, taxing existing exports to fund an export promotion agency may not be appropriate.

On the positive side, experiences in several successful countries underscore the importance of maintaining a competitive real exchange rate, especially for several initial years after an export push has begun. Beginning with a depreciated exchange rate and holding the real value of the currency in check for several years has been a hallmark for nearly all countries that have managed to increase their export growth rate significantly over a sustained period. This approach allows time for products to penetrate several geographic markets, for exporters to develop transportation and other economies of scale, and for entrepreneurs to learn about new markets.

ANNEX 7A: EXPORTER AND IMPORTER COVERAGE

Table 7A.1 Importers Covered

Argentina	Greece	Oman
Australia	Guatemala	Panama
Austria	Honduras	Paraguay
Barbados	Hong Kong, China	Peru
Belgium and Luxembourg	Iceland	Philippines
Belize	India	Portugal
Bolivia	Indonesia	Singapore
Brazil	Ireland	Spain
Canada	Israel	St. Lucia
Chile	Italy	Sweden
Colombia	Jamaica	Thailand
Costa Rica	Japan	Trinidad and Tobago
Cyprus	Jordan	Tunisia
Denmark	Korea, Rep. of	Turkey
Ecuador	Malaysia	United Kingdom
Egypt, Arab Rep. of	Mexico	United States
Finland	Morocco	Uruguay
France	Netherlands	Venezuela, R. B. de
Germany	New Zealand	

Table 7A.2 Exporters Covered

Argentina	Indonesia	Pakistan
Bangladesh	Ireland	Poland
Brazil	Jamaica	Portugal
Burkina Faso	Kenya	Singapore
Cameroon	Korea, Rep. of	Sri Lanka
Chile	Madagascar	Taiwan, China
Dominican Republic	Malawi	Tanzania
Ecuador	Malaysia	Thailand
Egypt, Arab Rep. of	Mali	Trinidad and Tobago
France	Mauritius	Tunisia
Ghana	Mexico	Turkey
Guatemala	Morocco	Uganda
Guinea	Mozambique	Uruguay
Honduras	Niger	Zambia
Hungary	Nigeria	

ANNEX 7B: TECHNICAL ANNEX

Dealing with Censored Data in Econometric Estimates

As is common in studies of survival, the available data are censored. First, we observe flows in the first year of our sample but do not know for how long they have been in existence. Second, we observe flows in the final year of our sample but do not know how long they will continue to exist. The problem of right-censoring is easily resolved by the Kaplan-Meier and Cox estimation procedures applied in this chapter that extract the valuable information contained in these observations while avoiding bias. For example, a right-censored observation that is three years old at the cutoff year of the sample still gives valuable information about survival in its first two years of existence but should not be counted as a failure event in year three. Left-censoring presents a more serious problem. The literature provides some suggestions for procedures to deal with left-censoring,[11] but most of them rely on either quite extensive assumption or supplementary data that are not available in our case. Thus, for this preliminary work, our approach is simply to examine two sets of results, one where we simply ignore left-censoring and one where we drop all left-censored observations as a robustness test. A second issue is that duration or time-to-event data are typically skewed and making assumptions about underlying distributions is difficult. Hence, applying standard parametric statistical methods is unlikely to be appropriate.

Defining Indicators of Export Survival

Based on Keifer (1988), the probability distribution of duration can be defined as $F(t) - \Pr(T < t)$.

This specifies the probability that a random variable T is less than a value t. The corresponding density function is $f(t) = dF(t)/dt$.

The survivor function is most commonly used in analyzing duration data: $S(t) = 1 - F(t)$.

This gives the probability that T will equal or exceed some value t. Another useful function is the hazard function, $\lambda(t) = f(t)/S(t)$, which shows the rate at which spells will be completed at time t, conditioned on their lasting until t.

Define h_j as the number of export flows that are observed to have completed spells of duration t_j, for $j = 1$, and K as the number of years in our sample, 21. Define n_j as the number of flows that are at risk at time t_j. The Kaplan-Meier estimator is the nonparametric maximum likelihood estimate of $S(t)$ and takes the form $\hat{S}(t_j) = \prod_{i=1}^{j} (n_i - h_i)/n_i$, which is essentially obtained by equating the estimated conditional probability of completing a spell at t_j with the observed relative frequency of completion at t_j. The corresponding estimator for the hazard function is $\hat{\lambda}(t) = h_j/n_j$.

Dependent Variable Used in Investigating the Determinants of Export Survival

Following many studies of duration data and the Besedes and Prusa (2006) study of U.S. imports, we implement a semiparametric approach to the hazard function in order to analyze the determinants of the longevity of trade relationships. We estimate a Cox proportional hazard model, which assumes that variables influencing longevity have a proportionate impact on the base hazard function, that is, a change in variable z would increase or reduce the hazard function by the same factor in any period. The mathematical form of the hazard function in the Cox (1972) model is $\lambda(t, z) = \lambda_0(t)e^{\beta z}$, where $\lambda(t, z)$ is the hazard function, $\lambda_0(t)$ is the base hazard function, $\mathbf{z}$ is a vector of variables that have a proportional impact on the hazard function, and β is a vector of coefficients to be estimated that characterizes how $\mathbf{z}$ impacts the hazard function.

ANNEX 7C: RESULTS OF HAZARD RATE ESTIMATIONS

Table 7C.1 Semiparametric Results for Full Sample

	Hazard ratio					
Variable	**1**	**2**	**3**	**4**	**5**	**6**
VAL	0.828	0.860		0.860	0.859	0.867
	(0)*	(0)*		(0)*	(0)*	(0)*
DIST	1.088	1.107		1.108	1.101	1.115
	(0)*	(0)*		(0)*	(0)*	(0)*
BORDER	0.826	0.806		0.801	0.786	0.824
	(0)*	(0)*		(0)*	(0)*	(0)*
COMLANG	1.079	0.939		0.936	0.939	0.938
	(0)*	(0)*		(0)*	(0)*	(0)*
COLONY	0.895	0.948		0.953	0.951	0.843
	(0)*	(0)*		(0)*	(0)*	(0)*
EXP_PRODUCT		0.924		0.923	0.923	0.924
		(0)*		(0)*	(0)*	(0)*
IMP_PRODUCT		0.987		0.991	0.993	0.991
		(0)*		(0)*	(0)*	(0)*
TOTALTRADE		0.936		0.936	0.936	0.932
		(0)*		(0)*	(0)*	(0)*
PP			1.265	1.048	1.042	0.999
			(0)*	(0)*	(0)*	(0.779)
PR			1.226	0.971	0.969	0.947
			(0)*	(0)*	(0)*	(0)*
RP			1.111	1.048	1.046	1.034
			(0)*	(0)*	(0)*	(0)*
DE3					1.501	1.272
					(0)*	(0)*
REL_E					0.977	0.969
					(0)*	(0)*
PTA						0.925
						(0)*
AVTARIFF						1.001
						(0)*
DAVTARIFF						1.001
						(0)*
Number of observations	1,218,063	1,218,063	1,218,063	1,218,063	1,212,504	740,756

Source: Authors' calculations.

Note: VAL = initial export value; *DIST* = distance; *EXP_PRODUCT* = the value of all exports of the product by the exporter; *IMP_PRODUCT* = the value of all imports of the product by the importer; *TOTALTRADE* = the value of all exports between the export and the importer; *PP, PR,* and *RP* = dummy variables for exports from poor to poor countries, poor to rich, and rich to poor, respectively; *DE3* = a measure of the variability of the exchange rate; *REL_E* = a measure of deviation of exchange rate; *PTA* = membership in a free trade agreement; AVTARIFF and DAVTARIFF = measures of the average and the dispersion of tariffs. All specifications are stratified by product, left-censored observations included. Numbers in parentheses indicate the p-values; zero indicates a p-value of 0.0004 or less.

* Significant at the 1 percent level.

NOTES

1. A trade flow is the movement of a particular product to a specific market. The birth of a trade flow, one that was previously zero, entails a firm or firms entering that market for the product concerned. The death of a trade flow signifies that a firm or firms have exited from that market for the particular product. This chapter has benefited from discussions with Peter Walkenhorst.
2. Baldwin and Harrigan (2007) conclude that models of trade-based monopolistic competition are inconsistent with the presence of zeros and that those based on comparative advantage are not consistent with the observed tendency of zeros to decrease with the size of the import market. Models with heterogeneous firms (meaning that productivity differs among firms) and fixed entry costs to exporting (Melitz 2003) can be consistent with zero bilateral trade entries that decline with distance and size of the market. However, such models need to be amended to take into account product quality to explain another important observation—export prices increase with distance.
3. The importance of quality in influencing the pattern of bilateral trade flows has also been stressed by Schott (2004) and Hallak (2006).
4. The exporters and importers are listed in annex 7A. The need for consistent import data over 21 years means that most African countries and transition economies are absent from the importer group.
5. The econometric tests are complicated because we do not know how long flows in the first year of our sample have been in existence, nor for how long flows in the last year are sustained. These issues are briefly discussed in annex 7B.
6. For example, Brenton and Hoppe (2005) find that mirror statistics suggest the apparent export of a number of manufactured products from Sierra Leone, including electrical machinery, vehicles, and clothing. The export of passenger vehicles to Greece, to take one example, is simply not credible. Conversations with government officials, private organizations, and individual business persons confirmed that there was currently no significant manufacturing export capacity in the country. Thus, these apparent exports are either misclassified by product or origin (they could have been incorrectly allocated to the Sierra Leone country code in the process of compiling the relevant statistics) or they could be reexports of formerly imported products (including materials brought in by the peacekeeping forces of the United Nations or the Economic Community of West African States).
7. Caution is required with the tariff variables. We lose a large number of observations (almost 40 percent) from lack of data.
8. In some specifications, we stratify the sample, allowing for hazard functions to differ between the strata.
9. See annex 7B for further discussion.
10. These results are presented in detail in Brenton, Pierola, and von Uexküll (2007).
11. See, for example, D'Addio and Rosholm (2002).

REFERENCES

Alvarez, Roberto. 2002. "Determinants of Firm Export Performance in a Less Developed Country." Anderson Graduate School of Management, University of California, Los Angeles.

Araujo, Luis, and Emmanuel Ornelas. 2007. "Trust-Based Trade." CEP Discussion Paper 820, Centre for Economic Performance, London School of Economics, London.

Baldwin, Richard, and James Harrigan. 2007. "Zeros, Quality, and Space: Trade Theory and Trade Evidence." Working Paper 13214, National Bureau of Economic Research, Cambridge, MA.

Besedes, T., and T. Prusa. 2006. "Ins, Outs, and the Duration of Trade." *Canadian Journal of Economics* 104: 635–54.

Brenton, Paul, and Mombert Hoppe. 2005. "Trade Policy in Sierra Leone: Capacity, Strategy and Market Access." Paper prepared for the Sierra Leone Diagnostic Trade Integration Study, World Bank, Washington, DC.

Brenton, Paul, and Richard Newfarmer. 2007. "Watching More than the Discovery Channel: Export Cycles and Diversification in Development." Policy Research Working Paper 4302, World Bank, Washington, DC.

Brenton, Paul, Martha Denisse Pierola, and Erik von Uexküll. 2007. "The Life and Death of Trade Flows: Understanding the Survival Rates of Developing Country Exporters." World Bank Development Economics Group, Washington, DC.

Brenton, Paul, and Erik von Uexküll. 2007. "Product Specific Technical Assistance for Exports: Has It Been Effective?" World Bank, Washington, DC.

Cox, D. 1972. "Regression Models and Life-Tables." *Journal of the Royal Statistical Society* 34, no. 2: 187–220.

D'Addio, Anna Christina, and Michael Rosholm. 2002. "Left-Censoring in Duration Data: Theory and Application." Working Paper 2002–5, University of Arhus, Denmark.

Edwards, Huw. 2007. "Trade Search and Its Implications." Photocopy. Centre for the Study of Globalisation and Regionalisation, University of Warwick, Country, UK.

Hallak, Juan. 2006. "Product Quality and the Direction of Trade." *Journal of International Economics* 68: 238–65.

Keifer, Nicholas M. 1988. "Economic Duration Data and Hazard Functions." *Journal of Economic Literature* 26: 646–79.

Melitz, Marc. 2003. "The Impact of Trade on Intra-Industry Reallocations and Aggregate Industry Productivity." *Econometrica* 71: 1695–725.

Rauch, James. 1996. "Trade and Search: Social Capital, Sogo Shosha, and Spillovers." Working Paper 5618, National Bureau of Economic Research, Cambridge, MA.

———. 1999. "Networks versus Markets in International Trade." *Journal of International Economics* 48: 7–35.

———. 2007. "Development through Synergistic Reform." Working Paper 13170, National Bureau of Economic Research, Cambridge, MA.

Rauch, James E., and Joel Watson. 2003. "Starting Small in an Unfamiliar Environment." *International Journal of Industrial Organization* 21: 1021–42.

Schott, Peter. 2004. "Across-Product versus Within-Product Specialization in International Trade." *Quarterly Journal of Economics* 119: 647–78.

CHAPTER 8

PROMOTING NEW EXPORTS: EXPERIENCE FROM THE MIDDLE EAST AND NORTH AFRICA

Claudia Nassif

Over the past 15 years, many non-oil-exporting countries in the Middle East and North Africa have made great strides in liberalizing trade, stabilizing the macroeconomic situation, and improving the investment climate. Supported by a favorable external environment, they have enjoyed a remarkable export performance. In many of these countries, export growth outperformed the world average, reaching impressive yearly growth rates of 12–25 percent since 2000. Yet, with the exception of Tunisia, they reached only half the export growth recorded by other emerging economies. Consequently they have not strengthened their position in the world market, and their shares in global manufacturing exports were less than 0.2 percent in 2005. And although there has been some optimistic progress, especially in the discovery of new exports, exports remain generally concentrated on a few commodities.

Faced with the challenge of stepping up the development of exports, many governments in the region are looking for more proactive ways to promote exports. In this context, the question arises how export promotion can be designed to spur not only growth but also diversification. In an effort to better understand the processes underlying export diversification through new exports, the World Bank (2007) conducted an analysis of export diversification in the Arab Republic of Egypt, Jordan, Lebanon, Morocco, and Tunisia. As part of the analysis, 23 cases of successful export discoveries in the five countries were studied. The objective of the case studies was to learn what triggers or constrains the discovery of new exports at the firm level. More important, what makes an entrepreneur take the risk of exporting a new product that has no track record in the economy? And how do imitators pick up on the new export activity?

EXPORT DIVERSIFICATION IN "RESOURCE-POOR" COUNTRIES IN THE REGION

At the structural level, exports in the Middle East and North Africa are quite concentrated. Even the non-oil countries rely heavily on a few export commodities, and diversification levels are lower than in other countries with comparable income and size (figure 8.1). In addition, exports are generally unsophisticated. Compared with countries in other regions, the technological structure of exports in the "resource-poor" countries falls short—only 21.2 percent of exports, on average, entail medium or high technology, while almost 37 percent of exports in other emerging economies fall into these categories.[1] This technology structure hurts productivity in Middle Eastern and North African countries, which is low compared with other countries of similar income levels in other regions.

However, the trade structure in the resource-poor Middle Eastern and North African countries is undergoing changes, albeit slowly. This is also indicated by the rather unusual fact that export growth in many of the region's countries has been much more driven by the extensive margin, that is, the change in export flows resulting from export flows to new markets and new products (table 8.1). While the extensive margin contributed to just 17 percent of the export growth of all lower-middle-income countries, on average, and 24 percent of the growth of all upper-middle-income countries, it accounted for over 38 percent in countries of the Middle East and North Africa. This result is partly explained by the magnitude of decline in existing flows and the disappearance of exports of particular products to particular markets.[2] For example, if Egypt had maintained the existing export flows that actually declined or disappeared, export growth would have been more than 30 percent higher. But even discounting for statistical effects, the incidence of new export activities remains high (World Bank forthcoming).

Figure 8.1 Herfindahl-Hirschmann Index of Export Concentration, 1990 and 2005

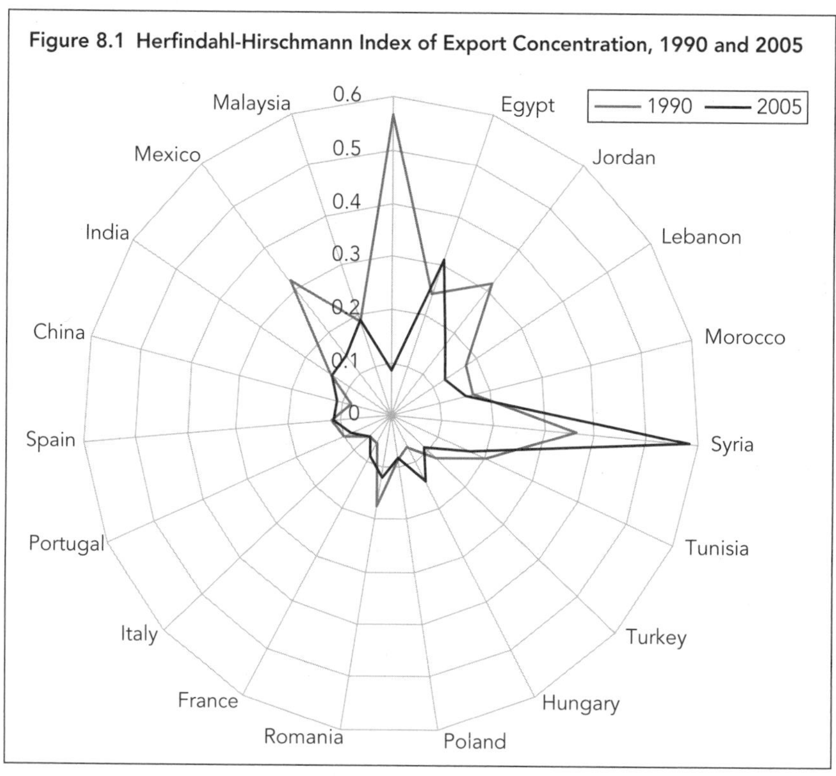

Source: World Bank 2007.

Note: The Herfindahl-Hirschmann index is a measure of the degree of product concentration, normalized to obtain values from 0 (minimum concentration) to 1 (maximum concentration). It implies that countries with an index closer to zero (middle point) are more diversified.

The differences in country outcomes are difficult to ascertain. They result partly from a proliferation of preferential trade agreements, especially with the European Union and the United States, and partly from responses to shifts in competition patterns on international markets. For some exports, such as pistachios in the Islamic Republic of Iran, the same product is responsible for a decline in some existing markets and an increase in others, which indicates trade diversion effects in traditional export markets. Finally, some countries in the region started with fewer export flows, which explains why exports at the extensive margin are more pronounced (World Bank forthcoming).

Table 8.1 Decomposition into Intensive and Extensive Margins of Export Growth, Selected Countries, 1995–2005 (percent)

Category	Algeria	Egypt, Arab Rep. of	Iran, Islamic Rep. of	Jordan	Lebanon	Morocco	Syrian Arab Rep.	Tunisia
Total intensive margin	4.6	26.0	–4.5	62.2	37.9	50.0	40.1	62.5
Increase of existing products to existing markets	57.0	57.2	61.1	78.1	81.8	110.6	99.6	101.6
Decrease of existing products to existing markets	–17.9	–19.1	–39.7	–9.0	–21.8	–47.2	–38.5	–25.0
Extinction of existing products to existing markets	–34.5	–12.1	–26.0	–6.9	–22.1	–13.4	–21.0	–14.2
Total extensive margin	95.4	74	104.5	37.8	62.1	50.0	59.9	37.5
New products to existing markets	28.3	10.1	26.4	12.7	14.9	4.5	19.3	8.4
Existing products to new markets	67.1	63.9	77.8	25	47	45.6	40.6	29.2
New products to new markets	0.1	0	0.3	0.1	0.1	0	0	0

Source: World Bank forthcoming.

CASE STUDIES: METHODOLOGY

The case studies are narratives based on interviews that included both standard and open questions. More than a hundred interviews were conducted with first movers and subsequent entrants. The selection of the case studies was based on a statistical identification and then through a reality test in which the selected exports were vetted with export and business associations.

The statistical identification of the export discoveries in the case studies follows the methodology by Klinger and Lederman (2009) described in chapter 5 of this book. For each country, export data at the 6-digit Harmonized System (HS) level between 1989 and 2004 were filtered for export discoveries. Export discoveries were defined as products that had not been sold abroad (or only in very limited amounts) at the beginning of the period but that were consistently exported in large quantities by the end of the period.

Identification of first movers and followers was fairly simple. In most cases, only a few firms were engaged in the export activity of interest. Since most of the businesses had started no earlier than 1990, information on diffusion was easy to track—for example, through interviews with industry analysts or business chambers. In all but two cases, information about the sequence of the development of industry was consistent across the different sources. To obtain the results discussed below, the case studies were examined for commonalities in observations, which in many cases were striking.

Obviously, this methodology is open to selection bias—23 case studies in five countries hardly make a case for a representative sample. The results should therefore be treated with the same caution applicable to all qualitative analysis.

Triggers for New Export Activities

Export discoveries can consist of genuine innovation, technological adaptation, customization, or licensed production of foreign-owned products. The case studies covered all of these types of innovation, with discoveries based on technology adaptation being the most frequent. The case studies found six possible triggers for export discovery.

- *An external, unpredicted shock:* An unanticipated event such as a war can change the profitability of existing businesses and forces firms to change strategy. This trigger might also include changes in global demand or supply that pushes multinationals to relocate part of their production to stay competitive.

- *Market evolution:* The emergence of a new market or a change in the existing market structure can create an opportunity for new business. Market liberalization is a key example.
- *Capacity to produce in excess of domestic demand:* A firm oriented toward a domestic market learns how to export its excess production.
- *Research:* A technology-oriented firm or person can commercialize a patented invention as a result of research.
- *News:* A discovery is driven by new information about business opportunities.
- *Random walk:* The rare case of high-risk entrepreneurs can create their businesses through trial and error or by seizing a one-time opportunity.

In many cases more than one trigger was at play. The most decisive trigger, however, was the combination of information about new business opportunities with an entrepreneur willing to take high risks and adopt new technologies and management techniques. Information normally came from business travels, from previous study, or from working experiences abroad. In a few cases, the process of obtaining information and translating it into business-relevant activities was supported by private sector networks. The similarity of the background, experiences, and attitudes of the entrepreneurs was striking, especially when contrasting them to the most predominant type of entrepreneur within their respective societies, who usually leads a family business and is conservative and rent seeking.

In contrast to characteristics associated with the individual entrepreneurs, the case studies did not establish a clear pattern of firm type or size. Discoveries occurred in small and large firms, and they occurred in firms that sold products domestically first and, through various iterations of production changes, learned to export. Sometimes newly discovered products were added to an existing export portfolio, and often firms were built up from scratch with the onset of the discovery. Most of the firms had one thing in common, however: they were all domestic in the sense that they were rarely a result of a foreign direct investment. This makes sense considering that foreign investors base their investment decision on existing comparative advantages for exports and factors that, among other things, include a certain skill level, infrastructure, or some local production experience. Investments are less risky in industries for which countries have already proven export or production capacity. Moreover, research and development activities that potentially could lead to the discovery of new products typically do not take place in subsidiaries or production facilities of multinational companies.

Having said this, foreign direct investment was nonetheless important in some cases to augment exports to a more significant level. In Jordan, for instance, foreign direct investment, attracted by the incentives provided in special economic zones, triggered a surge in textile exports. Similarly, motivated by domestic call-center activities, the government of Morocco heavily promoted the country as an attractive location for foreign investments, which subsequently contributed to the successful development of the new export sector; today Morocco is a front-runner in French-speaking call-center services. However, the role of foreign direct investment in export diversification, especially through the extensive margin, is contentious and remains underresearched.

Factors Constraining Development of New Export Activities

In an attempt to identify constraints to discoveries, first movers in the case studies were asked about the problems they faced at the earliest stage of the export development, which ranges from the initial idea to bringing the product to the export market for the first time. The inherent weakness of this approach is that it indicates the constraints only of entrepreneurs who were able to overcome them but not of entrepreneurs who failed to succeed for reasons other than those reported. However, failures are difficult to observe because the respective discoveries never emerged, so the constraints reported by the successful entrepreneurs can still be regarded as the best proxy.

The findings suggest that uncertainty is the major constraint in discovering new export activities. Uncertainty can be caused by a lack of information about demand in specific markets and about the price new products or services can command. Discovery may also be hampered when a firm has insufficient information about how to produce quality goods and services while maintaining price competitiveness. Neither type of knowledge is easy to obtain—simply because the product is new to the domestic economy and the knowledge does not yet exist. Gauging potential success in a new export business becomes a shot in the dark. The high cost of gathering the required information is thus the biggest hurdle in initiating a new export activity (Klinger 2007). Entrepreneurs in the case studies overcame these uncertainties in roughly four ways:

- Some entrepreneurs partnered with firms that had the required knowledge by entering a formal licensing agreement or forming a joint venture.
- In other cases uncertainty was resolved through subsidies from the input supplier, who was motivated by cultivating downstream demand.
- Often entrepreneurs simply assumed the higher risks and absorbed the costs of uncertainty alone.
- In a few cases, public support—in the form of export promotion, technical assistance for firm restructuring, or knowledge transfer—was critical, predominantly for the (few) entrepreneurs with no previous knowledge of the export business or foreign demand.

The case studies also found that exporters did not mention any policy-induced business constraints they suffered. The only pertinent investment climate constraint for new export discoveries in the case studies was limited access to finance. Almost all entrepreneurs reported difficulties in acquiring financial resources to start their new business within the domestic financial system. Although all the entrepreneurs eventually got the necessary financing—mostly from private resources—the financing constraints had several consequences, including delayed investment, high personal risk, and dependence on informal financial resources.

Except in the few cases mentioned above, public support played only a minimal role in the discovery process, although most entrepreneurs received support from export and investment promotion schemes or competitiveness programs at some point in the business cycle. One could therefore conclude that public support is not critical during the discovery phase. However, many entrepreneurs pointed out that initially public support was just not available to them, although they often felt that support was most warranted in the initial stages of business.

DIFFUSION AND THE FEAR OF IMITATION

From a social perspective, the imitation of a successful export discovery is desirable because it fosters the development of export sectors and economic growth. But as indicated in Klinger and Lederman (2009), the incentives for exporters to experiment might be lowered by the possibility that imitators will appropriate part of the returns produced by the new venture.

Free entry into the new market could thus undercut the incentive to search for new business opportunities—producing a market failure where the market produces fewer discoveries than is socially desirable.

But in stark contrast to the assumption that fear of competition discourages market entry, none of the first movers in the case studies regarded domestic followers as competitors. In fact, they often facilitated or even encouraged imitation though knowledge sharing and collaboration. The first mover and imitators in the call-center business in Egypt, for instance, regularly meet to discuss how to jointly organize trade fair participation and how to lobby for better telecommunication regulations; they even share business by lending each other agent positions. In Morocco, the first mover in strawberry exports openly shared information about farming techniques with neighboring farms. In another example from Egypt, medical equipment suppliers joined forces to target geographic markets, visit trade fairs in a group, and engage in national branding. To improve the image of Egyptian medical equipment abroad, the suppliers apply self-regulation and allow only quality-certified firms to participate in group marketing activities while helping each other to achieve the required certifications. How can this be explained?

One reason could be the limitations on the methodology, which does not allow observation of examples of failed export discoveries; information on failed discoveries would offer more insight on the question whether the appropriation problem led to market exit. Another explanation is that the first movers weighed the impact of appropriation by followers against the benefits of cooperation—such as building reputation in export markets, exploiting scale economies, or lobbying for better regulations or infrastructure improvements—and found the benefits greater than the losses.

While imitation in geographically limited domestic markets is a problem—with firms competing for input suppliers and buyers—the cost of imitation is less in export markets where firms compete without geographical limitations. Competition for imported inputs is relatively small, and international demand is theoretically unlimited. Some first movers conjectured, though, that competition could become more critical as production expands and input supply (especially labor) becomes scarcer for the individual producers.

The first movers in the case studies did fear competition from other countries, particularly countries with a strong market presence. Although the fear of imitation as a cause of market failure cannot be excluded, the cases imply that the benefits of cooperation or coordination can outweigh the potential loss from imitation.

The lack of coordinated or collective action might actually explain why export discoveries in many cases remained individual instances and have not contributed much to the development of new export industries. The diffusion process in the five study countries is fairly fragmented, with weak links between firms and public or private institutions or education facilities and research centers that could catalyze knowledge. Most of the followers interviewed for the case studies said that they did not act upon a signal from a first mover or even receive one. Instead, export discoveries occurred as parallel phenomena, with simultaneous market entry or the development of somehow differentiated products, triggered by the same set of similar factors that drove the "first mover." This finding implies that markets in these countries seem to lack the necessary transparency organization to enable (fast) information exchange. In the cases where direct foreign investment was a factor, investors received a general signal about the comparative advantages of the country, usually obtained through market studies. In the cases where followers acted upon signals, they were usually catalyzed by a cluster of firms, informal networks, or an association. This finding bears important implications for countries, like the five studied here, in which knowledge diffusion is hindered by weak private sector organization.

DESIGNING PROACTIVE POLICIES TO ENCOURAGE EXPERIMENTATION AND IMITATION

Exports will not diversify unless the economic environment is favorable to trade and investment. Diversification requires shifting resources across sectors or investing in new economic activity. This is unlikely to happen unless the economic environment allows for competitive production of goods and services. The primary objective of export promotion policy should therefore always be to reduce anti-export bias, macroeconomic imbalances, and behind-the-border constraints and to improve trade facilitation and access to services. Beyond these steps is a continuum of possibilities for proactive policies to foster export growth and diversification if externalities cause an underinvestment in productive activities. However, policy instruments, especially when the objective is to promote diversification through new export activities, need to be designed to address the specific constraints first movers face at the very early stages of the discovery process (from the idea to the market). This is not a trivial requirement: an assessment of the policy instruments used in the five countries studied here reveals that the eligibility criteria for most initiatives, such as matching grants for marketing activities, business development assistance, or even start-up schemes, favor exporters of traditional goods and services or those that are considered "strategic" in terms of their market potential.

Such policies may make economic sense because the observable and quantifiable returns on such interventions, assuming their effectiveness, are higher than the ones that could be expected from risky business activities new to the economy.[3] In this respect, governments act with the same logic as private investors, who calculate the risks against their expected returns. However, this approach naturally discriminates against new activities because their actual return consists mainly of externalities that are intangible in nature and difficult to measure, such as information about the feasibility and productivity of the respective activity. This approach also does not take into account the valuable information for the economy produced by the new activity even if it fails. Failures provide other firms with lessons on activities not to pursue or on how not to do business. In fact, it could even be argued that public support should be focused on promoting new activities. If the production or the marketing of a new export proved successful, the information about business viability and profitability should be, in the absence of other market frictions, incentive enough for imitators to invest even without subsidies of any kind.

Evidently, shifting a large amount of resources to more risky projects with outcomes that are difficult to measure might not be politically viable. It may also be difficult to establish the right balance between promoting growth in existing trade flows (which may have a large impact in the short and medium terms) and supporting new trade flows (with possible large impacts in the long term). Yet, in countries with low levels of diversification, it might be worthwhile to assess the incentives of export promotion programs and to evaluate their impact on both export growth and diversification. Shifting some of the export promotion resources for traditional activities to programs that favor new activities could help to achieve diversification objectives.

The way to encourage entrepreneurs to move into foreign and unknown fields is based on a very basic principle: reduce the cost of experimentation. There are different ways of doing this. In Egypt, for example, the private export association Expo-Link actively addressed producers of traditional products, identified those with a strong desire for change and entrepreneurial attitude, formed small business clusters, and pulled them into previously unexplored market segments by taking them on study tours abroad and bringing in international consultants to help transform the business. One successful example of this approach involved the furniture business, which has a long history of producing traditional, hand-crafted furniture. Here Expo-Link helped small-scale producers to move into the international market for modern, customized furniture for restaurants and hotels. In Tunisia, much success has been achieved with an export promotion program (box 8.1). Known as FAMEX, the program specifically addressed business innovation by providing matching grants and technical assistance only to firms with no previous export experience, to exporters of new products, and to exporters who sought to penetrate new markets.

Box 8.1 Tunisia Export Market Access Fund: FAMEX

The creation of the export market access fund known as FAMEX in April 2000 marked an important shift of focus for export promotion in Tunisia: away from a trade promotion organization model led by the government, to a public-private sector participatory approach. Acknowledging that it is firms, and not nations, that compete, the emphasis was on individual exporters and their associations. FAMEX helped individual firms implement a systematic strategy to enter, sustain, and expand export markets. The $10 million fund was set up by CEPEX (Tunisia's export promotion agency) with World Bank assistance, under private management consisting of international and local experts. It encouraged firms, especially small and medium enterprises, to enter export markets by covering on a temporary basis up to 50 percent of the cost of consultant services and by providing technical assistance. Services were offered by local consultants and international experts in response to demand from private firms.

In the five years that it existed, FAMEX assisted 700 firms to become exporters, export new products and services, or enter new markets. Estimates indicate that each $1 of FAMEX assistance generated more than $20 of additional exports. A recent survey also indicated that 60 percent of the firms that benefited from FAMEX assistance are now willing to pay, or are already paying, full market price for export services. In addition, a small export consulting industry has been created as a result of the program. As such, FAMEX served as a catalyst to develop business-to-business markets.

Source: Project documents provided by the Tunisian Export Market Access Fund (FAMEX).

The development of high-tech exports is intrinsically linked to the capacity of the national innovation system and its links to the private sector. The success stories of China and Taiwan, China, are in large part stories of a long-term strategy focus on fostering indigenous innovation and technology capacity. Some impressive, albeit still limited, results have been achieved in Jordan through public seed money for establishing a high-tech business incubator, iPark. The incubator provides a range of services including actively helping innovative entrepreneurs to tap into financial resources for research and development and to create strategic links to investors. Underlying the success of iPark is a business model that relies on achieving financial self-sufficiency through tenant rentals and revenue sharing. Egypt achieved some success, notably in textiles, through seed-financing of self-sufficient, industry-specific technology centers with smart business models based on buying expensive international knowledge and disseminating it at lower costs to domestic producers.

Fostering imitation without undermining the emergence of new export activities requires another set of instruments. As discussed earlier, imitation in the case study countries was often omitted in countries or industries with weak private sector organizations, and it occurred more frequently where clusters and networks helped to diffuse information. The lesson is to support collective action by creating clusters and networks and by strengthening the role of business associations in export promotion. Building on the experiences of Expo-Link, the Egyptian government has reformed its traditional export promotion model into a cluster-based system driven by the private sector. Incentives for coordinated and concerted action such as branding initiatives or knowledge sharing are provided through programs that fund export promotion activities to business clusters. Cluster creation in this system remains driven by the private sector, supported by Expo-Link. In fact, in some cases the formation of private associations emerged from the cluster activities that provided export promotion services to their members.

There is an obvious risk to rent-seeking behavior and state capture when firms coordinate their activities. This puts public support of collective action at odds with the objective of reducing barriers to export. These risks are real, and governments should be aware of them as they encourage firms to cooperate. However, the risks can be minimized by enforcing transparency, firmly fostering trade liberalization, and providing a regulatory balance between the creative industries' interest and society as whole.

CONCLUSION

The specific export diversification experience of the five countries in the case studies provides some interesting lessons. First, theory or empirical evidence does not always conform with realities on the ground even if it offers great guidance ex ante. In some countries, especially those with relatively few export flows, the extensive margin might play a larger role in growing exports than it does in other countries. The relevance of developing new exports or exporting to new markets should therefore not be underestimated. By the same token, in cases where social objectives seem to undermine those of individual initiative, solutions can be found to overturn fear of imitation if its benefits can be practically demonstrated.

Second, export diversification is a function of export growth. Among the five countries studied here, those with the most conducive environment for trade were also those that made the biggest progress in diversification. Achieving export diversification can therefore not be the only goal. At the same time, export promotion policies need to be carefully assessed for their ability to induce entrepreneurs to move into new products or markets that are associated with much higher risks than traditional export activities. At the least, export promotion policies should not undermine diversification efforts, by favoring one sector over another, for example, because its growth potential or economic relevance is considered to be higher.

Finally, institutional experiences, such as that of FAMEX in Tunisia, may be replicable in other countries if we can harvest the lessons. This, however, requires a rigorous evaluation of export promotion polices and instruments that has yet to be conducted in most countries of the world.

NOTES

1. Resource-poor countries are those countries where a majority of exports are not oil based.
2. The contribution of each margin to export growth is, because of the nature of such decomposition, influenced by the strength of the other margin. Weak growth at the intensive margin tends to elevate the contribution of the extensive margin.
3. Returns on interventions are measured, for example, by the number and volumes of contracts following participation in a subsidized trade fair or by the number of viable start-ups.

REFERENCES

Klinger, B. 2007. "Uncertainty in the Search for New Exports." CID Graduate Student and Postdoctoral Fellow Working Paper 16. Center for International Development, Harvard University, Cambridge, MA.

Klinger, Bailey, and Daniel Lederman. 2009. "Diversification, Innovation, and Imitation of the Global Technological Frontier." In *Breaking Into New Markets: Emerging Lessons for Export Diversification*, ed. Richard Newfarmer, William Shaw, and Peter Walkenhorst, 101–10. Washington, DC: World Bank.

World Bank. 2007. "Export Diversification in Egypt, Jordan, Lebanon, Morocco, and Tunisia." Report 40497-MNA, World Bank, Washington, DC.

———. Forthcoming. *Strengthening China's and India's Trade and Investment Ties to the Middle East and North Africa*. Washington, DC: World Bank.

CHAPTER 9

EXPORTING SERVICES

Aaditya Mattoo

Just as reductions in transport costs galvanized goods trade, reductions in communication costs and the digitization of services have transformed international trade in services. While industrial countries are still the largest exporters of such services, a number of developing countries are among the most dynamic. Since the mid-1990s, the business services exports of several developing countries, including Brazil, China, and India, have grown by more than 15 percent a year. Not all developing countries are participating, however; the exports of 70 small and poor countries have stagnated, and their share of services trade has halved. Even within India, services exports employ only a tiny fraction of the labor force, most of which is located in four states.

What determines the pattern of trade in services? And how much can these determinants be influenced by policy? Preliminary evidence points to the importance of endowments, institutions, and infrastructure and their interplay with technological change. As far as evolution of endowments is concerned, Sequeira (2003) finds that the richest countries are investing proportionally less than middle-income countries in engineering and technical human capital. A significant stylized fact emerges: the ratio of high-tech to low-tech human capital presents an inverted-U-shaped relationship with GDP (gross domestic product) per capita. Recent research also identifies institutions and social capabilities as sources of comparative advantage: customized services are more reliant on the quality of institutions, such as those that influence contract enforcement, than are standardized services for which there is a spot market and low-switching costs (Grossman and Helpman 2002, 2005).

Other research finds that the state of telecommunications, itself dependent on the quality of regulatory institutions and policy, has a significant influence on the pattern of trade (Freund and Weinhold 2002).

What of the poor regions? Because they are weak in institutions, infrastructure, and endowments of skills, there are doubts about whether they can engage in cross-border services trade any more successfully than they did in goods trade (Venables 2001; Winters and Martins 2004). If they cannot, there is a real danger of worsening inequalities, and even absolute declines in well-being as the few local resources of skills and capital migrate to more attractive locations.

This chapter examines the experience of developing countries in exporting services. It begins with a quick overview of the pattern of trade and services and then examines some of its determinants. The chapter then makes some observations about Brazil, which in some ways reflects the experience of several emerging exporters of services but is also quite unique. Next, the chapter looks at Zambia, a country that represents the many that have so far not been able to take advantage of the emerging opportunities. The final sections examine some alternative ways of trading services other than the cross-border trade, and how some of the impediments to trade in services might be addressed.

TRADE IN SERVICES: THE EMERGING PATTERN AND ITS DETERMINANTS

Industrial countries account for over two-thirds of global exports of business services, which include communication, financial, computer, and professional services, that is, all services other than transportation and travel (figure 9.1). Although most developing countries have only a small share of this global trade in services, Brazil, China, India, and a few others are achieving very rapid growth in business services exports.

Similar to goods trade, where reductions in transport costs and in tariffs have enabled countries to participate in different stages of production according to each country's comparative advantage (production networks), the growth in services trade has been driven by fragmentation. Dramatic reductions in communications costs and the possibility of digitizing a range of services have allowed each country to provide a portion of the services formerly bundled together in one location. For example, some years ago hospitals delivered a vertically integrated

Figure 9.1 The Pattern and Growth of Exports of Business Services

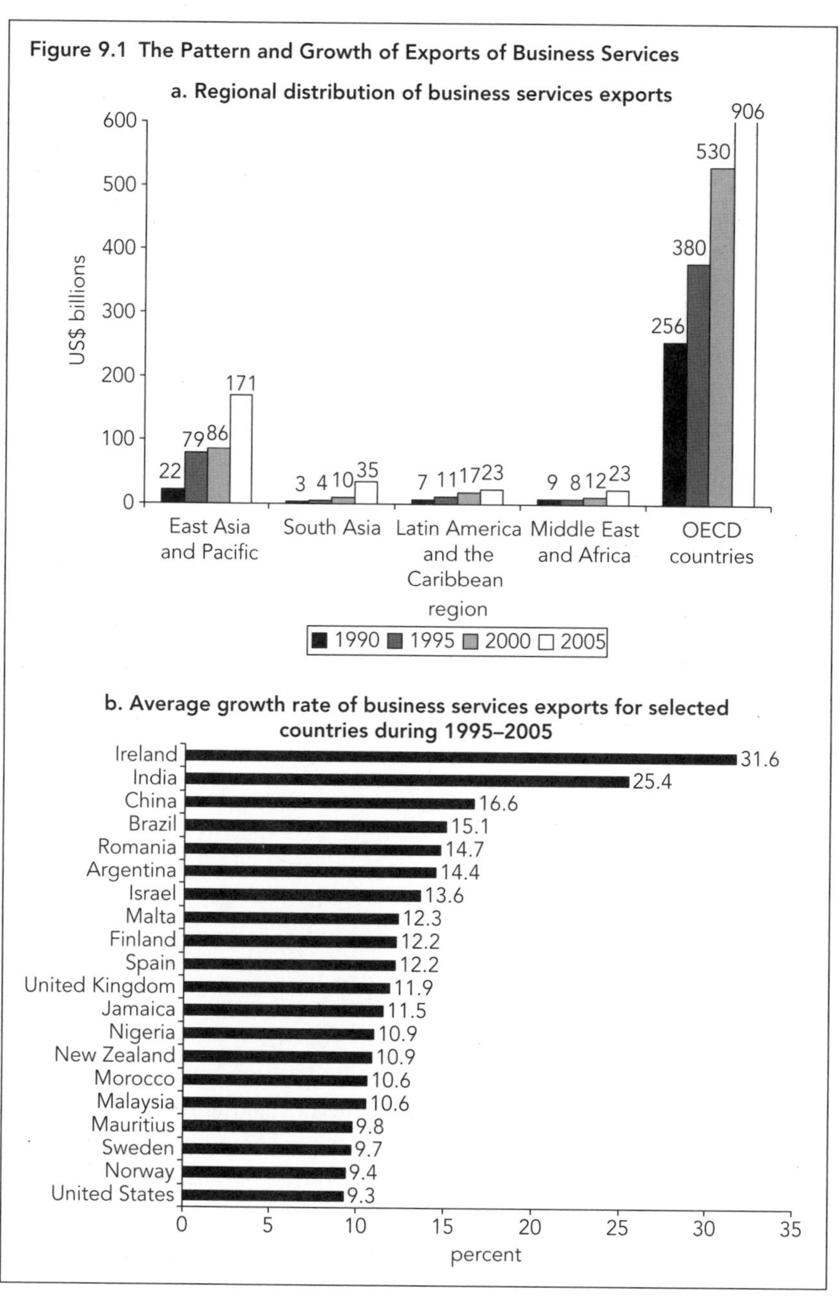

Source: International Monetary Fund (IMF) Balance of Payments Statistics database 2005.

Note: OECD = Organisation for Economic Co-operation and Development.

bundle of services produced on the spot. But today in a hospital in Europe, say, a call center might be operating from the Caribbean, the medical transcription might happen in India, payroll management might happen in the Philippines, and the web-hosting services might be produced in Ireland. Similar developments are occurring in other services, from architecture, where the preparation of basic designs is outsourced and the final stages are completed locally, to financial services, where a wide range of supporting data-processing and analytical services are being outsourced while the face-to-face dimension remains local. Just as in the case of goods, fragmentation has made it possible for countries to participate in services trade according to their comparative advantage in a specific stage of production. It is no longer necessary for them either to produce the entire service or to be excluded from services trade.

Determinants of Comparative Advantage

Preliminary evidence suggests that the determinants of comparative advantage in services include endowments (especially of human capital), infrastructure (especially relating to telecommunications), and institutions (especially regulatory and contract enforcing). While these determinants are given today, their future evolution can be influenced by current policy choices.

First of all, a number of services sectors, ranging from business services to banking and telecommunications, are significantly more skill intensive than most goods production. Skill intensity is defined here as the share of the total workforce of a particular sector that has tertiary education (figure 9.2a). Endowments of human capital are, therefore, a critical source of comparative advantage.

Less obvious is that services tend also to be more dependent than goods on institutions. The first reason for this dependence is their nature—services, being invisible, cannot be seen and inspected by consumers before they are bought and consumed. Imagine trying to identify, before obtaining their services, all the relevant characteristics of service providers such as doctors and banks. So consumers are much less informed about the true attributes of the services and the service providers than about the goods they purchase. In these circumstances, the existence of credible regulators provides consumers with vital reassurance, through certification and licensing mechanisms, about the quality of the services.

Figure 9.2 Importance of Skill Intensity

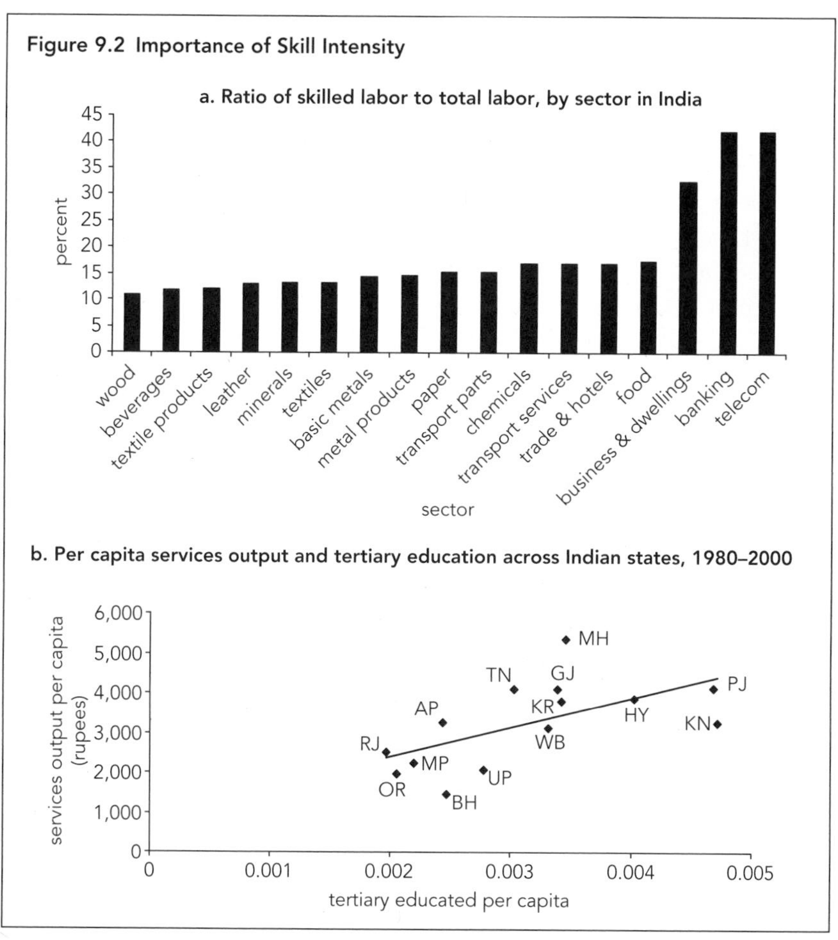

Source: Amin and Mattoo 2006.

Note: AP = Andhra Pradesh; BH = Bihar; GJ = Gujarat; HY = Haryana; KN = Karnataka; KR = Kerala; MH = Maharashtra; MP = Madhya Pradesh; OR = Orissa; PJ = Punjab; RJ = Rajasthan; TN = Tamil Nadu; UP = Uttar Pradesh; WB = West Bengal.

Second, unlike most goods, services tend to be customized, which means both the supplier and the consumer need to make relation-specific investments. Once these investments are made, there are big switching costs to moving to another supplier (or consumer). In these circumstances, the fear of ex post default can reduce the incentives to make ex ante investments. Therefore, contract-enforcing institutions arguably assume greater importance than they do for goods (figure 9.3a; see Amin and Mattoo 2006, for a more detailed discussion). For example, one's willingness to outsource the transcription of medical diagnosis or confidential financial information is going to be much greater if he or she has confidence in the privacy law of a particular jurisdiction.

India's experience provides some evidence that skill intensity and institutional dependence influence the pattern of services trade. States that have been most successful in creating institutions of higher learning have the highest per capita output of services (data on state-level services trade are not available) (figure 9.2b). Similarly, the states with stronger institutions (as measured by the inverse of the transmission and distribution losses of state electricity enterprises) have a higher services output per capita (figure 9.3b). Other research finds that the state of telecommunications, itself dependent on the quality of regulatory institutions and policy, has a significant influence on the pattern of services trade (Freund and Weinhold 2002). Note that India's openness to foreign firms has been a key determinant of its success in exporting information technology (IT) and related services; foreign firms were among the first to export services from India and created important spillovers in learning about services export production and identifying opportunities for exporting services. Today, as many as half of India's exports of IT-enabled services and a quarter of its exports of IT services originate from foreign firms based in India (World Bank 2004b).

Some Examples of Constraints to Growth in Services Trade

The analysis presented above sheds light on the constraints to the development of services in certain South Asian countries. Sri Lanka has nascent exports of IT-enabled services, with a particular niche in knowledge process outsourcing—in which high-value knowledge- and information-related work is carried out by highly skilled workers. The difficult security situation there deters foreign investment and outsourcing, however, and also requires precautionary measures that increase the cost of operation. Limited competition has resulted in high telecommunications costs (discussions with industry suggested that the cost of a dedicated line in Sri Lanka is twice as high as in India). Limited education and large-scale emigration have meant that skilled workers are scarce and expensive outside of certain areas such as accountancy; and space itself has become a constraint in Colombo,

Figure 9.3 Importance of Institutions

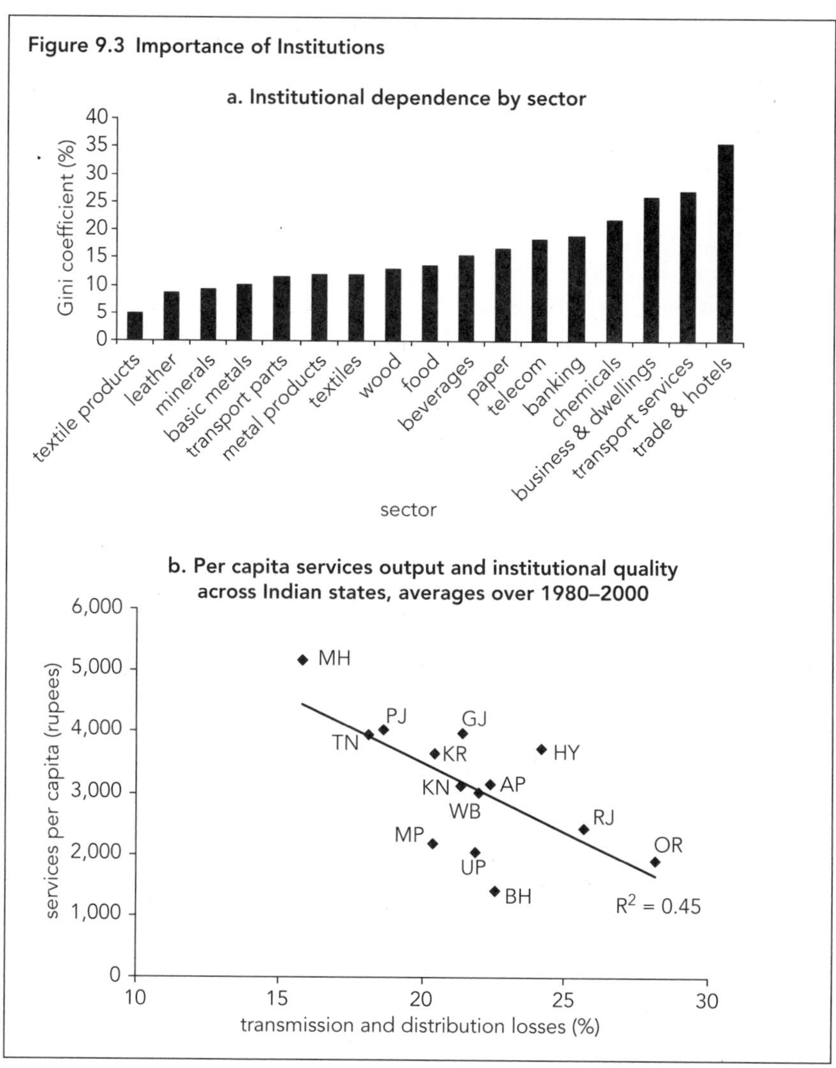

Source: Amin and Mattoo 2006.

Note: In figure 9.3a, institutional dependence is measured as the concentration of upstream and downstream transactions. AP = Andhra Pradesh; BH = Bihar; GJ = Gujarat; HY = Haryana; KN = Karnataka; KR = Kerala; MH = Maharashtra; MP = Madhya Pradesh; OR = Orissa; PJ = Punjab; RJ = Rajasthan; TN = Tamil Nadu; UP = Uttar Pradesh; WB = West Bengal. In figure 9.3b, per capita services and institutional quality are measured by transmission and distribution losses of public sector electricity undertakings.

where the infrastructure and skills are concentrated. The result is that even a successful company like Amba, which was founded in Sri Lanka, has chosen to expand not locally but in India and Costa Rica, according to company sources.

After virtual stagnation in the 1990s, Pakistan has seen significant growth since 2001 in business service exports, particularly software and IT-enabled services, as shown in data obtained from the State Bank of Pakistan and the Pakistan Software Export Board. But exports are still small in absolute magnitude and originate almost entirely in the three major cities of Islamabad, Karachi, and Lahore. Meetings with stakeholders in Pakistan suggested that while significant improvements have been made in access to telecommunications, access remains concentrated in urban areas. The high cost of office space (despite subsidies from the software export board) could be alleviated by a diffusion of economic activity, but this is prevented by, among other things, the geographical concentration of telecommunications infrastructure. Steps are being taken to increase the availability of appropriate skills (through reform of higher and vocational education), but these efforts may be frustrated by the persistently high rates of skilled emigration. A recurrent theme among Pakistani businesses is the belief that companies elsewhere are reluctant to outsource to Pakistan because of a negative external perception of the business and political environment there—and there is a strong awareness in Pakistan of the benefits of, and constraints to, collaboration with reputable Indian and international companies.

SUCCESSFUL ENGAGEMENT: THE CASE OF BRAZIL

Like India, Brazil experienced a striking increase in its revealed comparative advantage in business services during the 1990s. Both countries' former emphasis on import substitution led to heavy investments in institutions of higher learning. Those endowments of skills have interacted with the changes in technology to produce a new comparative advantage in business services exports (figure 9.4).[1]

For example, Brazilian companies such as Odebrecht were able to develop services for large turnkey construction projects, in part because of a captive domestic market and almost exclusive access to domestic government procurement and perhaps other implicit subsidies. The period of fiscal austerity led to a cutback on these implicit

Figure 9.4 Shifting Revealed Comparative Advantage in Brazil and India, 1990–2000

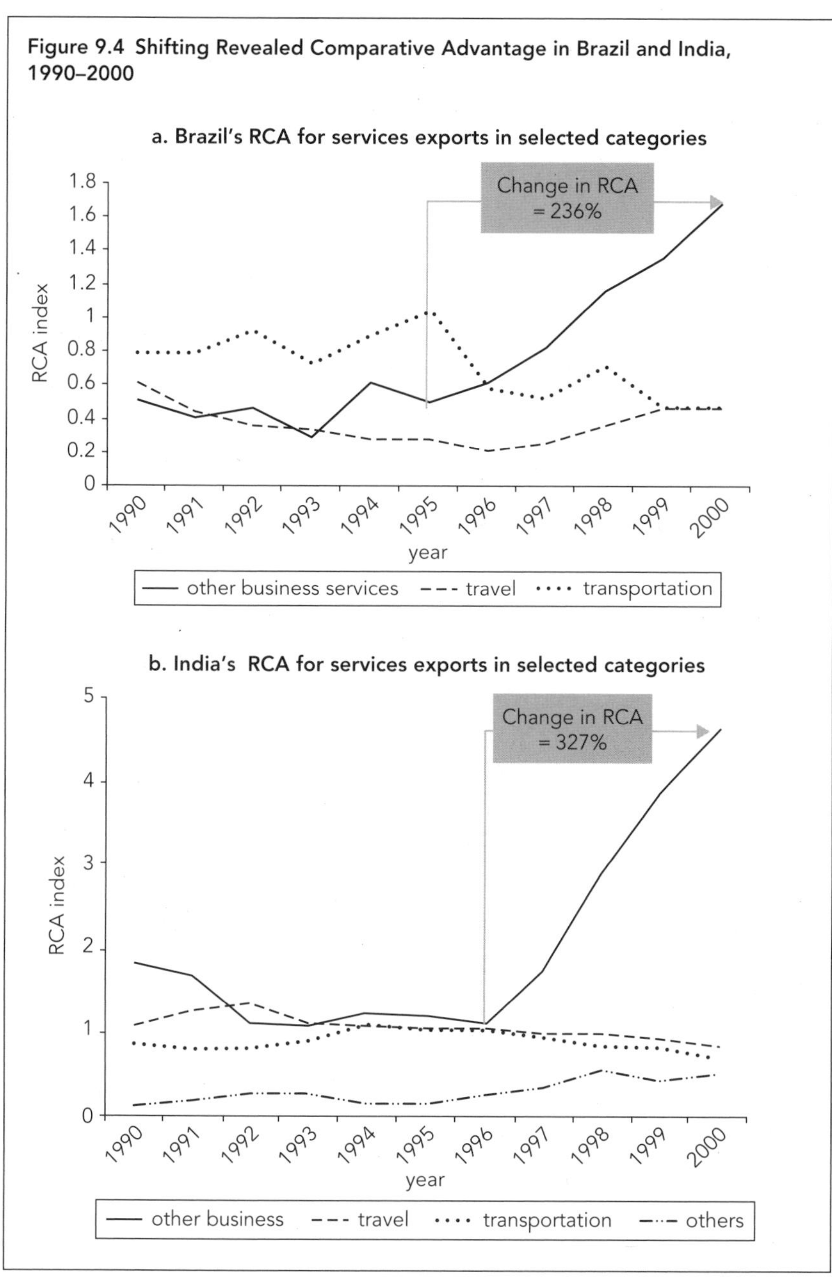

Source: IMF Balance of Payments Statistics database 2003.

Note: RCA = revealed comparative advantage.

and explicit subsidies from domestic operations to foreign operations, and the reach of Brazilian construction companies shrank. But the endowments of skills (and skill-generating institutions) in engineering, architecture, and other technical services remained and are now the basis for growing exports of professional services from Brazil (World Bank 2004a).[2]

COUNTRIES THAT ARE NOT PARTICIPATING: THE CASE OF ZAMBIA

Unlike Brazil and India, services exports from most small, poor developing countries have stagnated, and their share of services trade has halved. Zambia provides an instructive example. A simple cross-country regression shows that per capita GDP is significantly, and positively, related to the level of services exports per capita (table 9.1). But Zambia's low services exports do not stem only from low income: the coefficient on a dummy variable for Zambia in this equation is significant, and Zambia's services exports per capita are below the lower-bound of the confidence

Table 9.1 Zambia's Services Export Specialization in a Cross-Section of Countries

Variable	1	2
Zambia indicator	–0.300**	–0.032
	[0.139]	[0.235]
Log GDP per capita	1.123***	0.421***
	[0.052]	[0.125]
Log teledensity		0.655***
		[0.110]
Credit to private sector (as a percent of GDP)		0.224*
		[0.127]
Business climate (procedures required to open a business)		–0.452**
		[0.193]
Number of observations	108	108
	0.82	0.87

Source: Mattoo and Payton 2007.

Note: The dependent variable is log services exports per inhabitant in US$. Standard errors in brackets are robust and clustered on industries.

* Significant at the 10 percent level. ** Significant at the 5 percent level. *** Significant at the 1 percent level.

interval around the regression line shown in figure 9.5a. Adding other determinants of services exports provides some insight into Zambia's poor performance. After controlling for per capita GDP, the availability of communications facilities (proxied by teledensity), the depth of the financial sector (domestic credit to the private sector as a share of GDP), and the state of the business climate (number of procedures required to open a new business) are all significant determinants of services exports.[3] And introducing these variables means that the estimated coefficient on the Zambia dummy variable is no longer statistically significant (see table 9.1) and that Zambia is no longer an outlier (figure 9.5b).

Zambia's low levels of telecommunications, financial sector depth, and the business climate are directly related to policy choices. The insistence on maintaining a monopoly in the international telecommunications gateway through a prohibitive license fee has raised the cost of communication well above that in neighboring countries. Premature

Figure 9.5 Service Exports per Capita

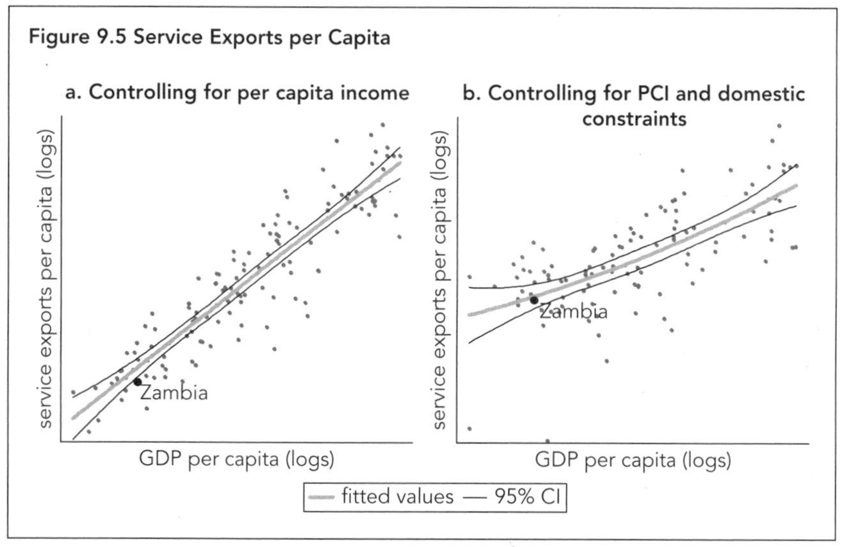

Sources: IMF Balance of Payments Statistics database; U.N. Comtrade (Commodity Trade Statistics Database); Bank of Zambia.

Note: PCI = per capital income; CI = confidence interval. Figure 9.5 is based on a regression equation across 109 countries, where services exports are the dependent variable. In figure 9.5a, GDP per capita is the explanatory variable. Figure 9.5b shows the same relationship as 9.5a, but after controlling for the influences of telecommunications infrastructure, financial depth, and a measure of the business climate. All variables are in logs.

liberalization of financial services in the 1990s, along with weaknesses in the institutional framework for financial transactions and heavy borrowing by the government, has depressed credit to the private sector to only 8 per cent of GDP, lower than in many sub-Saharan African countries and lower than the level in Zambia in 1990. The World Economic Forum's African Competitiveness Report ranks Zambia's legal framework as 72nd of the 102 countries that were surveyed (which includes only 11 of 25 African countries). Finally, fiscal austerity has eroded the quality of Zambia's once-reputable tertiary education system (not explicitly considered in the regression), where the enrollment ratio is now lower than that in most African countries (Mattoo and Payton 2007).

The dismal state of Zambia's services exports is reflected in the state of its tourism and accounting services, and potentially in roads. Despite Zambia's natural advantages, real growth of the travel and tourism sector in 2005 was 10 times faster in neighboring Botswana and Tanzania than in Zambia, differences that cannot be explained by the appreciation of Zambia's real exchange rate alone. Tourism accounts for 4 percent of Zambia's GDP, compared with about 10 percent for Botswana, Namibia, South Africa, and Tanzania, and for 3.7 percent of Zambia's employment, compared with more than 11–12 percent for Botswana and Namibia. Preliminary cross-country estimates suggest that because of weaknesses in its business climate and infrastructure, Zambia is receiving one-third fewer tourists than would be warranted by its fundamental endowments. While the Zambian Institute of Chartered Accountants produces a higher pass rate in the British accounting examination than many similar institutions in other countries, Zambia has been unable to attract substantial accounting students or provide training abroad, owing to the very limited number of professional educators.[4]

OPPORTUNITIES BEYOND CROSS-BORDER TRADE: ADDRESSING THE IMPEDIMENTS

Much of this discussion has focused on cross-border trade. But there are important new opportunities arising for countries that involve exporting services by attracting foreign consumers and by moving service providers to other countries.

Consumption Abroad of Health Care

Is health care so different from other goods and services that it cannot be regarded as tradable? Consumers certainly value both proximity and quality, but that has not prevented them from traveling abroad to obtain various treatments, such as cosmetic surgeries, rehabilitative care, alternative medicine, and in some cases, even eye and cardiac surgery. For example, in 2003, an estimated 50,000 medical tourists from the United Kingdom alone traveled to Cuba, India, South Africa, and Thailand for a variety of treatments (Mattoo and Rathindran 2006). If the possibilities of rest and recuperation, and even retirement are considered, then opportunities also exist for countries like Zambia, with their peaceful and congenial environment.

The high cost of health care in the United States relative to that in a number of other countries would seem to provide a strong incentive for trade. For example, roughly 400,000 inpatient knee surgeries are performed annually in the United States, each at a cost of more than $10,000; the same surgery costs less than $2,000 inclusive of travel at the best hospitals in Hungary and India. Even if only 1 in 10 patients who need 15 highly tradable, low-risk treatments went abroad, the estimated annual savings for the United States would be $1.4 billion (table 9.2). But surprisingly few Americans travel abroad for treatment, largely because health insurance plans do not cover treatment abroad or, when treatment abroad is covered, do not cover travel costs. Because these costs are usually greater than any out-of-pocket savings, the adequately insured have little incentive to travel, resulting in a strong "local-market bias" in the consumption of health care. If the terms of insurance coverage were made neutral to the location of the provider, and reimbursement were based on the costs of treatment inclusive of travel costs, then the consumer would have an incentive to travel if and only if there are any gains from trade. The scope for trade would be greatly enhanced if providers in destination countries were able to credibly signal improvements in health services by obtaining accreditation from health regulators in countries that are the source of patients. To avoid impairing the quality and availability of domestic health services, destination countries would need to use at least part of the revenues from increased inflows of foreign patients to ensure improved health care access for poorer domestic citizens.

Table 9.2 Estimating the Gains from Trade in Health Services for the United States

Procedure	U.S. inpatient price ($)	U.S. inpatient volume	U.S. outpatient price ($)	Estimated U.S. outpatient volume	Foreign price including travel cost ($)	Savings if 10 percent of U.S. patients undergo surgery abroad instead of at home ($)
Knee surgery	10,335	399,139	4,142	60,000	1,321	376,698,470
Shoulder arthroplasty	5,940	23,300	7,931	—	2,217	8,674,829
Transurethral resection of the prostate	4,127	111,936	3,303	88,064	2,413	27,029,437
Tubal ligation	5,663	78,771	3,442	621,229	1,280	168,834,441
Hernia repair	4,753	40,553	3,450	759,447	1,651	149,254,906
Skin lesion excision	6,240	21,257	1,696	1,588,884	805	153,078,349
Adult tonsillectomy	3,398	17,251	1,931	102,749	1,006	13,641,759
Hysterectomy	5,783	640,565	5,420	—	1,987	243,163,366
Haemorrhoidectomy	4,945	12,787	2,081	137,213	865	21,893,438
Rhinoplasty	5,050	7,265	3,417	42,735	1,936	8,590,926
Bunionectomy	6,046	3,139	2,392	41,507	1,502	5,120,817
Cataract extraction	3,595	2,215	2,325	1,430,785	1,247	154,681,706
Varicose vein surgery	7,065	1,957	2,373	148,043	1,411	15,350,137
Glaucoma procedures	3,882	—	2,292	75,838	1,086	9,143,374
Tympanoplasty	4,993	754	3,347	149,246	1,404	29,258,785
Total savings						1,384,414,741

Sources: Healthcare Cost and Utilization Project (H-CUP) database; Ingenix 2004; American Medical Association 2003; Vanbreda International; authors' calculations. Outpatient volume was obtained from the American Association of Orthopedic Surgeons, the American Urological Association, the National Center for Health Statistics, the Centers for Disease Control and Prevention, the American Society for Dermatological Surgery, the American Academy of Otolaryngology, the American Podiatric Medical Association, the American College of Phlebology, and Ethicon Endosurgery.

Note: Patient volume data pertain to 2002, while the prices pertain to 2004. — No data are available.

Moving People to Deliver Services

Developing countries can also export services through the temporary movement of service providers, whether it is to provide sophisticated information technology services or less sophisticated basic construction services. Such temporary movement arguably offers the neatest solution to the problem of how some forms of international migration are best managed, enabling the realization of mutual gains from trade while averting to a large extent the social and political costs in host countries and the brain drain from poor countries. However, the current options for most countries are either no migration or permanent migration of the skilled and usually, and unfortunately, the illegal migration of the unskilled.

Existing efforts to allow greater freedom of movement have taken place in the context of trade agreements, such as the World Trade Organization's General Agreement on Trade in Services (GATS). Such agreements involve the assumption of one-sided obligations, by the host country alone, to allow foreign service providers access to their markets, and have led to little liberalization (Mattoo 2005). If developing countries are to have greater opportunities for exporting services, and if the importing countries are to be able to realize the big cost savings and welfare improvements that could arise from allowing greater freedom of movement, cooperation between source and destination countries is vital. Such cooperation could pertain to unskilled movement, as is the case with the bilateral agreement between Canada and the Caribbean, or even the movement of skilled personnel, as is the case with the bilateral agreements between the Netherlands and Poland. Much can also be accomplished unilaterally, as has been demonstrated by the experience with the Philippine Overseas Employment Administration, or multilaterally, as is evident from the role of the International Organization of Migration as a broker from a number of developing countries to New Zealand.

Central to these arrangements (such as between Spain and Ecuador, Canada and the Caribbean, Germany and Eastern Europe) is the willingness of the source country to assume obligations, including premovement screening and selection, accepting and facilitating return, and commitments to combat illegal migration. In effect, the host country may be willing to allow increased access in return for cooperation by the source country in addressing security concerns, ensuring temporariness, and preventing illegal labor flows.

One approach to incorporating these elements in a multilateral agreement is for host countries to commit under the GATS to allow access to any source country that fulfills certain prespecified conditions—along the lines of mutual recognition agreements in other areas. Even if these conditions were unilaterally specified and compliance was determined unilaterally, it would still be a huge improvement over the arbitrariness and lack of transparency in existing visa schemes. Eventually, it would be desirable to negotiate these conditions (and even establish a mechanism to certify their fulfillment) multilaterally rather than in an unequal, non-transparent, and potentially labor-diverting bilateral context.

In the current GATS framework, when a country makes a market access commitment, it is obliged to grant a fixed level of access every year in the future regardless of domestic economic conditions. In contrast, bilateral labor agreements allow host countries to vary the level of access depending on the state of the economy. One example was a bilateral agreement between Germany and certain Eastern European countries, under which the quota on temporary migrants increased (decreased) by 5 percent for every 1 percentage point decrease (increase) in the level of unemployment. It may be desirable to consider GATS commitments along these lines, which allow necessary flexibility, albeit in a transparent, predictable, and objectively verifiable manner, and which would be a big improvement over the opaque economic needs tests that currently infest GATS schedules.

REGULATORY IMPEDIMENTS TO TRADE

Apart from explicit barriers, services exports from developing countries face newer, less transparent barriers, which take the form of restrictive regulation. Here there is a real challenge because the desire to export more services creates the pressure to harmonize standards with those at international levels or with the levels prevailing in export markets. A consequence can be that a country gravitates toward international standards and away from standards that are locally appropriate.

Qualification and Licensing Requirements for Professionals

The scope for international trade in professional services in particular has grown thanks to changes in demographics and patterns of investment in human capital. India, one of the largest exporters of skilled services, and the United States, one of the largest importers of skilled services, are two countries that mirror these broader global trends. But the scope for mutually beneficial trade is today inhibited by a number of domestic regulatory requirements, including qualification and licensing requirements.

It is possible to obtain a rough estimate of the financial cost of the regulatory burden on Indian professionals (accountants, architects, doctors, and engineers), noting, of course, that at least some of this burden may be necessary to remedy deficiencies in their education, training, and experience. Thus, on average, over the 1995–2000 period, 1,092 Indian doctors entered the U.S. medical system. Each incurred a cost of $4,640 to obtain a visa, take the three steps of the professional examination, and pay the licensing fee. Each had to go through a period of graduate medical education of between three and six years depending on the specialty and the state, irrespective of prior qualifications and experience. Then those on a J1 visa (most foreign doctors) were obliged to spend three years working in an underserved area at relatively low wages. Given that the average earnings of a doctor are shown by the census to be around $125,000, the earnings forgone by a foreign doctor are likely to be at least $100,000. The implication is that all the Indian doctors who entered in a particular year paid a regulatory tax of $114 million. Similarly, conservative estimates suggest that the 10,000 or so Indian professionals who entered just the four professions focused on here paid a "regulatory tax" of around $750 million.

This estimate needs to be qualified in several respects. At least some of the regulatory requirements may be justified by the need to ensure compliance with locally desired levels of competence. In fact, it is not just foreign professionals but also professionals from other U.S. states who must in some cases fulfill regulatory requirements imposed by a particular U.S. state. The heterogeneity of standards in a source country like India and the difficulty in observing true levels of professional competence also lend legitimacy to at least some of the regulatory requirements.

Furthermore, the regulatory constraint is not always binding. In particular, as noted above, the fragmentation of services facilitated by advances in information technology has made it possible to trade unregulated parts of services. In architecture, the preparation of basic plans and designs can be outsourced to individuals who have not been locally licensed, whereas conformity with local requirements and ultimate responsibility rest with the licensed professional. In legal services, research and documentation can be similarly outsourced, whereas representation in courts must be by a local firm. In accounting, bookkeeping can be outsourced, whereas conformity with local requirements and ultimate responsibility rest with the local professional. Thus, the market for "intermediate" services is increasingly contestable even though entry into the "final" stage is still affected by regulatory requirements.

How far can recourse to local "final" services help overcome regulatory barriers? To a large extent—if these services are supplied efficiently and competitively. The efficiency condition relates to whether the host country actually has a comparative advantage in the production of final services. The competitiveness condition would be fulfilled if the host country imposed no unnecessary barriers to entry into the final stage. If either condition is violated, the regulatory obligation to use local final services creates an excessive wedge between international service providers and local consumers, potentially hurting both.

Privacy Law

An issue that could have a profound effect on electronic commerce is privacy. In late 1998 the European Union issued a wide-ranging directive that aims to safeguard the privacy of personal data of EU citizens and prevent its misuse worldwide. It is backed by the power to cut off data flows to countries judged by the European Union not to have adequate data protection rules and enforcement. The directive caused friction with the United States, which accused the European Union of trying to impose laws beyond its own frontiers. A compromise was reached under which the United States agreed to set up arrangements for ensuring the privacy of personal data from the European Union, but the issue has not been fully resolved.

The issue could have an impact on developing countries' exports of data processing services and poses a difficult choice for these countries. If they choose not to enact laws deemed adequate, they could be shut off from participation in this growing market. In the absence of such laws and given the weakness of local legal systems, it might be difficult for private firms in developing countries to emulate U.S. firms such as Microsoft and credibly commit to meet the required high standards.

If they do enact stringent laws, it is unlikely that they could be made specific to trade with particular jurisdictions, and so the result could be an economy-wide increase in the costs of doing business. For instance, if private sector estimates generated in the United States are to be believed, information sharing saves the customers of 90 financial institutions (accounting for 30 percent of industry revenues) $17 billion a year ($195 for the average customer household) and 320 million hours annually (4 hours for the average customer household) (Glassman 2000). It is of course true that reporting of personal credit histories is critical to consumer credit, and, even in theory, excessively strict privacy laws could create significant asymmetries of information and affect the efficiency of markets (Kitchenman 1999). While there are good reasons to protect privacy, the desired level of such protection may differ across countries, and if trade is made conditional on the existence of "comparable" laws, then there might be a socially costly "race to the top."

Offshore Financial Services

The tax and regulatory regimes of several offshore financial services centers in the Caribbean have elicited increased scrutiny in recent years. For example, the Financial Stability Forum, which assesses conformity with international regulatory standards (including cross-border cooperation), placed many of the Caribbean offshore centers in the lowest category; the Financial Action Task Force (FATF), which is concerned with protecting financial systems from money laundering and criminal use, placed a number of Caribbean centers on its list of jurisdictions unwilling to cooperate with the FATF on a list of its own criteria; and the countries have also attracted the attention of the Organisation for Economic Co-operation and Development for tax practices deemed harmful.

While the regulatory objectives are legitimate, several concerns have been raised about these initiatives. Most developing countries have not participated in the development of the standards that are being applied, and the standards are not always applied uniformly. For example, the FATF applies the FATF 40 Criteria when conducting mutual evaluations of its members but uses a different standard, the FATF 25 Criteria, to assess jurisdictions that are not FATF members. In some cases, the assessment processes are not transparent. For example, the Financial Stability Forum does not specify how a country classified in a low category can improve standards and graduate to a higher category. And FATF deliberations determining "non-cooperative jurisdictions" are held in closed sessions. The evaluation processes are in some instances not voluntary and involve a "name and shame" approach to induce compliance.

These issues have provoked continuing discussions in the international financial institutions and other forums, but much work needs to be done before an international consensus can be established. The World Bank and the International Monetary Fund are assisting many jurisdictions to assess their compliance with international standards with the aim of helping them address any underlying weaknesses. Key in this is the Bank-Fund Comprehensive Financial Sector Assessment Programs and the Fund-led program of voluntary offshore financial center assessments. Several Caribbean offshore financial centers have endorsed these initiatives.

CONCLUSION

It would be unwise, even dangerous, to prescribe policies that would certainly enhance the growth of services exports. Policy makers simply do not know enough. But there are certain types of policy reform that would be generally beneficial and could create a more favorable environment for services exports. A first priority should be to allow greater competition, domestic and foreign, in the "delivery" services—telecommunications and transport—and to eliminate explicit and implicit barriers to entry in services more generally. India's experience shows that foreign investment can be a critical spur to the emergence of domestic capacity to export services. Second, the neglect of higher education must be remedied. There needs to be much greater openness to new entry in higher education, and possibly more support to the development of advanced education. Third, it is desirable to develop regulatory institutions that are capable of credibly signaling quality to foreign buyers, but that are at the same time sensitive to the needs of domestic consumers and capable of developing and implementing appropriate regulatory standards. Finally, the temporary movement of services providers remains a mode of delivery that is vital for developing countries in a range of services from health care to construction, and cross-border delivery will not in the foreseeable future be a substitute for the movement of individuals. Overcoming the powerful political barriers to greater openness to temporary migration may be possible through cooperation between source and destination countries.

NOTES

1. A revealed comparative advantage index for a sector is calculated by dividing the share of a particular sector's exports in that country's total exports of goods and services by the ratio of global exports in the sector to the total global exports of goods and services. An RCA index with a value greater than unity indicates a comparative advantage in the concerned sector, while a value less than unity indicates a comparative disadvantage.
2. Brazil has had mixed success in dealing with foreign restrictions on services exports. For example, Teleglobo circumvented the European Union's quotas on audiovisual services (and gained access to EU subsidies) by entering into joint ventures with Portuguese firms to distribute "telenovelas" (soap operas) in European countries. Establishing a local affiliate in a foreign country has also helped Brazilian firms in construction to evade local regulatory barriers and other forms of discrimination. By contrast, a limit on the number of soccer players who are not citizens of the extended European Economic Area has impeded the "export" of Brazil's soccer talent, a potentially large source of export revenue from professional player transfer fees (World Bank 2004a).
3. Information on the business climate is available for a large number of countries from the World Bank's Doing Business database.
4. Zambian transport companies have benefited from regional agreements that allow a company to provide transport services between two foreign countries only if the route passes through its own country. However, a liberalization of road transport could enable the more competitive South African firms to dominate regional trade and transport.

REFERENCES

American Medical Association (AMA). 2003. *CPT 2004: Current Procedural Terminology.* Chicago: AMA.

Amin, Mohammed, and Aaditya Mattoo. 2006. "Do Institutions Matter More for Services." Policy Research Working Paper 4032. World Bank, Washington, DC.

Freund, Caroline, and Diana Weinhold. 2002. "The Internet and International Trade in Services." *American Economic Review, Papers and Proceedings* 92 (May): 236–40.

Glassman, C. A. 2000. "Customer Benefits from Current Information Sharing by Financial Services Companies." A study for the Financial Services Roundtable, Washington, DC, December.

Grossman, Gene, and Elhanan Helpman. 2002. "Integration Versus Outsourcing in Industry Equilibrium." *Quarterly Journal of Economics* 117 (1): 85–120.

———. 2005. "Outsourcing in a Global Economy." *Review of Economic Studies* 72 (1): 135–59.

Ingenix. 2004. *DRG Expert 2005: A Comprehensive Reference to the DRG Classification System.* Salt Lake City, UT: Ingenix.

Kitchenman, W. F. 1999. "U.S. Credit Reporting: Perceived Benefits Outweigh Privacy Concerns." The Tower Group, Newton, MA.

Mattoo, Aaditya. 2005. "Services in a Development Round: Three Goals and Three Proposals." *Journal of World Trade* 39: 1223–38.

Mattoo, Aaditya, and Lucy Payton. 2007. *Services Trade for Zambia's Development.* London: Palgrave-Macmillan; Washington, DC: World Bank.

Mattoo, Aaditya, and Randeep Rathindran. 2006. "How Health Insurance Impedes Trade in Healthcare." *Health Affairs* 25: 358–68.

Sequeira, Tiago Neves. 2003. "High-Tech Human Capital: Do the Richest Countries Invest the Most?" *B.E. Journals in Macroeconomics.* Topics in Macro-Economics, www.bepress.com/bejm/topics/vol3/iss1/art13/.

Venables, Anthony J. 2001. "Geography and International Inequalities: The Impact of New Technologies." Paper presented at the Annual Bank Conference on Development Economics (ABCDE), May, World Bank, Washington, DC.

Winters, L. Alan, and Pedro M. G. Martins. 2004. "When Comparative Advantage Is Not Enough: Business Costs in Small Remote Economies." *World Trade Review* 3(3): 347–83.

World Bank. 2004a. "Brazil—Trade Policies to Improve Efficiency, Increase Growth, and Reduce Poverty." World Bank, Washington, DC.

———. 2004b. "Sustaining India's Services Revolution." World Bank, Delhi.

CHAPTER 10

TOURISM AS A STRATEGY TO DIVERSIFY EXPORTS: LESSONS FROM MAURITIUS

Olivier Cattaneo

Many developing countries have tried to use tourism as a vehicle for diversification. For some of them, this development strategy has proved to be an expensive failure, with the sector never taking off. For others there has been little development and poverty alleviation due to "leakages" and the capture of benefits by foreign investors. For a third group of countries, tourism has appeared to be a successful strategy for fostering growth and inclusive development. Moreover, in some cases it can be argued that the shift into tourism has overshot its diversification target and that exports are now excessively concentrated in the tourism sector, thus creating a need for greater diversification within tourism (that is, to diversify the tourism products offered) or out of tourism (that is, to develop trade of new goods or services).

By drawing largely on the example of Mauritius (World Bank 2006), this chapter analyzes the role and potential of tourism in exports diversification strategies. It discusses how countries at different stages of development and trade integration can use tourism as a vehicle for export growth and diversification, stressing at the same time that this opportunity is not equally available to all. A key lesson is that the government has a central role to play in providing stability, stimulating backward links, and preventing destructive externalities.

TOURISM AS A TOOL FOR DIVERSIFICATION

Tourism has played, and continues to play, a prominent role in the diversification and development strategies of many countries. Countries do stand, however, at very different stages of this diversification process. Countries at a preliminary stage of diversification are usually still highly dependent upon exports of one or a limited number of products but invest in experiments to discover new sources of trade and growth. Typically, at this stage, countries investing in tourism have relatively high growth rates in the sector (catch-up), but the share of tourism in economic activity remains low. For example, tourism accounted for only about 5 percent of Zambia's GDP and 4 percent of employment in 2005, but the government has ambitious plans to boost tourism to levels comparable with other tourism centers in sub-Saharan Africa, such as Botswana and South Africa where tourism accounted for more than 10 percent of GDP (Cattaneo 2007). The challenge for countries at this stage is to test the markets and find a niche or segment that will enable the country to attract a critical mass of tourists.

Countries at an advanced stage of diversification have a less concentrated structure of exports. Where tourism has become a major source of exports, the challenge is to make the sector's growth sustainable, that is, to develop the tourism product to meet the evolving needs and tastes of tourists; this challenge also corresponds to a phase of diversification within the tourism sector. At the same time, these countries should avoid becoming too dependent on the tourism sector: in the Maldives, for example, tourism represents more than three-quarters of exports and jobs. Before a critical stage of concentration is reached again, the country should explore other sources of trade and growth.

Mauritius is a good example of an economy at an advanced stage of the diversification process. Until the mid-1980s, Mauritius was primarily an exporter of agricultural products, but it then progressively diversified into textiles and clothing, tourism, and other services. In 1980, agriculture represented 54 percent of its exports and 16 percent of GDP; by 2004, this share had fallen to 16 percent of its exports and 6 percent of GDP. In the same period, its GDP per capita (measured in purchasing power parity in constant 2000 dollars) grew from $4,000 to $11,000. By 2004, none of the key sectors of the economy represented more than 30 percent of the country's exports (figure 10.1). The tourism industry is also well developed and largely contributed to reaching this stage of the diversification process: it generated export revenues of $431 million in 2005 and was projected to become the largest exporter in the country from 2006.

But Mauritius now faces daunting challenges posed by the elimination of market-distorting preferences that had favored the country's exports.

Figure 10.1 Exports in Mauritius, 1980–2004

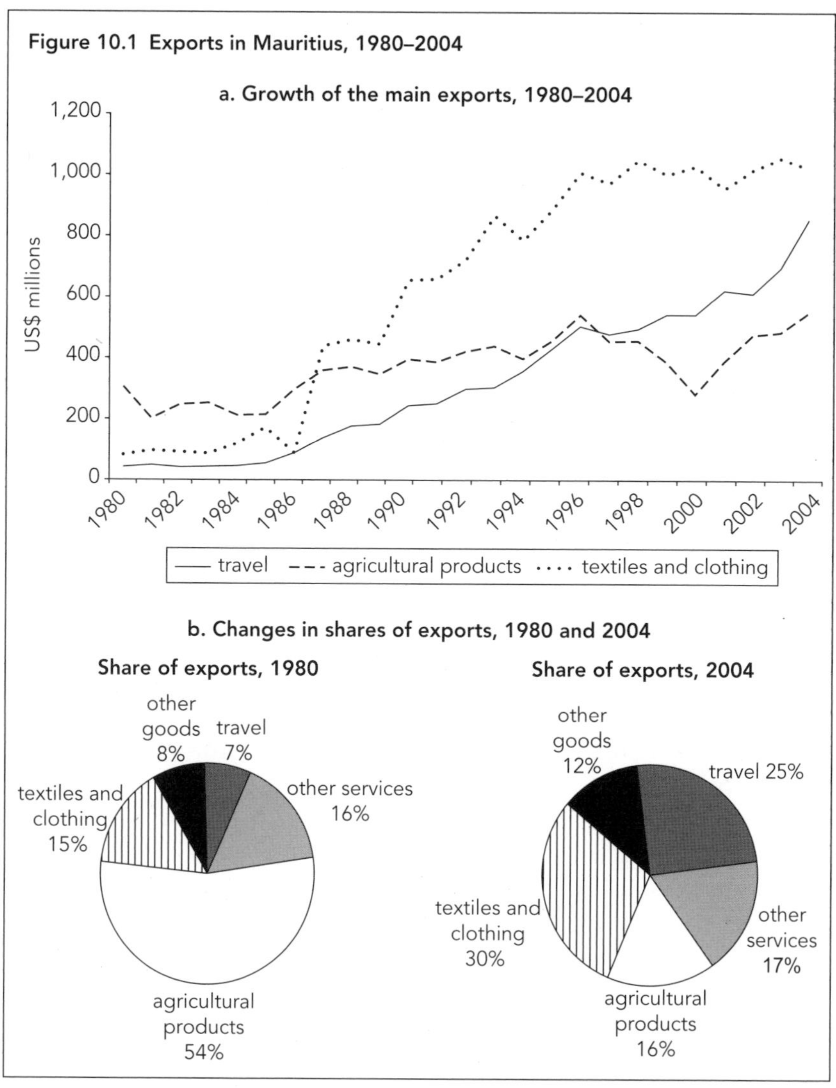

Source: Author's calculations, based on the World Trade Organization's International Trade Statistics database.

The phasing out of quotas imposed under the Multifiber Arrangement (replaced in 1995 by the Agreement on Textile and Clothing) and the reform of the European Union's sugar regime (which had guaranteed a high price for Mauritian exports) have led to stagnation and decline in

Mauritius' merchandise exports. At the same time, competition from Asian and Caribbean tourist centers is intensifying. Continued rapid growth is thus dependent on sustaining the tourism sector.

One strategy for maintaining a competitive tourism sector is to cut prices. For example, Mauritius has moved toward a policy of gradual liberalization of its air transport (by opening selective routes and including third-country carriers), which should reduce the cost of travel to the country. However, Mauritius has to strike the right balance between preserving its attractiveness for a traditional high-end clientele and reaching a critical mass of tourists. Another (complementary) strategy would be to diversify tourism activities: in addition to beach tourism (holiday), Mauritius is now trying to consolidate its position in the meetings, incentives, conferences, and events (or MICE) market. This business-related segment of the tourism market perfectly supplements the traditional beach holiday market: for example, the peak season for Indian business-related outbound tourism (May-July) corresponds with the low season for incoming tours into Mauritius, thereby facilitating availability and accessibility for visitors, and increasing the average occupation rate of hotel and business facilities. These diversification efforts into the MICE market coincide with heavy investments in telecommunications and technologies, with the aim of making a cyber-island of Mauritius—proactive policies for export diversification can thus cross-fertilize. Similarly, Mauritius is trying to tap into the market of medical tourism: Cuba has proven that a small island could become a major destination for tourists who do not have access to certain types of surgery in their home country. This market is growing, and Mauritius has started to develop its capacities in the field, relying on the advantages of a critical mass of tourists and an already existing health infrastructure.

But Mauritius also needs to avoid becoming too dependent on tourism receipts. Thus, the government should also pursue further diversification of goods production, for example, by shifting agricultural investments into products such as fruits, vegetables, or meat, which could supply the growing hospitality sector and the domestic market.

A TOOL NOT AVAILABLE TO ALL

Does the fact that many developing countries have successfully used tourism as a pathway to diversification make it an option available to all?

Countries with the necessary security and political stability, appropriate natural endowments, and sufficient environmental management capacities clearly have an advantage in developing tourism.

Security and Stability

Some countries might have the illusion of a tourism potential. In some others, tourism is a nonstarter. This is the case where political instability or insecurity, or both, prevail. The experience of Zimbabwe is very interesting in this regard. In 1999, Zimbabwe received more than 2 million tourists. Thereafter, however, the country began to experience a period of considerable economic and political upheaval: the worsening of human rights conditions and electoral frauds, among other problems, led to increasing international political isolation, while an escalation of violence added to the deterioration of the tourism climate. As a result, the number of tourist arrivals dropped by more than half in four years, with diversion to neighboring countries (including Namibia and Zambia).

Security and insecurity have several dimensions, from kidnapping, physical aggression, or theft to security of money transactions, fraud or corruption, food or transport security, health concerns, and natural disasters. Lack of security affects the willingness both of tourists to visit a country and of foreign operators to invest in the country. While politically stable, Mauritius is not immune from these security (including health security) issues: in 2005, the *chikungunya* (mosquito-borne illness) epidemics seriously affected the tourism industry in La Réunion, with some repercussions on neighboring Mauritius. Recent data released by the Mauritian authorities and hospitality associations estimate that the cost for the tourism sector of the *chikungunya* epidemics could have reached $39 million the following year. The number of French tourist arrivals shrank by more than 40 percent. However, the Mauritius Tourism Promotion Authority reacted swiftly and launched a new promotion campaign in France. This was also an opportunity for the country to diversify its target markets, considering that the epidemics did not have a significant impact on tourist arrivals from Italy, Germany, and South Africa.

Natural Endowments

Literature on tourism traditionally distinguishes between three types of countries: island, coastal, and landlocked. For the latter, attracting tourists can be more challenging, unless the destination is on a major road (air or land) to other tourist or business destinations. With the democratization of tourism (that is, the reduction of transport costs and the development of mass tourism), no country seems to be ab initio excluded from the tourism race. However, the cost of becoming a tourist attraction remains highly dependent upon natural (geographical, geological, historical, cultural) endowments. The nature of proactive policies needed to develop tourism exports varies accordingly: while Mauritius can develop a purely domestic strategy to attract tourists, landlocked countries will need to increase cooperation with their neighbors.

Mauritius has all the assets required to attract tourists, in particular white sand beaches, crystal clear water, and a hot climate. However, its geographical situation—relatively isolated in the Indian Ocean—makes it less accessible than some of its competitors, such as the Caribbean for the U.S. market. As a result, the cost and ease of air transport (number of direct flights or connections and frequency of flights) are essential to the development of tourism exports. Other countries, such as those in continental Africa, also have important assets but a higher cost of entry on the tourism market: a sustainable commercial exploitation of nature and wildlife requires heavy investments in infrastructure and basic services. At the other extreme, the example of Dubai shows that with sufficient resources countries can create tourism assets: massive investments can make a large shopping mall for tourists emerge out of the desert. The combination of oil money and a hub situation on major trade routes is unusual, however, and might be the unique recipe for Dubai's success.

Ensuring the Sustainability of Tourism

Tourism is often dependent on the availability of natural resources, but the growth of the tourism industry can pose a threat to the sustainability of these resources as well as impose environmental damage on the rest of the economy. Poor planning—such as allowing depletion of wildlife or excessive building on the coast—can destroy the attractiveness of the country, and the absence of management of natural resources can prevent a country from ever using its original tourism potential. Developing countries should therefore be careful not to miss their momentum for diversification in the tourism sector and should include sustainable tourism in their conservation plans.

Nature-based tourism of the kind developed in continental Africa, for example, is a double-edged sword: the main environmental threats reside in urban development (accommodation of tourists), transports networks (mobility of tourists), poor management of wildlife resources (issuing an excessive number of hunting licenses, for example), and the disturbance of wildlife by the presence of tourists in sensitive areas. On the other hand, it appears that the commercial value of wildlife (as an attraction for tourists) has created an incentive for better preservation and management of environmental resources. In Zambia, the establishment of national parks helped to preserve wildlife resources essential for tourism, for example, by curbing the poaching of elephants and rhinos.

Critics have stressed the environmental risks of mass tourism: for example, a World Wildlife Fund report on fresh water and tourism in the Mediterranean revealed that every tourist consumes between 300 and 850 liters of water a day, and the annual consumption of a golf course is around 1 million cubic meters a year—the equivalent of the water consumption of a city of 12,000 inhabitants. As a result, tourism has significantly affected the ecosystem of the region (de Stefano 2004). This type of tourism development could have a dramatic impact in developing countries where water resources are scarcer or less efficiently exploited. At the same time, new forms of tourism, such as ecotourism, have emerged that profoundly differ from 1970s practices. In Mauritius, for example, particular attention has to be paid to waste disposal and to conservation of the coral reef (damaged by unregulated tour operators).

THE IMPACT OF TOURISM ON THE DOMESTIC ECONOMY

Even in countries where tourism seems to be an accessible pathway to diversification, why invest in this sector rather than in another? Diversification experiments in various sectors are not necessarily mutually exclusive, but most of the developing countries have very limited resources, and priority should be given to sectors with the highest development (economic and social) potential.

The Direct and Indirect Impact of Tourism

The positive effects of tourism on the economy are usually captured by the concept of "tourism multiplier" (jobs and income), which is the sum of direct and indirect impacts (figure 10.2). Direct impacts are those arising from the original tourist expenditure (money spent on accommodation, for example). Indirect effects occur when a hotel buys inputs (goods and services) from other businesses in the economy or when hotel employees spend part of their wages to buy goods and services locally (Meyer 2006). The World Tourism and Travel Council estimates that, on average, tourism generates an indirect contribution to the economy equivalent to 100 percent of direct tourism expenditures. Estimations vary significantly from study to study, however, and there are no truly reliable data. Multipliers are also country-specific and even region-specific (it is, for example, estimated that the multiplier is higher in rural than urban areas). For Mauritius, the multiplier is slightly higher than 2, and tourism is estimated to have created close to 170,000 jobs (half of them in the tourism sector per se).

Data show that the level of expenditure varies greatly from country to country. For example, tourists leave five times more money behind in Mauritius ($126 a day, and $1,310 a tourist) than in Zambia. Several factors explain this gap, including the length of the stay, the level of development and prices in the host country, and the availability of services and goods to purchase. The level of expenditure also varies from one class of

Figure 10.2 Effects of Tourism: Direct and Indirect

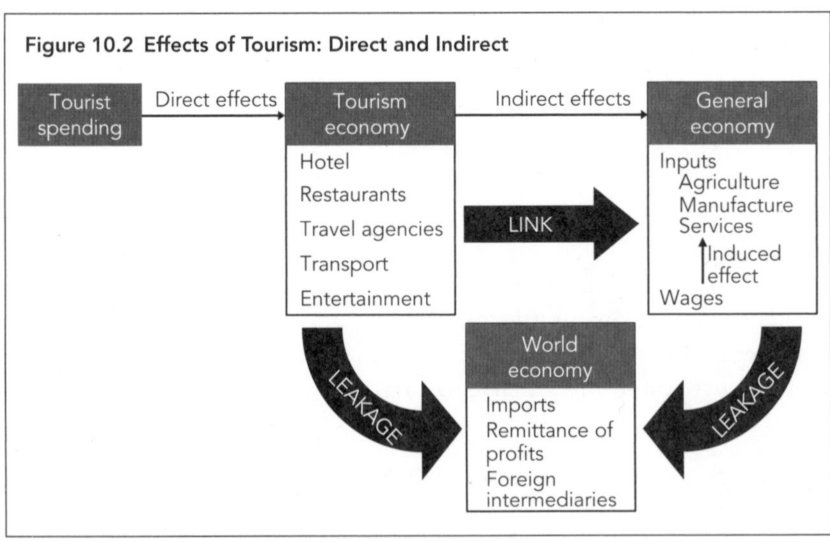

Source: Author's depiction.

tourists to another: backpackers spend less money on accommodation, food, and extras; tourists from the region spend less than American or European tourists. All those factors are intertwined: a certain level of comfort is required to attract the most exclusive clientele, and the poor quality of basic services (efficient telecommunications, proper roads and reliable transportation, access to reliable health care, and the like) can prevent a country from expanding beyond the regional or lower-end clientele. Therefore, a sector strategy should balance the cost of improving infrastructure (including hospitality facilities) with the direct and indirect receipts of tourism.

The weaknesses of tourism-driven growth are usually captured by the concept of "leakages," defined as the percentage of the price of the holiday paid by the tourist that leaves a destination (for example, imported inputs or profits remitted by foreign hotel groups) or that never reaches the destination, primarily because of the involvement of intermediaries (such as tour operators or transporters) often based in the developed countries. Here again, data vary considerably from source to source, and no data are truly reliable. For Mauritius, Jenner and Smith (1992) have estimated that up to 90 percent of gross tourist expenditure could be leaked. Obviously, the smaller the economy, the more leakages (caused by production capacity constraints). According to World Bank studies, leakages can be overestimated and should not obscure the overall positive economic impact of tourism; the studies also stressed that, while generating more criticisms in the tourism sector, leakages were a phenomenon observed in most sectors (Christie and Crompton 2001). In another study, English (1986) suggested that the net foreign exchange earnings from tourism were significant, ranging from at least 50 percent of gross expenditures within the country to as much as 90 percent in the most advanced developing countries.

Leakage can be reduced and links to the domestic economy increased by playing with different factors, including the improvement of production capacities of domestic industries, the development of stronger intersectoral links within the economy, the provision of a platform for efficient distribution of goods and services, and the enabling of domestic industries to compete successfully with their counterparts (Karagiannis and Witter 2004). The objective should not be to suppress leakage by all means, however; the example of Nigeria shows that strategies to reduce leakage by distorting competition and trade rules (by banning imports, for example) could have a rather negative impact.

A Vehicle for Exports and Diversification in Other Sectors

The debate on leakage stresses the tourism sector's high dependence on a wide range of inputs: both the tourism industry and tourists are important consumers of goods and services. This debate also reveals that while tourism is in itself a source of exports, it can be a vehicle for boosting exports in other sectors, for example, by bringing the foreign consumer to the local retailer or producer of handicrafts (see Lejárraga and Walkenhorst [2009], chapter 11 in this volume). Evidence shows that tourism development has positive externalities on certain up- and downstream sectors: it generates foreign demand for local goods and services, and it contributes to raising production standards, thereby enabling other sectors to export. In sum, the development of a local industry to serve the tourism sector can translate, in a second phase, into the exportation of the goods or services produced. That is, the tourism pathway to diversification has ramifications, facilitating diversification and exports in other sectors of the economy.

Some specific tourism activities have higher "export content" in other services or goods than others. For example, the Dubai tax-free zone is just such a platform for exports of diverse goods and services. Sectors like handicraft often primarily rely on tourism to "export." Medical tourism has a high "export content" in health services; for example, a Confederation of Indian Industry–McKinsey & Co. report (2002) estimates that medical tourism could generate about $2 billion by 2012 for India alone (with 3 million patients expected).

Tourism also facilitates trade, including by promoting higher-quality standards for goods and services and infrastructure (telecommunications and transportation, which contribute to trade facilitation). Hotels of international stature need high-quality products to have a uniform standard of services and utilities around the world. In poor or small island countries, hotels might need to import these products (certain foods, bed linens, toiletries, and the like) if local production is nonexistent or does not meet the required standards. With the development of the tourism sector and the increased demand for high-quality inputs, local industries have an incentive to adjust. Experience shows that foreign direct investment in sectors such as tourism and retail contributes to the adoption of international standards for both goods and services. In a second phase, those products can eventually be exported if, in addition to meeting international standards, they are competitively priced. Improvement of infrastructure prompted by tourism development is another channel through which tourism can help promote exports in other sectors.

In the health sector, medical tourism clearly has an impact on the level of standards: in Bangalore, India, for the first time, a multispecialty tertiary care hospital received the ISO 9001:2000 certification for quality management. Whether, in this specific case, local people actually benefit from the new standards is another issue, but nothing prevents an economy from developing two types of industries: one to produce at local standards meeting domestic needs and another to produce at international standards for the purpose of export. Eventually, when the latter industry becomes very competitive, it can contribute to improving local standards and quality of life (an example is the positive spillover effects of health services trade in the region of Marrakesh, Morocco).

CONCLUSION

Tourism has been and remains a pathway to development and export diversification for a number of countries at different stages of trade integration. This opportunity is not equally available to all, however, and certain conditions must prevail to enter the tourism market successfully. There is therefore an opportunity cost to investing in tourism development, in particular in countries with fragile security and political instability, few natural endowments, and poor environmental management capacity. Not all regions can—or should—invest billions of dollars in leisure and tourism as the Persian Gulf region has done. On one hand, tourism can have important spillover effects on the domestic economy and can constitute a vehicle for exports in other sectors. On the other hand, negative social and environmental externalities and the problem of leakage have tarnished the image of the sector. In practice, international hotel chains often prefer sourcing products locally when they can. The challenge for policy makers then is to create a business environment that brings international tourism operators and local producers together and enables the latter to meet the required product and marketing standards on a consistent basis.

One of the key features of tourism that distinguish Mauritius from less successful cases is the positive and proactive role of the government. First, in the early days, public authorities worked closely with private developers to release publicly regulated resources—particularly sugar lands—into tourism. The role of the government as coordinator of the tourism industry's development has continued since. Second, the government provided a stable and secure environment. Not only was sound macroeconomic management crucial to the industry's success, but so was the public effort to confront the potentially devastating effects of mosquito-born illnesses with fast and effective action. Third, the government has worked with the industry to minimize environmental damages that large-scale tourism could otherwise produce. Finally, the government has sought to deepen domestic linkages within the tourism industry and between it and other sectors.

Any diversification out of one sector leads to a higher concentration in another, which might subsequently lead to renewed diversification efforts. Thus, diversification can turn into a virtuous circle, if the country continues to discover and exploit new comparative advantages and thereby achieves higher levels of exports and income. However, diversification can also have adverse consequences, if the country moves its dependence from one sector to another that does not generate benefits that are widely shared throughout the whole economy. Whether diversification into tourism falls into the virtuous or the vicious category depends to a large extent on how well the sector is integrated with the domestic economy so that the latter can benefit from spillovers and the development of complementary goods and services sectors. In this context, policies to foster intersectoral links can make a decisive contribution.

REFERENCES

Cattaneo, Olivier. 2007. "Tourism: Unfulfilled Promises." In *Services Trade and Development: The Experience of Zambia*, ed. A. Mattoo and L. Payton. Washington, DC: World Bank.

Christie, Iain T., and Doreen E. Crompton. 2001. "Tourism in Africa." Africa Region Working Paper Series 12, World Bank, Washington, DC.

Confederation of Indian Industry and McKinsey & Co. 2002. *Healthcare in India: The Road Ahead.* New York: McKinsey & Co.

de Stefano, Lucia. 2004. *Fresh Water and Tourism in the Mediterranean.* Rome: World Wildlife Fund.

English, E. Philip. 1986. *The Great Escape? An Examination of North-South Tourism.* Ottawa: North-South Institute.

Jenner, Paul, and Christine Smith. 1992. *The Tourism Industry and the Environment* (EIU Special Report 2453). London: Economist Intelligence Unit.

Karagiannis, Nikolaos, and Michael Witter. 2004. *The Caribbean Economies in an Era of Free Trade*. London: Ashgate.

Lejárraga, Iza, and Peter Walkenhorst. 2009. "Fostering Productive Diversification through Tourism." In *Breaking Into New Markets: Emerging Lessons for Export Diversification*, ed. Richard Newfarmer, William Shaw, and Peter Walkenhorst, 197–210. Washington, DC: World Bank.

Meyer, Dorothea. 2006. "Caribbean Tourism, Local Sourcing and Enterprise Development: Review of the Literature." Pro-Poor Tourism Working Paper 18, Pro-Poor Tourism Partnership, London.

World Bank. 2005. *Development through Tourism: The World Bank's Role 1966–2005*. Washington, DC.

———. 2006. "Mauritius: From Preferences to Global Competitiveness." Report of the Aid for Trade Mission, Washington, DC.

CHAPTER 11

FOSTERING PRODUCTIVE DIVERSIFICATION THROUGH TOURISM

Iza Lejárraga and Peter Walkenhorst

In many low-income countries, tourism is an important economic activity and often one of the largest earners of foreign exchange. Indeed, a number of countries have used dynamic tourism growth as a means of diversifying away from an overwhelming reliance on commodity exports and of shifting toward trade in services (see, for example, Cattaneo [2009], chapter 10 in this volume). Yet simply fostering diversification by growing tourism services may overlook a potentially even more important lever for diversification: using tourism as a vehicle to develop and diversify other parts of the domestic economy.

The key is to take advantage of the manifold links between tourism and other sectors. In addition to obvious connections to air and ground transportation, hotel accommodation, and tour-guiding services, enhanced tourism activities have upstream effects in the agrifood, handicraft, jewelry and cosmetics, and furniture and textile industries that can act as catalysts for quality improvements and economic development. Supplying international tourists means selling to foreign consumers without incurring export logistics costs or requiring the scale of activity expected by industrialized country supermarkets.

Meeting the demanding requirements of tourists from developed countries often involves substantial changes in local production and distribution systems. But once the higher standards are achieved on a consistent basis, the same production and distribution practices can be used to ensure compliance with sanitary and phytosanitary requirements in international markets and to adjust to the technical standards and design tastes of foreigners, enabling a developing country to launch or broaden exports to markets in industrialized countries. Hence, there can be learning spillovers that are not directly associated with tourism but that are indirectly transmitted through backward links. Examples of successful tourism-led export product developments include butterfly chrysalises in Costa Rica (box 11.1), wooden furniture in Egypt, and rum cakes in Jamaica.

Private firms in the tourism industry, such as hotel operators, have an obvious incentive to try to replace imports with local produce in order to offer fresh fruit, vegetables, fish, and meat to their customers and to give their facilities a distinct local appearance. However, public policy can often play an important role when there are coordination or information failures between the tourism industry and related sectors of the domestic economy. Policy can support private sector developments and promote the availability of sufficient local supplies at competitive prices for the tourism industry. Examples of policy interventions include the organization of supplier fairs, the monitoring and enforcement of food safety standards, and the review of the incentive regime to ensure that duty exemptions for international tourism operators do not leave potential domestic suppliers at a disadvantage.

More generally, entrepreneurs in the tourism economy have greater success in discovering and developing new productive activities where conditions enable them to read and implement critical signals from tourist demand. In particular, a low-cost business environment, high entrepreneurial capital, and an open trade regime foster greater links between the tourism economy and the productive apparatus of the general economy. When greater links exist between the tourism sector and other sectors of the domestic economy, it is easier for new producers to learn about potential opportunities and take advantage of the established infrastructure, distribution channels, and local reputation with buyers.

This chapter traces ways to leverage tourism for economic diversification in several stages (figure 11.1). It then looks at the empirical evidence on the relative importance of different aspects of the policy environment that support tourism links with other sectors. Finally, it ventures some policy conclusions to enhance the diversification-promoting potential of tourism.

Box 11.1 Exports of Butterfly Chrysalises from Costa Rica

Although butterfly farming predates the advent of tourists in Costa Rica, it was only with the development of ecotourism in the mid-1980s that the country discovered it could commercialize its colorful butterflies and profitably export them to the rest of the world. Tourism has played a major role in the Costa Rican economy, contributing significantly to economic diversification and export growth. In 1984, the private company Suministros Entomológicos Costarricenses, SA (SECSA) undertook the first attempt to raise butterflies for commercial purposes. What had hitherto been a hobby for aficionados or a research activity for scientists became a new product for tourists. Butterfly exhibits began to be introduced in ecotours, and rural villagers across the country started to learn how to raise butterflies on their farms for the tourism industry, diversifying away from traditional cultivations, such as coffee.

Subsequently, SECSA and four firms learned how to package butterfly chrysalises in a way that conformed to national and international environmental laws and phytosanitary standards. Soon enough, a butterfly pupa could be shipped in a box and emerge as a butterfly 30 days later in the buyer's home. With this discovery, Costa Rica captured a unique niche and became the world's leading exporter of live neotropical butterflies, selling to zoos, research centers, and exhibits worldwide. Currently, SECSA works with 115 butterfly farms around the country, and it is estimated that 200 Costa Rican families earn their main income through the butterfly business. Unit prices range from $1.75 to $200 per chrysalis, and the butterflies are shipped to 20 export destinations, notably the United States, the European Union, Canada, Mexico, and Switzerland. In 2007, Costa Rica's butterfly exports amounted to almost $1.5 million.

The biodiversity Costa Rica enjoys is hardly unique in the region. Its two neighboring countries—Nicaragua and Panama—boast the exact same richness in butterfly species. Etymologically, Panama means "abundance of butterflies." The question to ask, then, is why the two countries did not manage to commercialize them. Clearly, part of the answer is the absence of a significant tourism market that could catalyze and sustain the discovery. Tourism is small in both Nicaragua and Panama, and without it, there is hardly any internal demand: local consumers do not pay to see butterflies or buy a pupa to take home.

Inspired by the success of Costa Rica, Nicaraguan producers have tried to imitate the butterfly export capability. Yet, without an internal demand, the production costs (such as high temperatures needed to raise pupae) have proven to be prohibitive, and these efforts have been unsuccessful. Much of the demand for butterflies in foreign markets is seasonal—covering the months of April-September when it is warm in the developed countries of North America and Europe. During the rest of the year, the butterfly farms cannot be maintained to cover costs—except in Costa Rica, where hundreds of daily tourists sustain the butterfly industry.

Source: Authors, based on information from the Foreign Trade Corporation of Costa Rica (PROCOMER) and Internet sources.

Figure 11.1 Tourism: A Major Stimulant for New Product Discovery

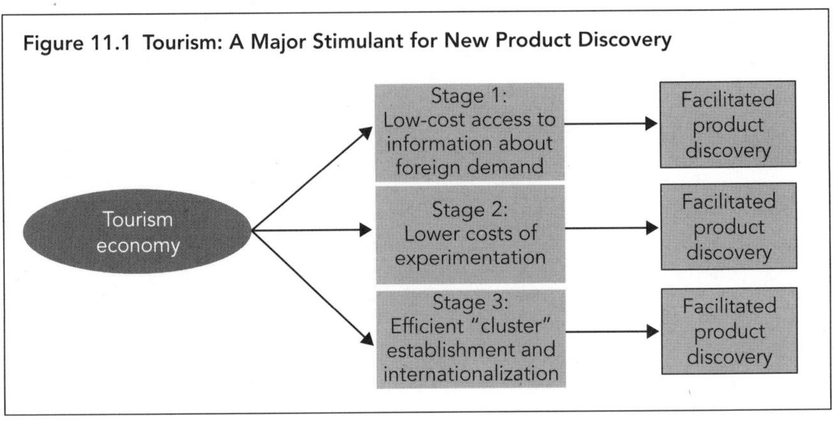

Source: Authors' depiction.

ACQUISITION OF INFORMATION ABOUT FOREIGN DEMAND

How does an entrepreneur in a developing country acquire information about foreign demand, and, without this knowledge, how can an entrepreneur go about discovering what to produce and export abroad? Rauch and Watson (2002) contend that one of the greatest sources of uncertainty concerning trading possibilities is the existence of international demand for a product. Such uncertainty is heightened in developing countries, where—given the lower purchasing power and less sophisticated tastes of local consumers—domestic demand is an inadequate indicator of demand in developed-country markets. In this context, learning about foreign demand is an expensive and complex venture involving an extensive process of market research, trade fairs, and other undertakings that most public and private entities in developing countries are ill-equipped to perform.

Tourism generates virtually cost-free information about international demand within borders. In effect, a consumer from a developed country who vacations in a developing country serves as a valuable signaling device about existing and potential demand in international markets. By observing the preferences tourists reveal through their economic behavior, in particular their purchasing choices, local entrepreneurs can garner key information about the characteristics of foreign demand, such as the types of goods and services that foreign consumers prefer, the quality and technical specifications required, and the willingness of foreign consumers to pay for a particular good or service.

Crucially, this information is furnished to local entrepreneurs at little or no cost: tourism subsidizes the market research required to launch new exports. Entrepreneurs who use tourism as a discovery channel are constantly learning and updating information about demand across borders, an opportunity that either is not available to entrepreneurs or is available only at high costs. Furthermore, the uncertainty about the existence of foreign demand—an uncertainty that tends to hinder the discovery activity—is overcome in the tourism context, where international demand for a product is not an open question mark, but already exists within the host developing country.

EXPERIMENTATION WITH NEW PRODUCTS

Once information about foreign demand has been acquired, how does an entrepreneur determine to what specifications he or she should produce a good? This second phase of the discovery process involves learning about the expected profitability of producing a new good. Indeed, the cost of production given a local setting is a priori unknown to the entrepreneur. Unveiling this information, what Hausmann and Rodrik (2003) refer to as "cost discovery," entails a process of experimentation. In some instances, entrepreneurs experiment with how to produce an entirely new product; in other instances, they learn how to adapt and commercialize existing products in a manner that appeals to foreign consumers. High costs of experimentation may abort the discovery process altogether, even when requisite information about foreign demand is available.

Tourism reduces the costs and risks associated with experimentation in notable ways. First, the kinds of "new goods" channeled through the tourism economy are ones in which the minimum efficient scale of operation is lower than in most other modern sectors. Therefore, it is not necessary to formally establish a firm and hire labor to test new goods in the market. On the contrary, most of the initial trial-and-error dynamic unfolds in a preestablishment phase, through self-employment or small-scale informal operations. As a result, experimentation costs do not typically entail large-scale investments.

Second, tourism-led entrepreneurs have the opportunity to test their trial products on a foreign market without incurring the transaction costs associated with exporting the product. In effect, the tourism market can be viewed as a within-the-border export market. In the process of learning about productive capabilities, entrepreneurs benefit from testing their trials on an "international market" that is not subject to tariffs and other cross-border fees. Time is also money, and testing trial products on foreign consumers in the tourism economy avoids costly delays in customs, making the trial-and-error process quicker and more dynamic. In addition, proximity to the foreign consumer allows entrepreneurs to observe directly the outcome of their experimentation efforts, enabling them to identify the successes or shortcomings of the trial products.

Finally, the level of risk associated with this phase of the discovery process is significantly mitigated in the presence of the tourism market, given that entrepreneurs will generally be able to sell their trial products to international tourists and thus cover their costs. The opportunity to make a profit from trial products in the tourism economy will in turn help finance the continuance of new trials, rendering the experimentation process sustainable. Therefore, regardless of the relative success or failure in discovering a new export, entrepreneurs will generally be able to cover the costs incurred by their investments in learning through experimentation.

ESTABLISHMENT AND POSTESTABLISHMENT

How does an entrepreneur in a developing country turn a successful market trial into a mature product and world export? Following a period of experimentation, those entrepreneurs whose goods pass an initial profitability market test strive to establish and solidify operations. This phase involves learning about scale, marketing, and reputation needed to internationalize (Zeufack, Fafchamps, and El Hamine 2002; Izquierdo, Jacques, and Olarreaga 2003). Access to international markets will generate a new source of demand for the new product, allowing entrepreneurs to achieve scale and lower their marginal costs of production. Arguably, in the absence of robust local demand, failure to internationalize a new product may lead to the death of the discovery. Yet there is a big leap to be made from experimentation to export-oriented establishment. Even when a new profitable product is identified in the experimentation phase, the promise of internationalizing the discovery can be easily stifled by ineffectual establishment.

The dynamics of the tourism economy provide a vehicle for cost savings in the phase of establishment and postestablishment. The tourism economy is composed of a group of interrelated firms and institutions that tend to agglomerate around a geographically proximate space. In this sense, tourism is touted as being a natural cluster—a term coined by Porter (1998) to define a constellation of interconnected firms in a particular field, linked by commonalities and complementarities. The collocation benefits and spillover effects that emerge from tourism clusters render establishment more efficient.

As a member of a cluster, a tourism-led entrepreneur can learn about productivity more quickly and at lower cost by observing other firms' business know-how and capitalizing on informational spillovers. In addition, membership in the cluster endows the entrepreneur with a marketing brand and other reputational effects that facilitate visibility and the placement of products in both local and international markets. An isolated firm, in contrast, would have to devote far more resources to learning and logistics to achieve a similar level of competitiveness. Thus, the agglomeration economies of tourism lower transaction costs and create incentives for investments in new activities.

TOURISM AND EXPORT DIVERSIFICATION: PANEL DATA EVIDENCE

Do countries that have specialized in tourism develop a more diversified economic structure over time? If tourism provides powerful incentives for local entrepreneurship, developing countries that attract significant levels of tourism might be expected to show a greater occurrence of new products and exports. Therefore, the number and variety of goods in the host economy would increase as a result of such discovery.

For empirical verification, the statistical relationship between tourism specialization and productive diversification can be investigated. Given that disaggregated production data do not exist, export data are generally used to proxy economic diversification. The latter is measured through the Herfindahl index of activity concentration. Moreover, a country's degree of tourism specialization can be defined as the ratio of annual tourism receipts to GDP; 63 developing countries have tourism receipts equal to at least 0.05 percent of GDP, a minimum threshold suggesting the existence of tourism activity. This sample was used to assess the relationship between tourism specialization and productive diversification from 1993 to 2003, the most recent decade for which data are available (figure 11.2).

The estimation results suggest that a 1 percent increase in tourism specialization between 1993 and 2003 is associated with a 0.11 percent increase in the export diversification index over the same period. This relationship is significant at the 1 percent level ($p = 0.00$). Additional empirical tests, such as fixed-effect panel data regressions, yield a similar relationship between tourism specialization and export diversification. Therefore, the empirical evidence supports the notion that countries that have experienced an increase in tourism activity have also exhibited an increase in the diversification of their exports over this period. While the depicted association and available data do not make it possible to determine causality, the question why some countries have been considerably more successful in leveraging tourism to discover new products and exports than others with similar levels of tourism activity merits further analysis.

Figure 11.2 Correlation of Tourism Specialization with Export Diversification

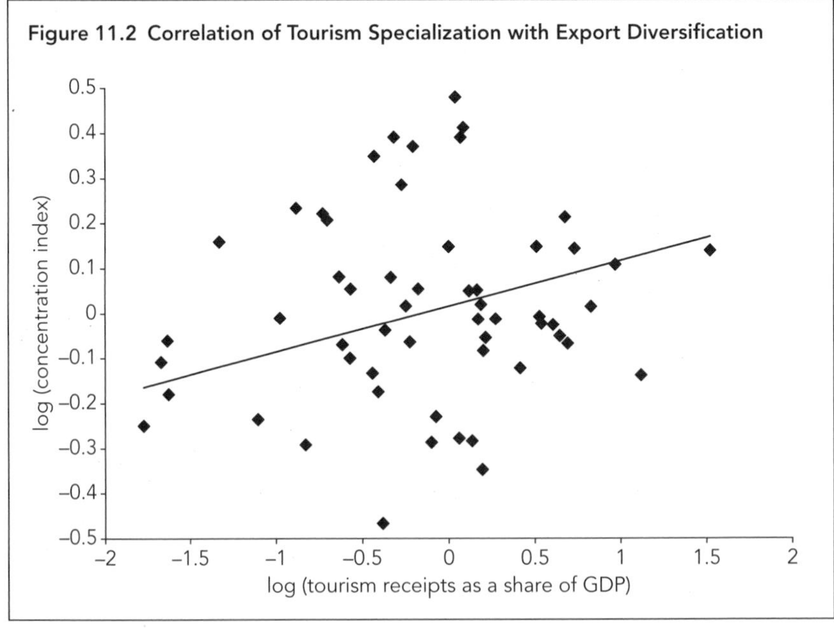

Source: Authors, based on data for 1993 to 2003 from the World Tourism Organization and from U.N. Comtrade (Commodity Trade Statistics Database).

THE ROLE AND DETERMINANTS OF TOURISM LINKS

In particular, it is worth exploring the conditions under which tourism can enhance discovery-cum-diversification in the host economy. One explanation that merits consideration highlights the role that tourism links play in catalyzing the discovery of new products. Links can be defined as the network of intersectoral supply relationships between the tourism economy and the rest of the productive sectors of the domestic economy. When such networks exist between tourism and the rest of the economic activities of the host country, it is easier for local entrepreneurs to collect the signals on foreign demand that are enshrined in the tourism economy. In this regard, tourism links serve as a mechanism for the transmission of information to local producers. The more links that exist between tourism and the general economy, the greater the potential for international buyers and local sellers to come together—ameliorating information gaps and coordination failures, while leveraging the opportunities for experimentation and discovery of local entrepreneurs.

The successful broadening and deepening of links, then, is an integral part of making tourism work for economic diversification. These networks facilitate collaboration among local producers in the agricultural, manufacturing, and services sectors, forging clusters of businesses that, while producing complementary types of goods, share the common objective of catering to a foreign consumer. In the absence of links between the tourism economy and other productive sectors of the host economy, tourism may fail to foment a discovery response from local entrepreneurship. Moreover, it will not stimulate a coordination dynamic among local producers. In light of these spillovers, a critical question from the perspective of a social planner in a tourism-recipient country is what—if any—conditions can be optimized to foster such links as a means to strengthen incentives for new productive activities.

Country conditions that might explain cross-country variations in tourism linkages can be broadly grouped into five domains: natural endowments, level of socioeconomic development, institutions, business environment, and policy (regarding trade, for example). These domains, in turn, can be conceptualized hierarchically based on their relative amenability to public policy over the long, medium, or shorter term (figure 11.3). The available literature on tourism links, largely based on country case studies, suggests that each of these five domains plays an influential role in harnessing or hobbling links.

Figure 11.3 Determinants of Tourism Links

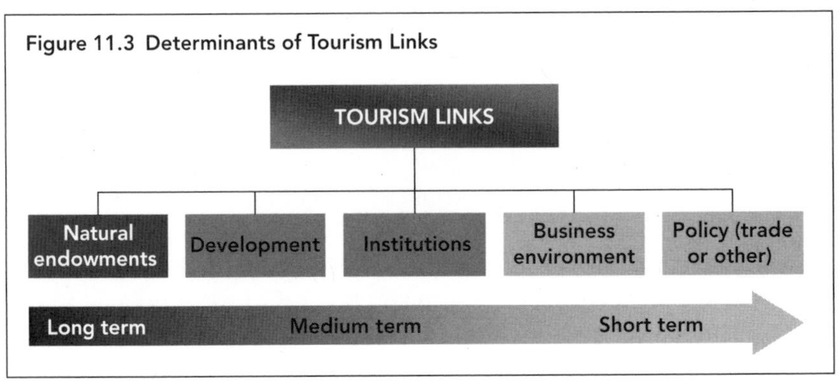

Source: Authors.

IDENTIFYING WHAT MATTERS MOST: CROSS-COUNTRY EVIDENCE

What country-specific factors matter most? This question can be addressed empirically by drawing on the Tourism Satellite Accounts research from the World Travel and Tourism Council, which provides data on the indirect and direct effects of tourism spending in 151 countries. The strength of tourism links is measured as the ratio of indirect to direct effects, that is, how much of a unit of tourist spending in the tourism economy (for example, for hotels, tour operators, souvenir shops, and the like) reverberates through tourist demand to nontourism sectors of the economy. The stronger these links are, the more solid the demand and supply networks that exist between the tourism economy and other domestic sectors of the host economy will be.

The regression of the tourism links variable on indicators representing the five domains suggests that fixed or semifixed factors of production, such as land, labor, or capital, have less influence on the extent of tourism links than is generally supposed (Lejárraga and Walkenhorst 2007). By contrast, variables related to the entrepreneurial capital of the host economy are of notable explanatory significance. The human development index (HDI), which is used to measure a country's standard of living, is significantly and positively associated with tourism links. One plausible explanation for this is that tourists from developed countries may feel more comfortable and thus may be inclined to consume more in a host country that has a lifestyle to which they can relate. Beyond income levels, the HDI measures the relative achievements of countries in the areas of health and education. Therefore, a higher HDI reflects a healthier and more educated workforce, and thus indicates the quality of local entrepreneurship. Related to this point, it is important to underscore that the level of participation of women in the host economy also has a significantly positive effect on tourism links. In sum, enhancing local entrepreneurial capital and incorporating women into this capital will strengthen the local economy's preparedness to leverage discovery opportunities.

Another notable observation deriving from the analysis concerns the relevance of informal institutional arrangements in the formation of links. Formal institutions and their regulatory control of the market, proxied by the size of the government and price controls, were not found to have significant effects on relationships between tourism and other sectors of the economy. Despite the importance of democratic governance, this was not identified as a key determinant either. On the other hand, the prevalence of informal institutions does appear to be significantly associated with stronger links. While at first sight surprising, this finding accords with the clustering dynamics noted above, in which links are formed on the basis of self-enforcing "relations-based" governance. Also, informal structures cost less than formal, rules-driven institutional frameworks for entrepreneurship. Hence, formal regulations can deter the spontaneous and cost-driven incentives for cluster formation.

Formal types of institutions that do matter are institutions for policing and vigilance. As would be expected, the results show that countries with a higher incidence of violence or crime have significantly fewer tourism links. Indeed, the coordination of discoverers in tourism clusters depends fundamentally on trust among local entrepreneurs—and trust can hardly flourish in an environment characterized by social conflict. Equally important, the perception of violence on the part of tourists and hotels will dissuade tourists from venturing beyond the safe boundaries of the "enclave" hotel resort. Finally, hotel managers and other foreign investors in the tourism economy will be less inclined to maintain productive relations with the host economy in the absence of predictability and stability. Therefore, investments in institutions that maintain safety—and a perception of safety—in the host economy may be critical for spawning coordination.

While all country domains play a role in fostering or hindering tourism links, the business environment has an overriding influence on them. After controlling for a country's natural endowments, level of development, and institutions, which are the less amenable domains, the business environment on its own explains almost 20 percent of cross-country variations in tourism links. In particular, the level of corporate taxes in the host economy has the most significant adverse effect on the formation of links, in conformity with the lower-cost motivation underlying tourism-led discovery. Also, a widespread use of the Internet has a positive effect in the ability to orchestrate coordination.

Finally, the results suggest that maintaining an open trade regime is critical for the emergence of tourism links. This underscores the importance of not protecting inefficient economic activities and of opening potential products for tourism demand to competition. Although trade barriers may indeed serve to prod investors in the tourism economy to procure domestic goods, they will also hinder the competitiveness of local producers. Shielded from imports, local producers will not have the incentives to meet the international quality standards of the products needed by the tourism economy. Quality standards, and not just costs, will likely inform the procurement decisions of the tourism economy.

POLICIES TO PROMOTE DIVERSIFICATION THROUGH TOURISM

Tourism represents a "low-cost road" for discovering what one is good at producing and exporting abroad. Along this road, local entrepreneurs enjoy free information about international demand, a trial-and-error process for testing new products free of transaction costs, and attractive cost savings for establishment and internationalization. Therefore, to the extent that local entrepreneurs are able to read the signposts that are enshrined in the within-the-border international market of the tourism economy, this road can represent a cost-effective channel to catalyze investments in new economic activities.

What can policy makers in developing countries do to harness the already existing tourism market to promote new exports? Several things.

- *Provide an adequate policy framework for the tourism economy.* Enhancing the business environment by lowering the cost of doing business is the single most important agenda governments can undertake. Policy enhancements might include reviewing and reforming corporate taxation and labor regulations and facilitating Internet access. Measures that have a direct impact on the marginal cost of production seem to be more critical than other aspects of the business environment, such as promoting access to finance or foreign direct investment. In addition, the informal nature of clusters and networks in which tourism discoveries emerge may not require strong regulatory market controls.

- *Enhance signals from the tourism economy.* Perhaps the first thing that governments need to be mindful of is that the road from the tourism economy to the local economy needs to be clear. An environment characterized by crime and poverty will deter investors and visitors in the tourism economy from interacting with the local economy, making tourism an "enclave" economy with limited potential for the emission of informational signals to local producers. Governments often focus on investments in hard infrastructure, such as roads and airports, but fail to understand that lack of security measures and failure to clean up depressed areas surrounding tourism centers are just as important if the industry is to interact with the wider economy.
- *Make it easier for entrepreneurs to read the signals from the tourism economy.* The best way to help local entrepreneurs collect signals from the tourism economy is to empower them with the capability to do so. This means identifying potential supply industries to the tourist sector and then encouraging potential buyers of local products (such as large hotels and travel agents) to meet with potential suppliers to help overcome information deficits on both sides of the market. Also, measures aimed at enhancing the quality of entrepreneurial capital, such as investing in training and health, will yield more tourism-led discoveries. Relatedly, initiatives to encourage the participation of women in tourism-related entrepreneurship have the potential to generate new activities because women play an important role in commercializing the local cuisine and traditional culture.
- *Rely on competition rather than protection to drive productivity.* Using protectionist policies to encourage tourism-led discoveries is likely to be counterproductive. Although high tariffs on certain products may prod hotels and the tourism industry to procure locally, lack of competition from imported goods can ultimately hinder local producers from achieving the requisite international standards tourists will demand. Standards, rather than costs, tend to prevail in the purchasing decisions of the tourism industry. Moreover, competition can encourage exit of resources—firms and labor—that are not productively deployed and shift them into more productive areas of the economy. Therefore, a tourism-led discovery and any links that may result from it will be valuable only if they are efficient.

When tourism-demand signals are emitted, captured, and executed successfully, the new discoveries that can emerge—provided that these are efficient—will increase the overall productivity levels of the host economy. In particular, given that tourism absorbs mostly unskilled entrepreneurs outside the urban centers, this discovery channel often provides rural villagers, women, and indigenous communities with an opportunity to participate in the economic life of the export basket of the country.

REFERENCES

Cattaneo, Olivier. 2009. "Tourism as a Strategy to Diversify Exports: Lessons from Mauritius." In *Breaking Into New Markets: Emerging Lessons for Export Diversification*, ed. Richard Newfarmer, William Shaw, and Peter Walkenhorst, 183–95. Washington, DC: World Bank.

Hausmann, R., and D. Rodrik. 2003. "Economic Development as Self-Discovery." *Journal of Development Economics* 72: 603–33.

Izquierdo, A., M. Jacques, and M. Olarreaga. 2003. "Information Diffusion in International Markets." Research Department Working Paper 488, Inter-American Development Bank, Washington, DC.

Lejárraga, I., and P. Walkenhorst. 2007. "Diversification by Deepening Linkages with Tourism." Paper presented to a workshop on Export Growth and Diversification: Incentive Regimes and Proactive Policies in the Export Cycle, March 15, World Bank, Washington, DC.

Porter, M. E. 1998. "Clusters and the New Economics of Competition." *Harvard Business Review* 76 (Nov/Dec): 77–89.

Rauch, J., and J. Watson. 2002. "Entrepreneurship in International Trade." NBER Working Paper 8708, National Bureau of Economic Research, Cambridge, MA.

Zeufack, A., M. Fafchamps, and S. El Hamine. 2002. "Learning to Export: Evidence from Moroccan Manufacturing." Policy Research Working Paper 2827, World Bank, Washington, DC.

CHAPTER 12

EXPORT PROMOTION AGENCIES: STRATEGIES AND IMPACTS

Daniel Lederman, Marcelo Olarreaga, and Lucy Payton

Institutionalized efforts to promote exports have a long tradition. The first export promotion agency (EPA)—still existing—was created in 1919 in Finland; in the mid-1960s such agencies became a widely used instrument to boost exports and reduce trade deficits. Yet by the early 1990s, their efficiency began to be questioned (Hogan, Keesing, and Singer 1991). EPAs in developing countries were criticized for lacking strong leadership, being inadequately funded, hiring staff that was bureaucratic and not client oriented, and suffering from government involvement.

Part of the blame for the failure of the early EPAs was put on the import-substituting trade regimes that prevailed at the time. Overcoming such a strong antitrade bias was probably too much to ask of any specialized agency. However, more than a decade later, the trade environment has significantly changed in the developing world, and some EPAs have evolved substantially. In this context, the objective of this chapter is to provide an assessment of the strategies and impacts of today's EPAs on national exports.

THE RATIONALE FOR EPAS AND PREVIOUS ANALYSIS

The aim of EPAs is to help (potential) exporters find markets for their products, as well as to provide exporters with a better understanding of products demanded in different export markets. One can divide the services offered by EPAs into four broad categories:

- Country image building (advertising, promotional events, but also advocacy)
- Export support services (exporter training, technical assistance, and capacity building including regulatory compliance, information on trade finance, logistics, customs, packaging, and pricing)
- Marketing (trade fairs, exporter and importer missions, and follow-up services offered by representatives abroad)
- Market research and publications (general, sector- and firm-level information such as market surveys, on-line information on export markets, publications encouraging firms to export, and importer and exporter contact databases).

The economic justification for government involvement in export promotion is based on the theory of asymmetric information and other market failures. Important externalities are associated with the gathering of foreign market information related to consumer preferences, business opportunities, quality, and technical requirements. Private firms alone will not provide foreign market information, as companies hesitate to incur research and marketing costs that can also benefit competitors. Yet the argument for public funding of EPAs ideally should be based on a comprehensive assessment of the social costs and benefits associated with the activities of the agencies. Unfortunately, program evaluation of EPAs on economic welfare grounds is difficult, if not impossible. Thus, often—if not always—evaluations of EPAs stop short of an assessment based on welfare grounds and focus instead on the more modest objective of assessing whether exports have increased or whether new markets have been opened.

The bulk of the empirical literature that has looked more closely at the effectiveness of export promotion has focused on agencies in developed countries, particularly the United States. The literature has taken two broad approaches. One relies on surveys of random samples of exporters and potential exporters, asking which programs they have used, their opinions of these programs, and the success they have had in exporting. Kedia and Chhokar (1986), for example, found that export promotion programs in the United States have little impact, largely because of a lack of awareness of their services. Seringhaus and Botschen (1991) surveyed the opinion of nearly 600 firms in both Austria and Canada and found that use of export promotion services was low and that the programs were not addressing the needs of exporters.

Gençtürk and Kotabe (2001) tested the link between program usage and export performance in a sample of 162 U.S. firms and found that usage of export programs increased profitability but not sales, a finding suggesting that there were no externalities across firms and that export programs represented a mere transfer from agencies to the exporting firm. Gençtürk and Kotabe also found that experienced exporters benefited from government programs more than did new exporters in terms of profitability. Despite their criticism of existing programs, these studies do support the argument that EPAs are a response to a genuine need of small and medium-size firms and that they can be crucial for export success.

In terms of the types of programs, institutional set-up, and financing that are more likely to succeed, Alvarez (2004) provided evidence from a survey of 295 small and medium-size sporadic and permanent exporters in Chile. While trade shows and trade missions did not affect the probability of being a successful exporter, a program of exporter committees showed a positive and significant impact. Such committees are made up of groups of firms with common objectives in international business, which cooperate on research, marketing, and promotion.

Macario (2000) identified the policies that determine successes and failures in Brazil, Chile, Colombia, and Mexico. On the basis of interviews with successful exporters, she set out a number of recommendations for export promotion agencies: they should be directed at firms with new products or that are entering new markets; they should emphasize cost-sharing to ensure that programs are used only by those truly dedicated to export; support should be given for a maximum of two or three years so that it does not turn into a subsidy; and programs should be submitted to external evaluation. She also found that agencies work best when they are subject to a mix of public and private management.

There are very few, if any, cross-country statistical assessments of EPAs. An exception perhaps is Rose (2007), who estimates the impact that the presence of an embassy or consulate may have on bilateral trade using a gravity model. Rose argues that as communication costs have fallen, foreign embassies and consulates have lost much of their role in decision making and information gathering, and therefore are increasingly marketing themselves as agents of export promotion. In a sample of 22 exporting countries, 8 of which are developing countries, and around 200 potential trading partners, he found that for each additional consulate abroad, exports increase by 6 to 10 percent.

A SURVEY-BASED ASSESSMENT OF EPAS

Embassies and consulates—although certainly relevant—are arguably not the core agencies for export promotion; many countries have special organizations devoted to this task. During 2005, a global survey of these agencies was undertaken as the empirical basis for the cross-country analysis presented here. Our goal in conducting the survey was twofold: first, to determine whether EPAs are having an impact on exports; and second, to identify the activities and institutional structures of agencies that seem to have positive effects on exports.

The survey contained five parts: institutional structure, responsibilities of the agency, the strategies followed, resources and expenditures, and activities and functions. Below we provide summary statistics by region. The surveys were sent to 116 countries that had operational EPAs, and 92 answered (of which 4 responded that they could not complete the survey). Each of the 88 surveys that we were able to use was followed up with phone conversations to confirm and clarify some of the answers.

Using the survey data, we disentangled the effects of export promotion agencies, their structure, responsibilities, strategies, resources, and activities on overall exports in order to understand what works and what does not. The first step was to explore whether there is any correlation between export promotion budgets and exports. Figure 12.1 provides a plot of exports per capita on EPA budgets per capita. There is a clear positive correlation between these two variables.

The figure also provides the predicted value obtained from the corresponding locally weighted regression, which provides us with some prima facie evidence about which agencies are underperforming in terms of exports per capita given their budgets. For example, Rwanda (*RWA*) would be expected to have a much higher level of exports given the budget of its EPA (underperformer), whereas the Irish agency (*IRL*) would be expected to have a lower level of exports (overperformer).

An interesting feature is that the curve flattens at very high budgets. Most of the countries among this group of high-budget agencies are developed countries. A test for heterogeneity between developed and

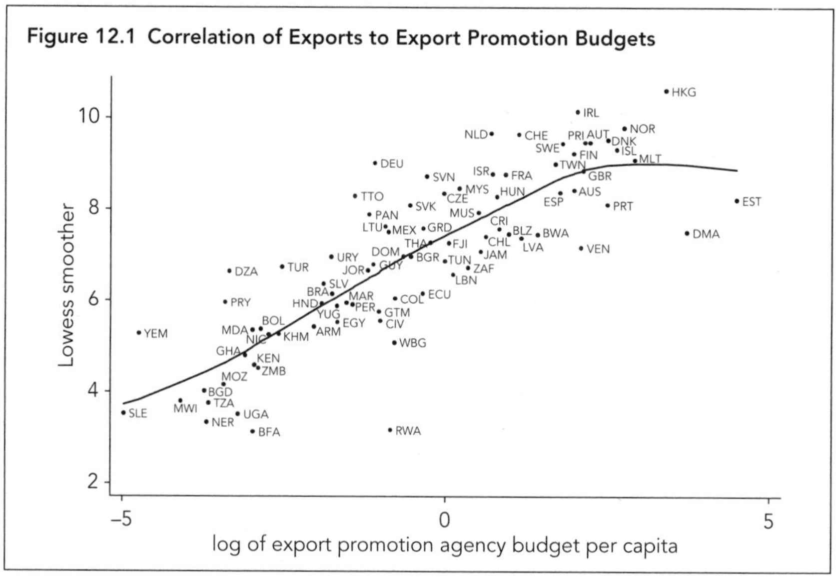

Figure 12.1 Correlation of Exports to Export Promotion Budgets

Source: Authors' calculations using data from the survey and World Bank World Development Indicators database.

Note: The Lowess smoother used involves running a locally weighted regression of the log of exports of goods and services per capita on the log of the export promotion agency budget per capita for small subsamples of data (we used the STATA 9 default options). Bandwidth = .8. ARM = Armenia; AUS = Australia; AUT = Austria; BFA = Burkina Faso; BGD = Bangladesh; BGR = Bulgaria; BLZ = Belize; BOL = Bolivia; BRA = Brazil; BWA = Botswana; CHE = Switzerland; CHL = Chile; CIV = Côte d'Ivoire; COL = Colombia; CRI = Costa Rica; CZE = Czech Republic; DEU = Germany; DMA = Dominica; DNK = Denmark; DOM = Dominican Republic; DZA = Algeria; ECU = Ecuador; EGY = Arab Republic of Egypt; ESP = Spain; EST = Estonia; FIN = Finland; FJI = Fiji; FRA = France; GBR = United Kingdom; GHA = Ghana; GRD = Grenada; GTM = Guatemala; GUY = Guyana; HKG = Hong Kong, China; HND = Honduras; HUN = Hungary; IRL = Ireland; ISL = Iceland; ISR = Israel; JAM = Jamaica; JOR = Jordan; KEN = Kenya; KHM = Cambodia; LBN = Lebanon; LTU = Lithuania; LVA =Latvia; MAR = Morocco; MDA =Moldova; MEX = Mexico; MLT = Malta; MOZ = Mozambique; MUS = Mauritius; MWI = Malawi; MYS = Malaysia; NER = Niger; NIC = Nicaragua; NLD = Netherlands; NOR = Norway; PAN = Panama; PER = Peru; PRI = Puerto Rico; PRT = Portugal; PRY = Paraguay; RWA = Rwanda; SLE = Sierra Leone; SLV = El Salvador; SVK = Slovakia; SVN = Slovenia; SWE = Sweden; THA = Thailand; TTO = Trinidad and Tobago; TUN = Tunisia; TUR = Turkey; TWN = Taiwan, China; TZA = Tanzania; UGA = Uganda; URY = Uruguay; VEN = República Bolivariana de Venezuela; WBG = West Bank and Gaza; YEM = Yemen; YUG = the former Yugoslavia; ZAF = South Africa; ZMB = Zambia.

developing countries by dividing the sample accordingly shows that the positive correlation is driven by developing-country data, and the correlation between exports and the budget of export promotion agencies is unclear within the subsample of developed countries.

EPA BUDGET SIZE AND EXPORTS

For a more careful econometric analysis, we controlled for numerous determinants of exports that may also be correlated with export promotion budgets. The control variables we considered are GDP per capita, an index of trade restrictiveness imposed on imports, an index of trade restrictiveness faced by each country's exports in the rest of the world, volatility of the exchange rate, an indicator of the regulatory burden that measures the average number of days it takes to comply with all necessary regulations to export goods, the geography-determined trade to GDP ratio, and regional dummies for Eastern Europe and Asia, Latin America and the Caribbean, the Middle East and North Africa, Sub-Saharan Africa, and members of the Organisation for Economic Co-operation and Development (OECD). A description of the model and detailed estimation results are contained in Lederman, Olearraga, and Payton (2007).

Across several specifications, the EPA budget has a positive and statistically significant effect on exports. In the subsample of developing countries, the effect is slightly smaller, although the difference is not statistically significant. A quick back-of-the-envelope calculation suggests that the effect of an additional $1 of EPA budget generates around $200 of additional exports, calculated at the median value both in the full sample and in the subsample of developing countries. This estimate seems large, but the elasticity at the median of the sample explains only 8 percent of the median country exports.

The finding is within the range of estimates by Rose (2007) discussed earlier, which suggests that the presence of a consulate or embassy engaged in export promotion leads to a 6–10 percent increase in exports. Also, the estimations are not welfare calculations, and such "returns" may be consistent with a welfare loss associated with an EPA's activities, as discussed earlier. In any case, these are encouraging numbers, when measured in terms of export returns. On the other hand, low estimated elasticities suggest that there are strong diminishing returns to scale. Consequently, large expansions of EPAs' budgets may not be desirable.

Concerning other variables controlled for, GDP per capita, and the geography-determined trade to GDP ratios have a positive and statistically significant effect on exports per capita. The trade restrictiveness of the rest of the world faced by exporters and the volatility of the exchange rate have a negative and statistically significant effect on exports per capita.

The burden of export regulations is negative and significant in the full sample but not in the subsample of developing countries.

We also explored the heterogeneity of the effect of export promotion budgets across regions and levels of income by allowing the coefficient to vary by geographic region and by level of income (GDP per capita). In terms of region heterogeneity, Eastern Europe and Asia, Latin America, and Sub-Saharan Africa are the regions where the export promotion budgets seem to have the strongest impact on exports and where the results are also statistically different from zero. For OECD members and the Middle East, the coefficients are not statistically different from zero. A quick back-of-the-envelope calculation suggests that for each $1 invested on export promotion there are $100 of additional exports in Eastern Europe and Asia, $70 in Latin America and the Caribbean, $38 in Sub-Saharan Africa, and $5 in the OECD member countries; for the Middle East and North Africa, there are $53 fewer exports. But it is important to recall that the estimates for the OECD and Middle East countries are not statistically different from zero. Also, the estimates for the other three regions are not statistically different from each other.

Across income levels, the estimates suggest that at low levels of development the effect of EPA expenditures on exports may be negative, but this rapidly increases with the level of income. There seems to be an inverted-U-shaped relationship between the effect of EPA budgets on the log of exports per capita and the size of EPA budgets per capita. This suggests, everything else equal, that returns may be smaller at very low or high levels of EPA budgets than at intermediate levels. That is, beyond a certain level of EPA budgets, around $1 per capita, the marginal returns of EPA budgets are negative. Thus, at very low budgets, a budget increase is likely to increase the efficacy of the EPA, but at larger budgets, further increases may be counterproductive.

EPA INSTITUTIONAL CHARACTERISTICS AND EXPORTS

To explore the types of institutional structures, strategies, and activities that are more efficient than others in export promotion, we added respective survey-based variables to our basic econometric specification. The findings suggest that exports increase with the share of the EPA executive board seats that are held by the private sector. But exports also increase with the share of EPA funding coming from the public sector. This finding implies that publicly funded agencies directed by the private sector are the best performers. After all, the rationale for export promotion is about externalities, and it may be difficult to raise private sector funding when benefits are diffuse.

The proliferation of agencies dedicated to export promotion within a country (the degree of decentralization of agencies) hurts exports. A single and strong EPA seems to be the most effective. Moreover, the extent to which EPAs focus on particular sectors or subsectors in their activities varies (figure 12.2). It turns out that exports are higher when the strategy of the agency is to focus on nontraditional exports or on some sector-specific component, rather than focusing just on overall exports. Note, however, that by sector focus, we mean broad aggregates (agriculture, manufacturing, services, tourism, and the like) rather than

Figure 12.2 Strategies or Goals of Export Promotion Agencies, by Region

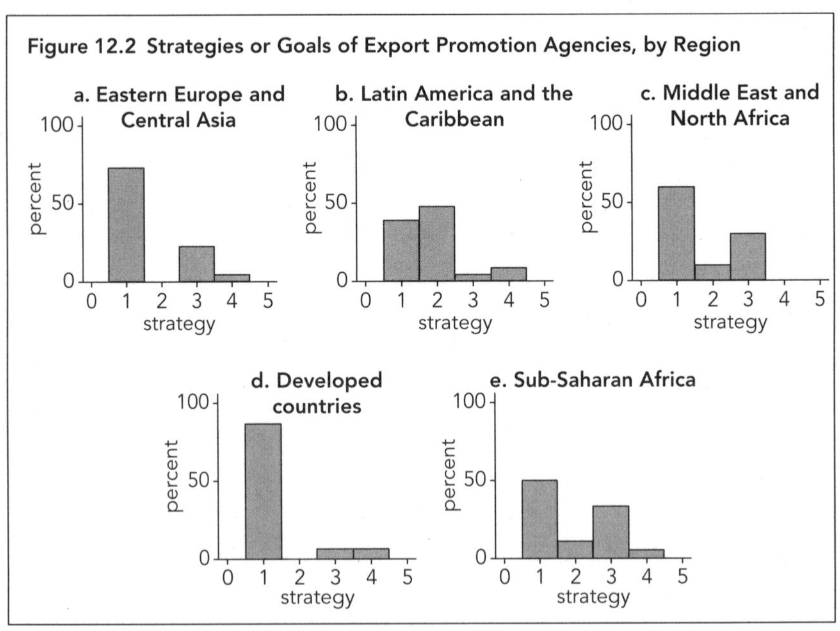

Source: Authors' calculations.

Note: A value of 1 indicates that the agency's strategy is to promote overall exports; a value of 2 indicates that the goal of the agency is to promote nontraditional exports only; a value of 3 indicates that the agency aims at promoting specific sectors; and a value of 4 indicates that the agency aims at promoting industrial clusters and other objectives.

specific products. Also, this effect is not statistically different from zero for the subsample of developing countries.

The allocation of expenditures among country image, export support services, marketing, and market research does not seem to matter in the subsample of developing countries. However, in the full sample, exports fall with the share of the budget spent on research and increase with the share of the budget spent on export support services (although the latter effect is not statistically significant). This provides weak evidence for thinking that onshore activities may be more productive than offshore activities.

Exports increase with the share of the budget spent on large clients and decline with the share of the budget spent on established exporters, indicating that the focus should be on large firms that have the potential to export but are not yet exporting. This finding holds both for the full sample and for the subsample of developing countries.

The more interesting differences between the full sample and the subsample of developing countries concern the use of EPAs' office representations abroad. They have a positive and statistically significant effect in the full sample, but a negative and statistically significant impact in the subsample. Thus, the evidence provides little support for funding foreign offices by EPAs in developing countries and implies that there may be lessons to be drawn from the use of foreign offices by developed-country EPAs.

CONCLUSIONS

Earlier analysis has argued that EPAs in developing countries were not effective because they lacked strong leadership, had inadequate funding, were too bureaucratic, and were not client oriented, with heavy government involvement. Moreover, they also had to overcome strong antitrade biases to be effective. Yet, over the past decade, the structure and activities of EPAs changed, and trade policies became more export oriented. Our estimates suggest that today's EPAs are having an impact on national exports. For every $1 in the EPA budget, there is an additional $100 of exports in Eastern Europe and Asia, $70 in Latin America and the Caribbean, $38 in sub-Saharan Africa, $5 in OECD countries, and –$53 in the Middle East and North Africa, although the last two estimates are not statistically different from zero. On average, exports increase with

EPAs' budgets, even though our estimates suggest that at levels around \$1 per capita, the marginal efficiency may become negative.

What works and what doesn't? Our estimates suggest the following:

- EPAs should have a large share of the executive board in the hands of the private sector, but they should also have a large share of public sector funding. In other words, full privatization of EPAs does not seem to work. A single and strong EPA should be preferred to the sometimes-observed proliferation of agencies within countries.
- EPAs should focus on nontraditional exports or have some broad sector orientation, rather than attempt to promote exports overall.
- EPAs should also focus on large firms that are not yet exporters, rather than on small firms and established exporters.
- Also, EPA offices abroad have a positive effect on exports in the full sample but a negative impact in the subsample for developing countries, suggesting that agencies in developing countries are better off focusing on onshore activities and probably have something to learn from the experience of developed countries with EPA office representations abroad.

Last but not least, words of caution are warranted. First, regarding the methodology used to derive these conclusions, cross-country regressions cannot fully capture the heterogeneity of policy environments and institutional structures in which agencies operate, without running out of degrees of freedom. To complement our study and provide adequate policy advice, case studies are needed. Second, the large average "returns" to EPA expenditures do not provide a justification for those budgets on welfare grounds; that will require some measurement of the externalities and net benefits associated with export promotion. Moreover, larger returns may be obtained by investing those resources in improving the overall business climate (infrastructure, education, and the like), and we do not provide such an analysis. The analyses discussed in this chapter do provide guidelines for institutional design, objectives, and activities of EPAs that can help maximize the impact of EPAs on exports. Finally, the evidence of diminishing returns to scale in EPA budgets, and of negative marginal returns above certain levels, suggests that small (but not tiny) is beautiful when it comes to EPAs.

REFERENCES

Alvarez, Roberto. 2004. "Sources of Export Success in Small and Medium-sized Enterprises: The Impact of Public Programs." *International Business Review* 13: 383–400.

Gençtürk, Esra, and Masaaki Kotabe. 2001. "The Effect of Export Assistance Program Usage on Export Performance: A Contingency Explanation." *Journal of International Marketing* 9 (2): 51–72.

Hogan, Paul, Donald Keesing, and Andrew Singer. 1991. *The Role of Support Services in Expanding Manufactured Exports in Developing Countries.* Washington, DC: Economic Development Institute, World Bank.

Kedia, Ben, and Jagpeep Chhokar. 1986. "An Empirical Investigation of Export Promotion Programs." *Columbia Journal of World Business* 21: 13–20.

Lederman, D., M. Olarreaga, and L. Payton. 2007. "Export Promotion Agencies: What Works and What Doesn't." Policy Research Working Paper 4044, World Bank, Washington, DC.

Macario, Carla. 2000. *Export Growth in Latin America: Policies and Performance.* Boulder, CO: Lynne Rienner Publishers.

Rose, Andrew K. 2007. "The Foreign Service and Foreign Trade: Embassies as Export Promotion." *World Economy* 30 (1): 22–38.

Seringhaus, F., and G. Botschen. 1991."Cross-National Comparison of Export Promotion Services: The Views of Canadian and Austrian Companies." *Journal of International Business Studies* 22 (1): 115–33.

CHAPTER 13

SPECIAL ECONOMIC ZONES AND ECONOMIC DIVERSIFICATION: SOME EVIDENCE FROM SOUTH ASIA

Aradhna Aggarwal, Mombert Hoppe, and Peter Walkenhorst

Many developing countries operate spatially confined economic areas in the form of export processing zones, special industrial zones, or free trade zones. They experiment in these areas with infrastructure, regulatory, and fiscal policies that are different from those implemented in the domestic economy. In particular, special economic zones (SEZs) offer a more investor-friendly business environment and are seen as vehicles to attract foreign investment, create employment opportunities, and introduce advanced technology.

Nevertheless, the role of SEZs for economic development has been a controversial topic. Many case studies find that SEZs have been successful in terms of the dynamics of economic activity and employment. Yet this overall optimistic impression might stem partly from sample bias in that researchers pay little attention to nonperforming zones that stagnate and perish, and so their fate remains untold.

Major changes to the external environment of SEZs in low-income countries have taken place in recent years. On the one hand, fiercer competition for foreign direct investment has emerged from East Asia. On the other hand, multilateral liberalization and the proliferation of preferential trade agreements have opened up new export opportunities (Rolfe, Douglas, and Kagira 2004; Cling, Razafindrakoto, and Roubaud 2005). These countervailing forces have further accentuated the differences between well-performing SEZs and sluggish ones.

SEZs contribute to diversification through two pathways. First, by attracting manufacturing activities to predominantly resource-based developing countries, SEZs add to the diversity of economic activities by virtue of their existence. Second, SEZs can stimulate the domestic economy through productive links. These can be vertical, by increasing demand for intermediate goods that are produced in the domestic economy, or horizontal, by demonstrating the feasibility of manufacturing nontraditional products.

In this context, the central development questions concern the institutional factors that have been instrumental in determining the relative performance of SEZs, and the extent to which the two types of pathways exist and can best be harnessed for the diversification of the domestic economy. This study addresses the two questions by assessing and comparing the experiences with special economic zones in Bangladesh, India, and Sri Lanka. These three South Asian countries were chosen as case studies because they have similar socioeconomic and cultural environments, they have been operating SEZs for several decades, and they make data on institutional characteristics and economic performance available.

The analysis first compares the policies and characteristics of SEZs in the three South Asian countries, with a focus on factors that might explain differences in performance. It then looks in more detail at trade patterns of SEZs in comparison with the rest of the domestic economy and across zones and to investigate the extent to which SEZs have been the engines of economic growth and export diversification in different sectors. The chapter summarizes the findings of a firm survey on the relative importance of different elements of the zone environment for SEZ performance, before presenting some concluding remarks.

CHARACTERISTICS OF SPECIAL ECONOMIC ZONES IN SOUTH ASIA

City-based free zones with policy objectives and approaches similar to modern SEZs were in place for Gibraltar and Singapore as early as 1704 and 1819, respectively (FIAS 2008). While not dating back quite as far, export processing zones in South Asia have a long tradition. The first such zones were established in India in 1966, in Sri Lanka in 1979, and in Bangladesh in 1983 (Aggarwal 2005). All three countries have subsequently added several new zones, and total employment in the zones has increased over time to more than 100,000 workers in each country. Similar to worldwide trends, most currently operating zones focus on labor-intensive, assembly-oriented activities, such as apparel, electronics, and electrical goods, with women making up the majority of the workforce.

The institutional environment in which SEZ firms operate is shaped by a number of elements and has evolved over time. The most important factors include economy-wide characteristics, such as macroeconomic stability, labor skills, and wage levels, as well as zone-specific aspects, such as incentive regimes, infrastructure quality, ease of linking into local production networks, and zonal governance. The combination of these factors has a determining influence on the production and investment decisions of firms, with different elements naturally carrying differing weight for particular investors and industries.

Fiscal incentives often receive substantial attention as a means of attracting investors to SEZs. A comparison of respective measures and exemptions across the three countries reveals, however, that the fiscal policies toward SEZ enterprises are rather similar to each other (table 13.1). From the perspective of a multinational investor, the incentive packages in the three surveyed economies seem to largely neutralize each other, making it likely that nonfiscal aspects of the SEZ environment are more crucial as determinants of investment decisions. Incentives might, however, be more important factors when choosing between these and other countries with substantially different incentive packages.

A second critical element for any export-oriented activity is adequate physical infrastructure. Developed land and ready-made factory shells cut down on start-up time for industrial operations, the available utility services are generally of superior quality within SEZs, and zones tend to be better connected to the transport systems compared with the connections available in the wider domestic economy.

However, it is not clear whether the incentives granted to SEZ firms even in apparently successful zones, such as tax breaks or subsidized infrastructure, can always be justified on a cost-benefit basis (Madani 1999; Engman, Onodera, and Pinali 2007). For example, detailed analysis suggests that governmental infrastructure investments in the export processing zones in the Philippines, which have demonstrated strong performance according to headline export indicators, have not been justified by the outcomes in terms of employment, tax receipts, and foreign exchange earnings (Jayanthakumaran 2003).

Table 13.1 Fiscal Incentives in South Asian Special Economic Zones

Incentive	Bangladesh	India	Sri Lanka
Income tax exemption	10 years; 50 percent exemption afterward; 3-year personal exemption	Up to 10 years, including 5 years for offshore banks	10 percent for 2 years, 15 percent thereafter; thrust industries still exempt up to 20 years; total exemption for gems and jewelry exporters
Profit tax rate	100 percent deduction for first 10 years;	100 percent deduction for first 5 years; 50 percent deduction for next 5 years	20 percent tax on offshore transactions
Excise duty	Exempt	Exempt	Exempt
Customs duties	Exempt	Exempt	Exempt
Securities transaction tax	Exempt	Exempt	Exempt
Service tax	Exempt	Exempt	Exempt
Remittances	Full repatriation of invested capital, profits, and dividends	Full repatriation of invested capital, profits, and dividends	Full repatriation of invested capital, profits, and dividends
Dividend distribution tax	3-year exemption; 10 percent tax rebate with 20 percent dividend declaration	Exempt	Exempt for nonresident shareholders for lifetime; 15 percent tax during holiday for resident shareholders
Local sales tax/Value added tax	Exempt (for capital assets)	Exempt	Exempt
Central sales tax	Exempt	Exempt	Exempt

Duty rebate schemes	No	Yes	Yes, on raw materials imports
Royalties exemptions	15 percent withholding tax	10 percent withholding tax	15 percent withholding tax
Interest tax	Exempt (for borrowed capital costs)	Exemption on offshore deposits	Exempt (for borrowed capital costs)
Customs duty exemption	Up to 10 years	Up to 10 years	Up to 10 years
Tax holidays for SEZ developers	10 years	10 consecutive years during first 15 years	10 years
Minimum alternate tax	Exemption for developers	Exemption for developers, for units	Exemption for developers
Capital gains tax	Exemption on asset transfers	Exemption on asset transfers	Exemption on transfer of shares to nonresidents
Property tax	30-year land lease	30-year land lease	30-year land lease
Payroll tax	Up to 3 years	Up to 5 years	Up to 3 years
Stamp duty	Exempt (on land transfer)	Exempt	Exempt
Depreciation (machinery, etc.)	Up to 10 years	100 percent exemption during tax holiday	Up to 10 years
Backward zone development	50 percent subsidy on land, factory rent (30 percent cash incentives for development of agro-based industry)	5–10 years exemption for development in undesirable location	5–8 years exemption for development in undesirable location

Source: Shah 2008.

Moreover, international experience suggests that the use of incentive packages, even if these are generous, cannot offset the disadvantages of poor location or lack of infrastructure connectivity (FIAS 2008). Indeed, accessibility to international port and airport facilities can be a major problem for zones that have been established with the aim of introducing manufacturing activity into rural regions. All three South Asian countries have SEZs that are located in less-developed regions and are sometimes 100 kilometers or more away from seaports or major commercial centers. This remoteness is often synonymous with a lack of high-quality social infrastructure, such as residential accommodation, health and education institutions, and recreational facilities, making it difficult to attract expatriate investors and staff. It is not surprising then that zones in less-developed regions have generally underperformed in generating employment and exports in comparison with more easily accessible SEZs that are located near major cities (Aggarwal 2005).

Yet a thorough cost-benefit analysis also has to take vertical and horizontal links between the SEZs and the domestic economy into account. Theoretical analysis suggests that indirect benefits from SEZ investments can spread to the domestic, or mainland, economy through purchasing relationships, if the SEZ technology is expressing constant returns to scale and the purchased goods are not traded internationally (Din 1994; Yabuuchi 2000). In this case, the additional demand from SEZ firms leads to a strengthening and expansion of the respective intermediate goods–producing industries on the mainland. This structural shift entails economic diversification, if the industries in question are nontraditional.

With respect to horizontal links, empirical research on the Dominican Republic suggests possibilities for significant knowledge transfers from multinational to domestic firms within an SEZ (Rhee, Katterbach, and White 1990). In subsequent analysis on Malaysia, it was found that the spillovers were not confined to the SEZs, but that indirect benefits extended into the domestic economy beyond the zone. Johansson and Nilsson (1997) reported that successful SEZ enterprises demonstrated to domestic firms how to produce, market, sell, and distribute manufactured goods on the world market and thereby acted as catalysts for the diversification and growth of production and exports.

All three South Asian countries allow SEZ firms to sell a certain percentage of their output on the domestic market if they pay the applicable duties and taxes. India's regime is particularly generous, allowing sales of up to 50 percent of total output on the domestic market provided producers maintain positive net foreign exchange earnings over a five-year period. In Bangladesh and Sri Lanka, the share of production that can be sold within the countries amounts, respectively, to 10 percent and 20 percent. Moreover, the SEZs link with the wider domestic economy through purchases from local support industries, such as banking, transport, telecommunications, and catering. In Bangladesh, purchases from local suppliers corresponded to about 26 percent of the value of total sales of SEZ firms.

One notable trend in worldwide SEZ development over the past 15 years has been the growing importance of zones that are privately owned, developed, and operated (FIAS 2008). Across the three countries, privately and publicly managed SEZs, as well as domestically and foreign-owned zones, coexist. In the case of Sri Lanka, there is a marked differentiation in the activities of zones by ownership status. Domestically owned companies are relatively more active in food, beverage, and tobacco exports, as well as in exports of services. Jointly held companies have a strong presence in services exports, in paper products and printing, as well as in exports of nonmetallic mineral products. Foreign-owned firms account for nearly 90 percent of exports of fabricated metal, machinery, and transport equipment. Exports of textiles, wearing apparel, and leather are distributed in roughly equal shares across the different forms of ownership.

TRADE PERFORMANCE AND EXPORT DIVERSIFICATION

Assessing the trade performance of SEZs in South Asia and their role for export diversification presents considerable statistical challenges. In particular, when comparing export data from the zones with export data for the whole economy, as reported in U.N. Comtrade (Commodity Trade Statistics Database), one runs into problems of time inconsistency. Data for the SEZs in Bangladesh and India are reported in financial or operating years (2002/03, for example), while trade data that are accessible through U.N. Comtrade are reported by calendar year. Moreover, SEZs use generic descriptions of exports that are not necessarily in concordance with classification systems used to record trade data. For example, the researcher is often confronted with broad and poorly defined terms such as "electronic hardware" or "agro products," which make trends in exports performance of these sectors in the SEZs difficult to compare with the performance of the same sectors outside the SEZs. Assessing the performance of SEZs in

India is particularly difficult, because trade flow data are available only since 2000, and these export data are highly aggregated, making the comparison with world trade data virtually impossible at the product or sectoral level.

Keeping these data limitations in mind, the share of SEZs in a country's exports can be an indicator of the relative importance of the zones. In India, SEZ exports corresponded to a modest 5 percent of total exports during the early 2000s, while the corresponding share reached one-fifth in Bangladesh and one-third in Sri Lanka (table 13.2). It should be noted, however, that India has embarked on a major expansion of its zone program, with the adoption of a new SEZ law in 2005. This new framework has led to a surge in development of mostly privately owned and managed zones, with the number of SEZs increasing from 11 in 2005 to 191 in 2007. Once these new zones are fully operational, the share of SEZ exports in total exports is bound to increase markedly.

The role SEZs have played in export performance and productive diversification varies across sectors and products. Some of the sectors in Bangladesh, India, and Sri Lanka in which substantial exports from SEZs can be observed were already outward-oriented before SEZs were set up. Analysis of trade data shows that in these cases, SEZ exports have often grown alongside existing exports. Examples of this pattern in Bangladesh are exports of footwear and leather (figure 13.1), knitted products, and clothing. Similar developments can be observed for Sri Lankan exports of wearing apparel and leather; nonmetallic mineral products; and food, beverages, and tobacco. The available data do not make it possible,

Table 13.2 Share of Special Economic Zone Exports in Total Exports (percent)

Year	Bangladesh	India	Sri Lanka
1973	n.a.	0.14	n.a.
1979	8.0	0.59	n.a.
1985	1.5	4.86	27.8
1990	3.4	4.23	35.2
1995	9.9	4.07	31.1
2000	17.9	5.41	28.8
2001	19.5	5.62	29.5
2002	19.7	5.27	32.3
2003	21.3	—	33.2

Source: Aggarwal 2005.

Note: n.a. Not applicable; — not available.

Figure 13.1 Exports of Footwear and Leather from Bangladesh, 1972–2003

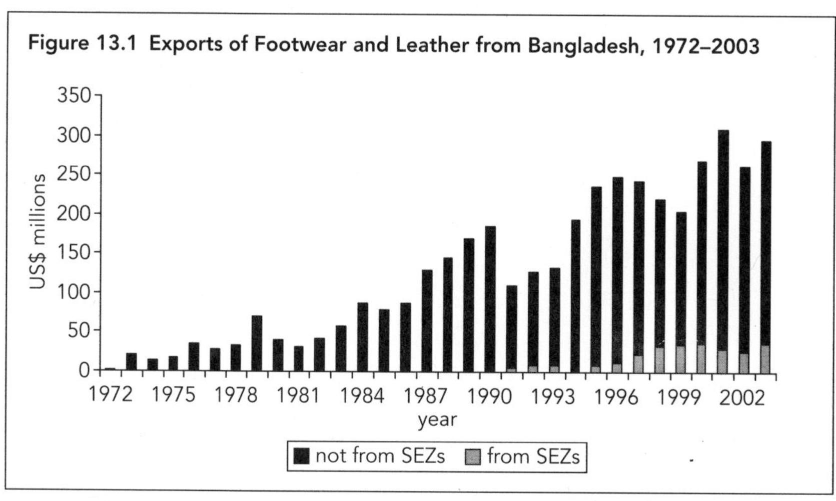

Sources: U.N. Comtrade; Aggarwal 2005.
Note: SEZs = special economic zones.

though, to determine whether the SEZ exports were generated from new operations or from firms that used to produce in the domestic economy but relocated to the SEZ to take advantage of the incentives provided there. Yet the coexistence of SEZ and non-SEZ exports suggests that the business environment in the zones has not been so much more favorable as to induce a complete shift of certain production processes to the SEZs.

In some sectors, however, large-scale shifts toward SEZs have occurred. An example is Sri Lanka. During the 1970s, the total exports of the chemicals, petroleum, coal, rubber, and plastics industries amounted to about $50 million a year, with virtually no exports originating in firms registered for SEZ status with the Board of Investment (BOI). Exports then increased to about $150 million in 1990, of which about $20 million came from BOI-registered firms. During the 1990s, exports of these goods from BOI firms started to increase strongly, while overall exports remained constant. By the early 2000s, only BOI-registered firms were exporting. Without detailed firm-level information, it is not possible to determine whether the shift toward SEZ-based operations merely boosted rents and profits of the BOI companies, or whether the SEZ status and related incentives have enabled otherwise unprofitable industries to continue operations in the country, thereby contributing to a greater diversity of economic activities than would otherwise be observed.

For some products, the zones have played an initiating role by adding "new" products to the overall export portfolio. In these cases, SEZs have directly contributed to productive diversification and export growth at the extensive margin, that is, in exports of new product lines. Figure 13.2 shows the exports of tents from Bangladesh, which grew dynamically throughout the 1990s based on SEZ operations. The situation is very similar for exports of camera parts, fishing reels, and golf equipment, which started in 1991 and originated nearly entirely in the country's SEZs. There might be a number of additional "new" products, but the high level of aggregation of available SEZ trade data makes it difficult to identify cases where firms start to export new products. Often new, specialized product categories are grouped together with existing products. One would hence not observe the export of a new product but rather an increase in the size of exports in an already existing category.

Perhaps also as a result of the high level of aggregation, the data do not provide evidence of any new product introductions in the domestic economy. For example, there is no case where a product was first exported from within a SEZ and then later also from the domestic economy. Hence, export diversification based on links from SEZs to the domestic economy does not seem to be a prominent feature of South Asian SEZs.

Figure 13.2 Exports of Tents from Bangladesh, 1972–2003

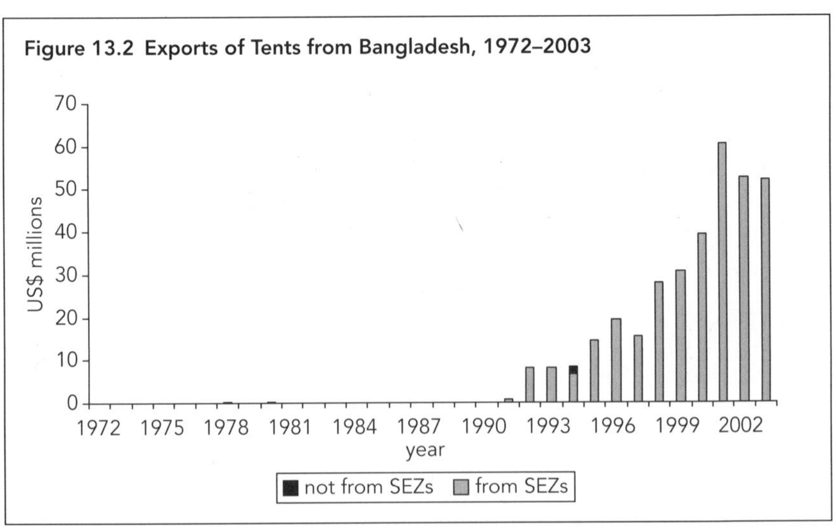

Sources: U.N. Comtrade; Aggarwal 2005.

FIRM-LEVEL PERCEPTIONS OF SEZ PERFORMANCE

The role SEZs can play for export diversification and economic growth depends on the extent to which the zones can help to remedy market and government failures in the wider domestic economy. This section summarizes perception data from a firm survey that was administered in SEZs in Bangladesh, India, and Sri Lanka to complement the "hard" data obtained from economic and trade statistics. Information on the relative subjective importance of different elements of the incentive, infrastructure, and regulatory environment of SEZs was collected from identical surveys administered across zones in the three countries, with almost 300 responses from firms.

The survey responses are summarized in figure 13.3. In all three countries, firm representatives rated the physical infrastructure in the zone, the proximity to ports and cities, tax concessions, and zone governance as of

Figure 13.3 Relative Importance of Different SEZ Elements

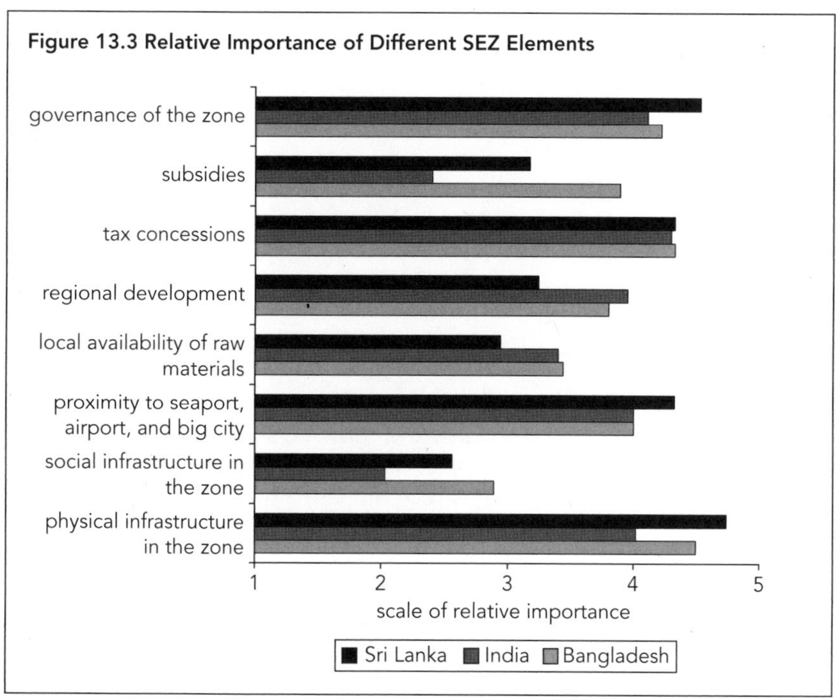

Source: Aggarwal 2005.

Note: On the scale, 1 means least important and 5 means most important. SEZ = special economic zone.

high and nearly equal importance for investment decisions. Hence, to be successful, SEZs will need to provide a package of favorable elements of the business environment, rather than addressing single constraints in the wider domestic economy of the three countries. On the other hand, social infrastructure within the zones (such as housing for workers, day care, and schooling), the availability of raw materials nearby, the state of economic development of the surrounding region, and direct subsidies are seen as relatively less important for success, and have not featured prominently in the investment decisions of existing SEZ enterprises. However, these features might carry more weight for other investors.

Complementary findings from the firm surveys on the quality of the physical infrastructure, zone governance, and fiscal advantages show that firm representatives see the SEZ environment as being clearly superior to that in the wider domestic economy (Aggarwal 2005). Remarkably, the surveyed firms in Bangladesh reported the highest level of overall satisfaction with the quality of the existing SEZ packages. This observation coincides with Bangladesh's receiving the least favorable ratings among the three countries in economy-wide assessments of the fiscal system, physical infrastructure, and governance and corruption, as measured by the World Bank's investment climate assessments, Doing Business surveys, and governance indicators. Hence, SEZs can play a potentially prominent role in least-developed countries that face a multitude of severe impediments to private sector–led development.

CONCLUDING REMARKS

Bangladesh, India, and Sri Lanka have a long tradition of operating export processing zones. The favorable fiscal, infrastructure, and regulatory conditions under which firms in these zones operate have made it possible to attract substantial foreign direct investment and thereby bring new economic activities and employment opportunities to the countries. Although data limitations make it challenging to evaluate the institutional characteristics and trade performance across zones and countries, the comparative assessment attempted in this study yields several findings. In particular, zone location, access to and quality of infrastructure, and the governance structure of the zones seem to influence the performance of SEZs.

Moreover, the effect of SEZs on diversification varies across types of activities. In some sectors, SEZ activity adds to already-existing exports in the countries, in others it absorbs production and exports previously performed in the domestic economy, and in a third set it brings entirely new production processes to the country. Available trade data do not suggest the existence of strong links between SEZs and the domestic economy that would lead to SEZ-induced export product discoveries by firms outside of the zones, even though all three South Asian countries allow SEZ firms to interact with producers in the domestic economy and to sell parts of their output on the domestic market.

Evidence from firm surveys suggests the importance of the ability of SEZs in South Asia to address simultaneously constraints in the wider domestic economies with respect to fiscal incentives, physical infrastructure, accessibility, and governance. SEZs can thereby serve as a policy tool to overcome coordination problems across several policy areas. The three South Asian countries have been successful in providing a business environment in the zones that is markedly superior to that in the wider domestic economy across the crucial dimensions. This has made it possible for them to maintain and expand SEZ activity, thereby retaining and attracting industries that might otherwise not exist in the countries.

More generally, intangible factors often influence the success or failure of SEZs. For example, in Trinidad and Tobago the fear of unsteady labor relations has been seen as a reason why investors find SEZs there relatively unattractive compared with other zones in the Caribbean (Willmore 1996). In Africa, many SEZs have suffered from a lack of sociopolitical and economic management skills that have made it impossible for governments to address the multiple challenges of establishing SEZs, such as providing high-quality infrastructure, government services, and human capital (Watson 2001). One clear lesson from existing SEZ development experience is that zones can be a tool to pilot and accelerate reforms on a larger scale, but they cannot be substitutes for countrywide trade and investment reforms (FIAS 2008).

REFERENCES

Aggarwal, A. 2005. "Performance of Export Processing Zones: A Comparative Analysis of India, Sri Lanka, and Bangladesh." Working Paper 155, Indian Council for Research on International Economic Relations, New Delhi.

Cling, J.-P., M. Razafindrakoto, and F. Roubaud. 2005. "Export Processing Zones in Madagascar: A Success Story under Threat?" *World Development* 33: 785–803.

Din, M. 1994. "Export Processing Zones and Backward Linkages." *Journal of Development Economics* 43: 369–85.

Engman, M., O. Onodera, and E. Pinali. 2007. "Export Processing Zones: Past and Future Role in Trade and Development." OECD Trade Policy Working Paper 53, Organisation for Economic Co-operation and Development, Paris.

FIAS (Foreign Investment Advisory Service). 2008. *Special Economic Zones: Performance, Lessons Learned, and Implications for Zone Development*. Washington, DC: World Bank.

Jayanthakumaran, K. 2003. "Benefit-Cost Appraisals of Export Processing Zones: A Survey of the Literature." *Development Policy Review* 21: 51–65.

Johansson, H., and L. Nilsson. 1997. "Export Processing Zones as Catalysts." *World Development* 25 (12): 2115–28.

Madani, D. 1999. "A Review of the Role and Impact of Export Processing Zones." Policy Research Paper 2238, World Bank, Washington, DC.

Rhee, Y. W., K. Katterbach, and J. White. 1990. "Free Trade Zones in Export Strategies." Industry Series Papers 36, World Bank, Washington, DC.

Rolfe, R. J., D. P. Douglas, and B. Kagira. 2004. "Footloose and Tax Free: Incentive Preferences in Kenyan Export Processing Zones." *South African Journal of Economics* 72: 784–807.

Shah, S. 2008. "Special Economic Zones in South Asia: A Comparative Analysis of Bangladesh, Sri Lanka and India." Kennedy School of Government, Harvard University, Cambridge, MA.

Watson, P. S. 2001. "Export Processing Zones: Has Africa Missed the Boat?" Africa Region Working Paper 17, World Bank, Washington, DC.

Willmore, L. 1996. "Export Processing in the Caribbean: Lessons from Four Case Studies." Working Paper 42, United Nations Economic Commission for Latin America and the Caribbean, Santiago.

Yabuuchi, S. 2000. "Export Processing Zones, Backward Linkages, and Variable Returns to Scale." *Review of Development Economics* 4 (3): 268–78.

CHAPTER 14

INFRASTRUCTURE AND DIVERSIFYING THROUGH BETTER PRODUCTS

Torfinn Harding

Among the many ways to diversify exports, improving quality and moving to closely related products within an industry are especially important. It is widely believed that high-quality infrastructure is a part of economic development (World Bank 1994; Bogetić and Fedderke 2006; Duflo and Pande 2007). Intuitively it is not hard to make the case that better infrastructure can increase economic efficiency, and many studies do indeed find a positive association between infrastructure investments and growth. Other studies have shown that inadequate infrastructure can impede export diversification (see, for example, Cadot, Carrère, and Strauss-Kahn 2007). Here I consider whether better infrastructure can improve the quality of goods produced, thus increasing diversification within export product lines, as evidenced by higher export unit values. Unit values of the same export product vary greatly across countries and tend to be higher in countries with a relative abundance of capital and skills and for firms that use relatively capital-intensive production techniques.[1] The interpretation is that countries at high levels of development produce goods of higher quality than countries at lower levels of development (Hummels and Klenow 2005). Countries exporting more sophisticated goods are, in addition, found to grow faster (Hausmann, Hwang, and Rodrik 2007). Infrastructure investments are a potentially important avenue toward export diversification and growth.

This study argues that better infrastructure policies, resulting in improved infrastructure (quality and quantity), can lead to an improvement in products, either by improving the quality of existing products or by upgrading to closely related products within the same narrow industry. I have two mechanisms in mind. Better infrastructure may increase manufacturing productivity, and higher manufacturing productivity may increase product quality and unit values. Better infrastructure may also reduce trade costs. Shorter delivery times, for instance, can be valued by buyers, thus earning higher unit values.

Despite high levels of attention to export quality both in the economics literature and in policy debates, and despite the plausible positive role infrastructure may play in upgrading export quality, I am not aware of any other studies investigating the effects of infrastructure on export unit values.

To analyze the effects of infrastructure improvements on export unit values, I exploit data on infrastructure services reforms in 10 Eastern European countries. In the period studied, 1989–2000, these economies went from being governed by central planning to becoming open market economies. Service industries were not regarded as important during the era of central planning (Eschenbach and Hoekman 2006), and the countries studied have massively reformed these sectors since 1989. Moreover, the 10 countries are all now members of the European Union, and the variation in my data on service sector reforms is interpreted as exogenous variation, driven by preparation for EU membership. I use indexes on the extent of reforms in three infrastructure sectors: electric power, roads, and telecommunications. Examples of the reforms in question are improved regulatory regimes and increased competition in the generation of electric power and road provision. I analyze export unit values at the 4-digit product level. In total, I explore variation across more than 30,000 observations of unit values of exports.

My findings are consistent with higher export unit values attributable to infrastructure sector reforms. Reforms in all three of the studied sectors are significantly and positively correlated with unit values. Across products, better roads seem to be particularly important for differentiated products. A measure of general service reforms (including reforms of both financial and infrastructure sectors) is found to be significant. Reforms of financial sectors alone do not seem, however, to have a positive association with unit values.

EXPORTERS AND INFRASTRUCTURE REFORM

In regard to exporters, infrastructure effects can be considered along two lines. Better infrastructure may increase the productivity of the production process and thereby the quality of the products exported. Better infrastructure may also facilitate trade, by reducing time costs, for instance; this can also be interpreted as a quality improvement of the products exported. I now go through evidence on both mechanisms in more detail.

Infrastructure and Manufacturing Productivity

Infrastructure service sectors provide manufacturers with important inputs such as power, transport, and telecommunications. Nadiri and Mamuneas (1994) argue that several types of public capital are important for enhancing productivity in the private sector, of which the quality and size of the network of infrastructure are among the most important. They estimate the effects of publicly financed infrastructure and capital for research and development on the cost structure of twelve 2-digit U.S. manufacturing sectors. Although their estimated effects are smaller than the previous literature had reported, they find that infrastructure affects productivity positively.

Röller and Waverman (2001) focus specifically on telecommunications infrastructure and economic growth. They argue that the economic returns to telecommunications investments are much larger than just the direct returns, because these investments positively affect communication between firms. Improving telecommunications systems lowers the transaction costs of ordering, gathering information, and searching for services. Better telecommunications services can, for example, increase firms' ability to engage in new productive activities, the authors argue.[2] Their estimates, using a simultaneous structural model estimated for 21 developed countries over the period 1970–90, suggest positive effects of telecommunications infrastructure on aggregate output. Their results are also consistent with the existence of positive network externalities in telecommunications technologies.

Fernald (1999) looks specifically at roads and manufacturing productivity in the United States and interprets his results to suggest that public capital in the form of roads leads to higher productivity in (vehicle-intensive) manufacturing sectors. Yeaple and Golub (2007) find that provision of infrastructure, especially roads, helps to explain sectoral total factor productivity (comparative advantage) across 10 sectors and 18 developed and developing countries.

Findings by Esfahani and Ramirez (2003) suggest that power and telecommunications services make a substantial contribution to GDP in developing countries. Arnold, Mattoo, and Narciso (2006) use a sample of Sub-Saharan African firms and provide some indications "that firms in regions with more frequent power outages are less productive than others."

Arnold, Smarzyńska Javorčik, and Mattoo (2007) find positive effects of service sector reform on productivity in Czech manufacturing firms and interpret their findings as "consistent with services sector liberalization, particularly foreign direct investment (FDI) inflows into the sector, being associated with improved availability, range and quality of services, which in turn contribute to improved performance of manufacturing firms using services as inputs."[3] Work on the link between service sector reforms and economic growth is provided by Eschenbach and Hoekman (2006). Utilizing the same data sources on service sector reforms that I used in this chapter, they find a positive association between services liberalization and economic growth in 24 transition countries over the 1990–2004 period.

Thus, a positive correlation between infrastructure services and indicators of economic development such as productivity and value-added growth is well established, although it may be hard to establish convincing causal relationships.[4]

Infrastructure and Trade Costs

Infrastructure can influence trade costs. Anderson and Wincoop (2004) suggest that of a total estimated tax equivalent trade cost for developed countries of 170 percent, 21 percent is transportation cost.[5] These transport costs include directly measured freight costs and a 9 percent tax equivalent attributable to the time value of having goods in transit.[6]

Limão and Venables (2001) estimate that poor infrastructure accounts for 40 percent of predicted transport costs for coastal countries and up to 60 percent for landlocked countries. While only a country's own infrastructure is relevant for coastal countries, the figure for landlocked countries can be broken down to 36 percent attributable to a country's own infrastructure and 24 percent attributable to transit infrastructure. In their analysis based on shipping company quotes of transporting a container from Baltimore, Maryland, to various destinations, they also estimate that transporting over land is about seven times more costly per unit of distance than transporting over sea. Bougheas, Demetriades, and Morgenroth (1999) find, in accordance with their theoretical model and based on bilateral trade for up to nine Western European countries, that infrastructure has a positive impact on the volume of trade. Shepherd and Wilson (2006) exploit data on minimum distance road routes for 27 European and Central Asian countries, and their results suggest a positive association between improvements in the quality of the road network and intraregional trade.[7]

The 9 percent time costs reported by Anderson and Wincoop (2004) are estimated for the United States for 1998 by Hummels (2001), who argues that faster ships and switching from shipping to air have reduced these costs from 32 percent in 1950. Djankov, Freund, and Pham (2006) find that a one-day delay in shipping a product reduces trade by at least 1 percent, or the equivalent of an extra distance of 70 kilometers on average. They find the effects to be larger for exports from developing countries and for time-sensitive products.

Summing Up: Infrastructure and Unit Values

Better infrastructure can positively affect the quality and efficiency of production processes. This channel is consistent with increased unit values of manufacturing exports because the quality of the export products is likely to be positively related to the productivity of exporters.[8] Better infrastructure can reduce trade costs. This channel is consistent with better infrastructure leading to higher unit values as buyers are willing to pay extra for fast and accurate delivery and perhaps also because exporters may keep some of the possible cost reductions in the form of higher unit values.

EMPIRICAL STRATEGY AND DATA

I estimate reduced form equations for diversification and unit values of exports. The explanatory variables of interest are infrastructure reforms in the electric power, roads, and telecommunications services sectors.

As is further explained below, the indexes of infrastructure policy reform used in this chapter measure the extent of policy reforms that have taken place in a given country at a given time. These are to be interpreted as stocks of policy reforms. Implementation of one new reform lifts the index permanently to a higher level. The assumption is that reforms lift the quality or quantity (or both) of infrastructure services available to exporters. I do not think this is a controversial assumption because bottlenecks—also in infrastructure—were common in centrally planned economies.[9] It is a task for future research to evaluate the exact channels through which infrastructure policies may affect the export characteristics in question. I interpret these infrastructure policies as instruments for infrastructure services and use them directly in the estimations. Having access to policy measures is an advantage in the sense that policy may be more exogenous than actual infrastructure. It may, on the other hand, come with the cost of larger measurement errors. To use the policy indexes as instruments for actual infrastructure outcomes in a two-step least squares estimation could be a way to bridge the two approaches.

Empirical Strategy

To test the effect of infrastructure reform on export unit values, I estimate an equation where the unit value of exports is the dependent variable, and independent variables include infrastructure reforms (in power, roads, or telecommunications), lagged export values, tariffs into high-income countries, control variables (lagged GDP per capita, inflation, and investment climate index), and dummy variables to control for all time-invariant characteristics that affect the average level of unit values in a specific sector in a specific country as well as for common shocks across countries.[10] Products are defined at the 4-digit SITC (Standard International Trade Classification) level. The variables and their sources are described below.

The Country Setting and the EBRD Indexes

To investigate the link between infrastructure and export unit values, I take advantage of the transition experience of 10 Eastern European countries.[11] Since around 1990, they have gone from being centrally planned economies to becoming open market economies. Eschenbach and Hoekman (2006) describe how Marxist thinking focused on material inputs, while service inputs were left with relatively low priority. Bottlenecks in transportation and low-quality telecommunications were two consequences of these policies. The potential for improvements in these sectors appeared to be large and the transition experience through the 1990s did indeed involve reforms of sectors providing infrastructure services. The European Bank for Reconstruction and Development (EBRD) has published yearly indexes of the extent of such reforms for each of the 10 countries.[12] These indexes vary from a minimum score of 1 to a maximum score of 4.3. A description of what these indexes measure is found in the appendix of Eschenbach and Hoekman (2006).

An electric power sector achieving a score of 4.3 on the index would be characterized by, for instance, tariff charges reflecting costs, large-scale private player involvement, sound regulation, and full liberalization in both network access and electricity generation. For roads, a 4.3 score would include a decentralized road administration, competitively awarded maintenance assignments to private companies, and user charges reflecting full costs. Telecommunications sectors ranked at 4.3 would incorporate a coherent regulatory and institutional framework for dealing with tariffs, interconnection rules, licensing, concession feed, spectrum allocation, and regulation by an effective, independent entity. EBRD also publishes indexes for railroads and water and wastewater. I do not investigate the effects of railroads because of the low number of observations. The roles of water and wastewater for export unit values are not clear and are therefore not investigated specifically. All five sectors are, however, included in an aggregate measure of infrastructure reform that is calculated as a simple average of the five.

The 10 countries in question also reformed other aspects of their economies during the period of study. To capture these other reforms, I follow Eschenbach and Hoekman (2006) and construct an index reflecting general business climate reforms by combining the following six indexes published by EBRD: large-scale privatization, small-scale privatization, governance and enterprise restructuring, price liberalization, trade and foreign exchange system, and competition policy. To avoid capturing the reforms in these six areas in my estimates on infrastructure effects, I include the investment climate variable as a control variable in the regressions.

As a robustness check, I also estimate the model using reforms in financial sectors instead of infrastructure sectors. The financial sector index is constructed as an average of EBRD indexes on "banking and interest rate liberalization" and "securities markets and nonbank financial institutions," also as suggested by Eschenbach and Hoekman (2006). Figure 14.1 shows the indexes for reforms in infrastructure services and financial services, as well as the investment climate index for each of the 10 countries.

The 10 countries studied are now all members of the European Union. I interpret the reforms measured by the indexes discussed here as preparations for being eligible for EU membership. Accession to the European Union can be considered as an external mover of the policy changes. As reforms captured by both the investment climate index and the infrastructure indexes can be interpreted as preparations for EU membership, it is crucial to include the investment climate index in the regressions. To

Figure 14.1 Index of Reforms in Financial and Infrastructure Service Sectors and in Investment Climate for 10 Countries, 1989–2000

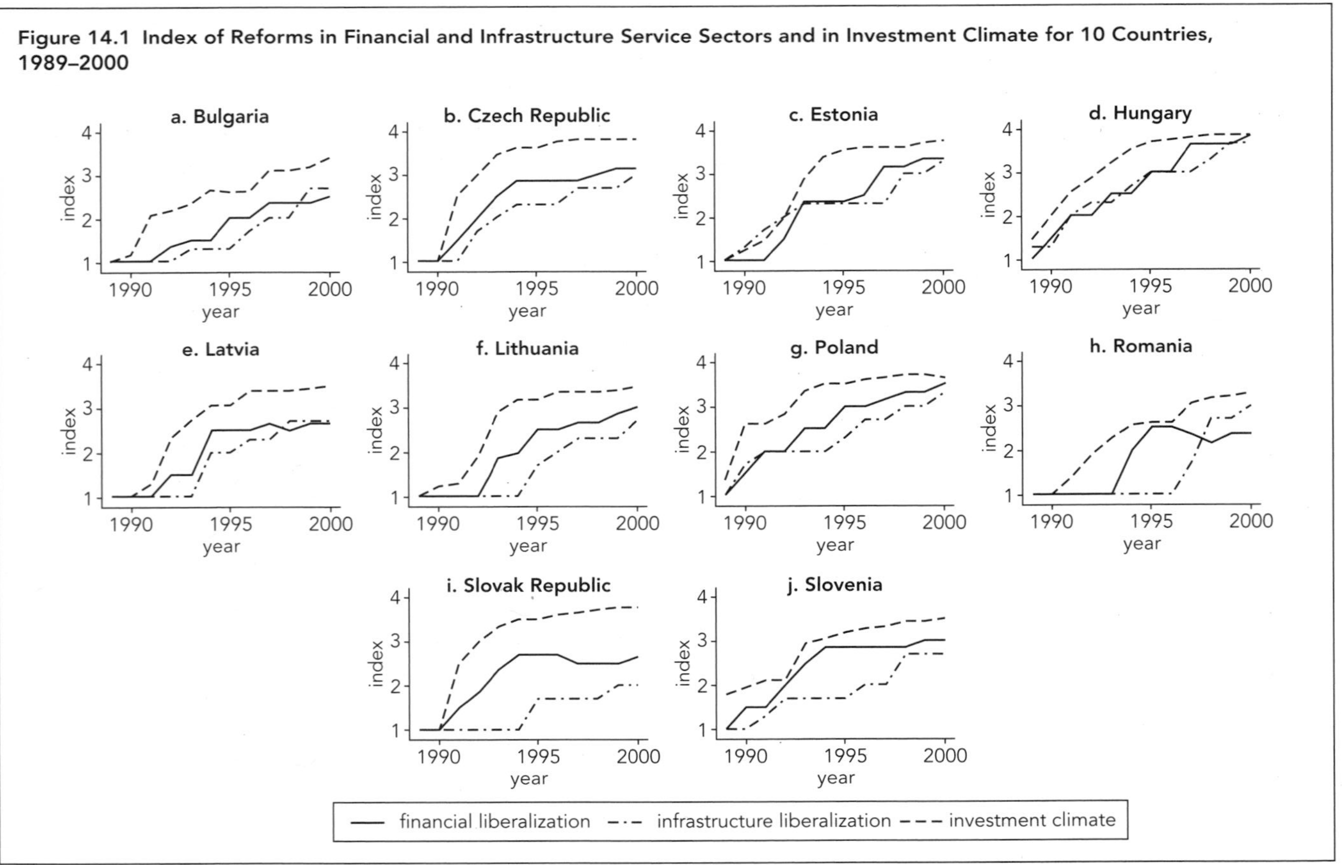

Source: EBRD 2007, see note 12 at the end of the present chapter.

identify the coefficient of the infrastructure reform variable, the variable must be exogenous (that is, uncorrelated with the error term) conditional on the controls included in the regression. Given that these countries were on paths of preparations for EU membership and that I control for other reforms through the investment climate index (as well as other aspects of these economies), it seems plausible that this requirement is satisfied.

Other Data

As did Harding and Smarzyńska Javorčik (2007), I use 4-digit SITC Rev. 2 classified export data compiled by Feenstra and others (2005), which are available from before my period start of 1989 until 2000.[13] I exclude products from agriculture and natural resource extraction activities.[14] Unit values are calculated by dividing the export value, measured in current U.S. dollars, by the quantity of exports.[15] GDP per capita, measured in current U.S. dollars, is found in the *World Development Indicators* (WDI) provided annually by the World Bank.[16] Inflation figures are measured in shares—0.01 means 1 percent inflation—and their source is the *International Financial Statistics* provided by the International Monetary Fund.[17] Tariffs are sector specific and calculated as a simple average of the tariffs a specific country met in high-income countries in the specific year. They are measured in percentage points and linearly interpolated to avoid an unnecessary loss of observations.[18] I use the classification developed by Rauch (1999) to identify differentiated products.

RESULTS: HIGHER UNIT VALUES ASSOCIATED WITH BETTER INFRASTRUCTURE

I have argued that there are reasons to expect better infrastructure services to increase the quality and therefore the unit values of exported products. To identify the effect of infrastructure on export unit values, I take advantage of the variation in infrastructure policies in 10 Eastern European countries.

Table 14.1 shows my estimates of the effects of electric power, roads, and telecommunications services on unit values of exports. The size of the effect in the three infrastructure sectors is similar: a one-point increase in the electric power index, say from 2 to 3, would increase unit values by between 5.3 and 7.0 percent.[19] A one-point increase in the road index gives a 6.5 percent

Table 14.1 Estimates of Effects of Infrastructure Reforms on Export Unit Values

Variable	1	2	3	4	5	6	7	8	9
Electric power	0.053*								
	[0.029]								
L electric power		0.070**							
		[0.029]							
L2 electric power			0.060**						
			[0.028]						
Roads				–0.005					
				[0.033]					
L roads					0.065**				
					[0.032]				
L2 roads						–0.008			
						[0.031]			
Telecommunications							0.076***		
							[0.020]		
L telecommunications								0.055***	
								[0.018]	
L2 telecommunications									0.014
									[0.017]
L export value product	0.546***	0.543***	0.564***	0.549***	0.558***	0.577***	0.555***	0.557***	0.577***
	[0.095]	[0.095]	[0.096]	[0.095]	[0.097]	[0.096]	[0.096]	[0.096]	[0.096]

Tariffs in high-income countries (simple average)	0.000	0.001	0.001	0.001	0.001	0.001	0.000	0.001	0.001
	[0.003]	[0.003]	[0.003]	[0.003]	[0.003]	[0.003]	[0.003]	[0.003]	[0.003]
L GDP per capita	0.141***	0.168***	0.192***	0.143***	0.127***	0.183**	0.130***	0.148***	0.174***
	[0.033]	[0.048]	[0.072]	[0.036]	[0.047]	[0.071]	[0.031]	[0.043]	[0.060]
EBRD investment climate	0.032	0.106	0.243**	0.125	0.105	0.216*	0.051	0.106	0.205*
	[0.057]	[0.076]	[0.110]	[0.084]	[0.076]	[0.110]	[0.076]	[0.088]	[0.104]
Inflation	–0.003	–0.004	–0.003	–0.005	–0.005	–0.003	–0.007	–0.006	–0.003
	[0.007]	[0.007]	[0.007]	[0.007]	[0.006]	[0.006]	[0.007]	[0.007]	[0.006]
Number of observations	32,603	31,588	30,529	32,603	31,588	30,529	32,603	31,588	30,529
R2	0.87	0.87	0.87	0.87	0.87	0.87	0.87	0.87	0.87

Source: Author's calculations.

Note: Robust standard errors in brackets (standard errors are clustered on country-year). Log unit values as dependent variable. L and L2 indicate one- and two-year lags. Tariffs are included in percent and linearly interpolated when missing values. Export value and GDP per capita are in the log form. The infrastructure measures and the investment climate measure are included as indexes going from 1 to 4.3. Inflation is included as percent/100. All estimations include product-year and country-sector fixed effects. The period is 1989–2000.

* Significant at the 10 percent level. ** Significant at the 5 percent level. *** Significant at the 1 percent level.

increase in unit values, while for telecommunications, a one-point increase leads to between a 5.5 and 7.6 percent increase in unit values (the effects of improved regulations in the electric power and roads sectors are illustrated in figure 14.2). For electric power, the estimated coefficients are significant when the index is included contemporaneously and with one and two lags, so reform in the sector supplying electric power services raises the unit values of the countries' exported products immediately, as well as having effects in the two succeeding years. For roads, I estimate that it takes a year for the change in unit values to show up. Effects of reforming policies toward telecommunications show up within the same year and the following year. These patterns seem reasonable. Changes in electric power supply and telecommunications may reach users of these services rather quickly. In these sectors a change in, for example, regulations could generate increased efficiency almost immediately. Enhancing the efficiency of roads may, on

Figure 14.2 Effect of Infrastructure Reforms on Export Unit Values, 1989–2000

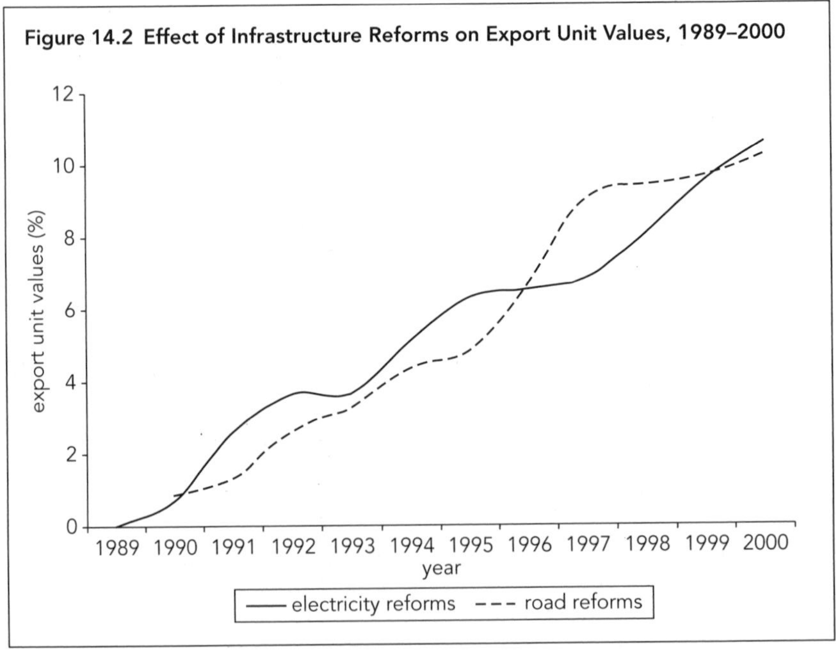

Source: Author's calculations.

Note: Based on the estimates of model 1 (electricity) and model 5 (roads), respectively, the graph shows the percentage increase in export unit values attributable to infrastructure policy reforms compared to contrafactual situations with no policy reforms (indexes set to 1 during the whole period).

the other hand, take more time, as the physical infrastructure is very different and perhaps more resistant to changes.

To get closer to what exactly is at work here, I investigate heterogeneity across products. Rauch (1999) classified products as differentiated or homogeneous.[20] I replicate the estimations of table 14.1 but now also include a variable interacting the infrastructure index in question with a dummy variable indicating whether the product is a differentiated product or not. These estimations (not presented to save space) indicate that the relationship between roads and unit values is present only for differentiated products, because the interaction variable turns out to be significant at the 1 percent level in all three versions (zero, one, and two lags), while the roads variable included separately turns out to be nonsignificant. The size varies between a 5.0 and a 6.6 percent increase in unit values for a one-point increase in the index. By contrast, reforms in power and telecommunications are estimated to affect differentiated and nondifferentiated products the same, as the interaction terms are not significant and the indexes are similar when included separately.

To follow the track of differentiated products one more step, I now replicate the estimations of table 14.1 with two changes: the inclusion of the interaction variables described in the last paragraph and the inclusion of country-year fixed effects instead of explicit country controls.[21] I can now identify only the interaction variables, which turn out very similar to the estimations described above. They are all significant at the 1 percent level, with the unit value increase varying between 5.5 and 7.2 percent given a roads index increase of one point. These results make me more confident in my estimation of the effect of roads on differentiated products.

Conceivably of greater importance, these results strengthen my confidence in the other estimates as well. A reason for caution toward the estimation results in table 14.1 is that other changes at the country level affecting unit values might not be included in the regressions, for example, a policy change not captured by the investment climate index. If such a policy change is correlated with the infrastructure measure, I could wrongly assign its effect to infrastructure. The country-year fixed effects used in this estimation control for any countrywide change over time, which completely removes the possibility of omitted variable bias caused by omitted time-variant country variables. The fact that the results for roads are almost identical with country-year fixed effects as with country controls indicates that the results are not driven by some reform not captured by my controls.

I will let it be a question for further research to understand exactly why roads clearly matter more for differentiated products than for other products. Rauch (1999) uses trade costs between Japan and the United States to glean some insights on the transportability of different products. This measure suggests that differentiated products are roughly twice as tradable as homogeneous products. On the one hand, such products are likely to be traded more. On the other hand, the quality of the road infrastructure might matter more than other types of transport for products that are expensive to transport.

In this chapter, I have focused on infrastructure services rather than financial services. Replacing infrastructure with a variable capturing the extent of service sector reforms in general shows a positive association between general service reforms and unit values. When this general service sector reform measure is broken into its two subcomponents, namely, the aggregate indexes on financial and infrastructure sectors, the infrastructure sector is significant while the financial sector is not. The positive association estimated between the extent of general service sector reform and unit values seems to be driven by the infrastructure component. This finding also supports the view that the results here are not driven by some other, correlated, reform.

CONCLUDING REMARKS

I am not aware of other studies estimating the relationship between infrastructure and unit values. The results of Harding and Smarzyńska Javorčik (2007) suggest that inflows of foreign direct investment (FDI) to the exporting sector (proxied by actively performed investment promotion policies) can increase unit values of developing countries with about 11 percent. FDI can contribute to bridging the gap between developing countries' and developed countries' unit values. The size of the estimates presented in Harding and Smarzyńska Javorčik (2007) is comparable to the ones presented in this chapter. For developing countries they do not find systematic differences in the FDI–unit value relationship between differentiated and homogeneous products. For developed countries, however, the link found—if any—between FDI and unit values seems to go through differentiated products.

Unit values of exports are in the previous literature found to be positively correlated with the level of development across countries. The results presented in this chapter suggest that the state of a country's infrastructure is one dimension of development that can help explain such a correlation. During the 1990s, the 10 new EU members studied went through massive policy changes aimed at improving their infrastructure services. I find the extent of these changes to be positively correlated with the unit value of products exported from these countries. This is consistent with the hypothesis that better infrastructure services increase the quality of the products exported. Better policies surrounding services of electric power and telecommunications seem to affect differentiated and homogeneous products in the same way. Better road service policies seem, on the other hand, to be related to higher unit values only for differentiated products.

As the debate on exports and growth turns away from exports as such, and toward quality and sophistication of export products, identification of the policy measures available to developing and transition countries capable of raising export product quality appears to be an important task for future research. Improving the infrastructure supply seems to be key.

NOTES

The author especially wants to thank Beata Smarzynska Javorcik and Jørn Rattsø for ideas and comments on this chapter. He also thanks Jon Fiva, Richard Newfarmer, Marte Rønning, and William Shaw for helpful remarks and suggestions along the way. For comments, the author can be reached at torfinn.harding@economics.ox.ac.uk.

1. Schott (2004) cites the example that both Japan and the Philippines export cotton shirts for men, but Japan achieves about 30 times as high a price as the Philippines does.
2. For more on the effects of telecommunications, see the literature references in Röller and Waverman (2001), who conclude that "preceding studies provide some evidence that telecommunications investment has positive effects on output."
3. See their literature section for more findings pointing in the direction of positive effects of general service sector reforms, level of service sector development, and economic development. See Sakakibara and others (1997) on the role of infrastructure for successful just-in-time production practices.
4. A positive correlation between infrastructure and economic development seems to be found in both developed and developing countries. See, for instance, Fernald (1999) for works on developed countries. Sachs and others (2004) seem to assign infrastructure a central role in the development process of the poorest countries. Esfahani and Ramirez (2003) provide another example from a developing-country context. Fernald (1999) and Esfahani and Ramirez (2003) emphasize that the direction of causality is often hard to identify in these studies. Infrastructure investments are likely to increase efficiencies and therefore GDP. At the same time, the demand for and supply of infrastructure services are likely to be affected by GDP.

5. Another 44 percent is attributable to border-related barriers and another 55 percent to retail and wholesale distribution costs (2.7=1.21*1.44*1.55) (Anderson and Wincoop 2004, p. 692).
6. See Hummels (2007) for more on transportation costs and trade.
7. See references within Shepherd and Wilson (2006) for more on effects of infrastructure and trade facilitation on trade.
8. Schott (2004) states that his data are inconsistent with an inverse relationship between unit values and producer productivity, which is the prediction of some new trade theory models.
9. For a discussion of socialist systems as resource-constrained economies, see Kornai (1979).
10. Country-sector fixed effects allow me to investigate changes in unit values within each country sector over time. For example, if the Czech Republic has constantly higher export values on car parts because of its geographical proximity to Germany, that premium will be completely absorbed by the country-sector fixed effects. Product-year fixed effects control for the fact that *different* products have different unit value levels, for instance, pencils and computers. They also control for shocks in product unit values that are common to all countries.
11. The 10 countries in the analysis are Bulgaria, the Czech Republic, Estonia, Hungary, Latvia, Lithuania, Poland, Romania, the Slovak Republic, and Slovenia. Bulgaria and Romania joined the European Union on January 1, 2007, while the others joined on May 1, 2004.
12. EBRD 2007 is a data file. For data description and downloading, see http://www.ebrd.com/country/sector/ econo/stats/index.htm.
13. For additional information on the data set, see http://cid.econ.ucdavis.edu/data/undata/FAQ_on_NBER-UN_data.pdf; and http://cid.econ.ucdavis.edu/data/undata/undata.html. I classify sectors according to the NAICS (North American Industry Classification System) 1997 and the concordance between 4-digit SITC Rev. 2 and NAICS 1997 is found at http://www.nber.org/lipsey/sitc22naics97.
14. Details on sectors included are available on request.
15. When there are multiple observations on value and corresponding quantities for a certain product-country-year observation (the quantity can be measured differently, for instance, a part by weight and a part by number of units), I calculate the unit value as a weighted average. Shares of total country-product-year value are used as weights. This is the strategy followed by Schott (2004).
16. http://publications.worldbank.org/WDI/.
17. http://ifs.apdi.net/imf/.
18. http://wits.worldbank.org/witsweb/.
19. This is found by the following calculation (let U indicate unit values and use column 2 as an example):

$$\begin{aligned}\ln U_t = 0.07 * Index_t \Rightarrow (U_t - U_{t-1})/U_{t-1} \\ = (e^{0.07*Index_t} - e^{0.07*Index_{t-1}})/e^{0.07*Index_{t-1}} \\ = (e^{0.07*3} - e^{0.07*2})/e^{0.07*2} = e^{0.07} - 1.\end{aligned}$$

20. Rauch divide products into three categories—differentiated products, products with a reference price, and products traded on organized exchanges. The latter two are, in other words, seen as homogeneous goods. I apply Rauch's conservative classification, which minimizes the number of goods classified as either reference priced or organized exchange.
21. I can include country-year fixed effects only when I pose variation in the effect of infrastructure across sectors or products. The interaction variable allows the infrastructure effect to be different for differentiated products than for other products. I have also investigated heterogeneity across sectors due to their intensity in marketing or research and development expenses and due to their dependency on external financing. No systematic patterns were found.

REFERENCES

Anderson, J. E., and E. van Wincoop. 2004. "Trade Costs." *Journal of Economic Literature* 42 (3): 691–751.

Arnold, J., B. Smarzyńska Javorčik, and A. Mattoo. 2007. "Does Services Liberalization Benefit Manufacturing Firms? Evidence from the Czech Republic." Policy Research Working Paper 4109, World Bank, Washington, DC.

Arnold, J., A. Mattoo, and G. Narciso. 2006. "Services Inputs and Firm Productivity in Sub-Saharan Africa: Evidence from Firm-Level Data." Policy Research Working Paper 4048, World Bank, Washington, DC.

Bogetić, Z., and J. W. Fedderke. 2006. "Infrastructure and Growth in South Africa: Direct and Indirect Productivity Impacts of 19 Infrastructure Measures." Policy Research Working Paper 3989, World Bank, Washington, DC.

Bougheas, S., P. O. Demetriades, and E. L. W. Morgenroth. 1999. "Infrastructure, Transport Costs and Trade." *Journal of International Economics* 47: 169–89.

Cadot, O., C. Carrère, and V. Strauss-Kahn. 2007. "Export Diversification: What's Behind the Hump?" CEPR Discussion Paper 6590, Centre for Economic Policy Research, London.

Djankov, S., C. L. Freund, and C. S. Pham. 2006. "Trading on Time." Policy Research Working Paper 3909, World Bank, Washington, DC.

Duflo, E., and R. Pande. 2007. "Dams." *Quarterly Journal of Economics* 122 (2): 601–46.

Eschenbach, F., and B. Hoekman. 2006. "Services Policy Reform and Economic Growth in Transition Economies." *Review of World Economics* 142 (4): 746–64.

Esfahani, H. S., and M. T. Ramirez. 2003. "Institutions, Infrastructure, and Economic Growth." *Journal of Development Economics* 70 (2): 443–77.

Feenstra, Robert C., Robert E. Lipsey, Haiyan Deng, Alyson C. Ma, and Hengyong Mo. 2005. "World Trade Flows: 1962–2000." Working Paper 11040, National Bureau of Economic Research, Cambridge, MA.

Fernald, John. 1999. "Roads to Prosperity? Assessing the Link between Public Capital and Productivity." *American Economic Review* 89 (3): 619–38.

Harding, T., and B. Smarzyńska Javorčik. 2007. "FDI and Unit Values of Exports." Oxford University, Oxford, U.K.

Hausmann, R., J. Hwang, and D. Rodrik. 2007. "What You Export Matters." *Journal of Economic Growth* 12 (1): 1–25.

Hummels, D. 2001. "Time as a Trade Barrier." Working paper, Purdue University, West Lafayette, IN.

———. 2007. "Transportation Costs and International Trade in the Second Era of Globalization." *Journal of Economic Perspectives* 21 (3): 131–54.

Hummels, David, and Peter J. Klenow. 2005. "The Variety and Quality of a Nation's Exports." *American Economic Review* 95 (3): 704–23.

Kornai, J. 1979. "Resource-Constrained versus Demand-Constrained Systems." *Econometrica* 47 (4): 801–19.

Limão, N., and A. J. Venables. 2001. "Infrastructure, Geographical Disadvantage, Transport Costs, and Trade." *World Bank Economic Review* 15 (3): 451–79.

Nadiri, M. I., and T. P. Mamuneas. 1994. "The Effects of Public Infrastructure and R & D Capital on the Cost Structure and Performance of U.S. Manufacturing Industries." *Review of Economics and Statistics* 76 (1): 22–37.

Rauch, J. E. 1999. "Networks versus Markets in International Trade." *Journal of International Economics* 48 (1): 7–35.

Röller, L.-H., and L. Waverman. 2001. "Telecommunications Infrastructure and Economic Development: A Simultaneous Approach." *American Economic Review* 91 (4): 909–23.

Sachs, J. D., J. W. McArthur, G. Schmidt-Traub, M. Kruk, C. Bahadur, M. Faye, and G. McCord. 2004. "Ending Africa's Poverty Trap." *Brookings Papers on Economic Activity* 1: 117–216.

Sakakibara, S., B. B. Flynn, R. G. Schroeder, and W. T. Morris. 1997. "The Impact of Just-in-Time Manufacturing and Its Infrastructure on Manufacturing Performance." *Management Science* 43 (9): 1246–57.

Schott, P. K. 2004. "Across-Product Versus Within-Product Specialization in International Trade." *Quarterly Journal of Economics* 119 (2): 647–78.

Shepherd, B., and J. S. Wilson. 2006. "Road Infrastructure in Europe and Central Asia: Does Network Quality Affect Trade?" Policy Research Working Paper 4104, World Bank, Washington, DC.

World Bank. 1994. *World Development Report 1994, Infrastructure for Development*. Washington, DC: World Bank.

Yeaple, S. R., and S. S. Golub. 2007. "International Productivity Differences, Infrastructure, and Comparative Advantage." *Review of International Economics* 15 (2): 223–42.

INDEX

Boxes, figures, notes, and tables are indicated by *b*, *f*, *n*, and *t*, respectively.

S

ECO-AUDIT

Environmental Benefits Statement

The World Bank is committed to preserving endangered forests and natural resources. The Office of the Publisher has chosen to print ***Breaking Into New Markets: Emerging Lessons for Export Diversification*** on recycled paper with 30 percent postconsumer fiber in accordance with the recommended standards for paper usage set by the Green Press Initiative, a nonprofit program supporting publishers in using fiber that is not sourced from endangered forests. For more information, visit www.greenpressinitiative.org.

Saved:

- 10 trees
- 7 million Btu of total energy
- 863 lb. of net greenhouse gases
- 3,583 gal. of waste water
- 460 lb. of solid waste